Henry Panasci—

At the pinnacle of your success, you don't need much, if any, advice on your PPR (you might've appreciated it when you were in college, or just starting up the career ladder), but perhaps you'll get a tidbit of good advice.

John Chestara

P.P.R.
(Personal Public Relations)

P.P.R.
(Personal Public Relations)

Using Public Relations Skills, Concepts, Techniques, and Strategies In Your Business, Career, Family and Social Life.

John A. Chestara

TROY, NEW YORK

P.P.R. (Personal Public Relations). Copyright © 1988 by John A. Chestara. Printed and bound in the United States of America. All rights reserved. No part of this book may be reproduced in any form or by any electronic or mechanical means including information storage and retrieval systems without permission in writing from the publisher, except in a reasonable manner, with proper credit, under what is commonly called *fair use*, to promote intellectual progress and public access to information, and by a reviewer who may quote brief passages in a review. Published by Sage Publishing Company, 26 Moonlawn Road, Troy, New York 12180, (518) 279-9487.

Although the author and publisher have researched all sources to ensure accuracy and completeness of information contained in this book, no responsibility is assumed for errors, inaccuracies, omissions, or any inconsistency herein. Any slights of people or organizations are unintentional. Readers should use their own judgment for specific applications to their individual needs.

Library of Congress Cataloging-in-Publication Data

Chestara, John A., 1926-
   P.P.R. (personal public relations)

   Bibliography: p.
   Includes index.
   1. Interpersonal relations. 2. Interpersonal communication. 3. Public relations. 4. Business communication. I. Title. II. Title: PPR (personal public relations).
HM132.C426 1988 302.3'4   88-18212
ISBN 0-929222-00-8

This book is dedicated to my dad, Michael, who taught me P.P.R. without knowing it; to my mother, Frances, who saw to it that I practiced it; to the many people along the way who added to my knowledge and experience; and to my wife, Gladys, who's made it a very rewarding concept to practice for almost forty years.

Contents

13 Introduction

PART ONE – Getting To Know

19 Chapter 1 – ...In Sheep's Clothing...

23 Chapter 2 – Only Marionettes Have Strings

33 Chapter 3 – Getting To Know The Product...YOU
How Do You See Yourself? 33/ The Physical You 34 / The Educated You 35/ You and Your Abilities 37/ You Are Unique And Special 38/ Personality – You Have One 40/ Shaping Your Personality 42/ Assessing Your Personality 43/ Six Self-Assessment Questions 44

47 Chapter 4 – Getting To Know The Consumers...Them
Fundamentals Of Human Behavior 48/ Perception (49), Motivation (51), Emotion (54), Learning Experience (55)

57 Chapter 5 – Your Publics-Who Are They?
Public Opinion 57/ Opinion Can Change 59/ We Have Many Publics 59/ Who Are Your Publics 61/ SPHERE I - These People can Affect My Happiness (61), SPHERE II - These People Can Affect My Career and Finances (63), SPHERE III - Members Of A Public Who Can Influence Sphere I or II (68)/ My Fellow - Workers

Public 69/ Learning About Specific Them 71/ Learning About Your Boss 71/ The Driver (72), The Expressive (73), The Amiable (73), The Analytical 74/ Assertive And Responsive Traits 74/ The Myers-Briggs Type Indicator 75

79 Chapter 6 – Motivation – Are There Buttons To Push?

What Motivates Them? 81/ A Dozen Motivational Buttons 81

1. Security	2. Good Health	3. Prestige
4. Possession	5. Status	6. Recognition
7. Approval	8. Responsibility	9. Belonging

10. Understanding 11. Accomplishment 12. Independence /Multiple Motivational Drives 83/ Why People Do What They Do 84/ Ambition 85/ Emotions Motivate People 86/ Motives In Conflict 87/ Self-Actualization 88/ Needs, Drives, Incentives 89/ The Art of Gentle Persuasion 89/ Positive Reinforcement 90/ 12 Positive Ways to Motivate 90/ 6 Ways To Turn People Off 91

PART TWO – Honing Your Communication Skills

97 Chapter 7 – Communicating With Them

How You Look 97/ How You Act 98/ How You Speak 98/ How You Write 98/ The Transmission Of Ideas 99/ Know The Other Person 102/ Know The Other Person's Language 102/ Know The Other Person's Concerns, Goals, Interests, Expectations 103/ Packaging Your Message 104/ Twelve "Roadblocks" To Communication 106/ Ten Psychological Considerations 113/ Consider The Six P's 116/ Fifteen Fundamentals Of Perception 118

121 Chapter 8 – Here's Looking At You

Communicating With Clothes - Viewpoints From The Experts 121/ Some General Rules 127/ From Molloy (for men) (127), From Molloy (for women) (128), from Fenton (for men) (128), The P.P.R. Way (129)

131 Chapter 9 – Actions Can Speak Louder...
Four Basic Reasons For Our Actions 131/ 1. Acting Subconsciously (132), 2. Acting from Ignorance (133), 3. Acting Unconsciously/Nonverbal Communication (134), (25 Nonverbal Communications Gestures 136), 4. Planned Communication (138)/ Consider Manners 139/ Manners - by an authority 141/ The Message Must Fit The Receiver 142

145 Chapter 10 – Say It Better...
The Sound Of Our Voice, The Choosing Of Words, And The Skills To Use Both 146/ Choosing Our Words (147), The Right Words (147), Pronunciation (149), The Sound Of Your Image (150)/ Speech Habits 151/ Listen! Listen! Listen! 152/ Plan! Plan! Then Rehearse 154/ Listening To Them 154/ Four Reflective Listening Techniques 155/ Conversation – Discussion Or Debate? 156/ Speech! Speech! 157/ Practice! Practice! Practice! 158

161 Chapter 11 – Write It Better
Four Essential Considerations 162/ Two Basic Formulas 162/ The Inverted Pyramid Formula 163/ The Pyramid Formula 164/ The Five W's And H 166/ An Example (167), Same Story— Ten Lead Sentences (169)/ Think AIDA 170/ The Outline 171/ Write! Check! Edit! Rewrite! 172/ Euphemisms 173/ When In Doubt-Simplify 173/ An Expert's Viewpoint 174/ Let's Review The Basics 177

179 Chapter 12 – Writing Memos, Letters, Speeches, Resumes...
Memos 179/ Writing A Better Memo (180)/ Letters 181/ Some General Guidelines (183)/ Notes 185/ Speeches 185/ Writing Your Speech 187/ Reports 188/ ... five steps (188)/ Precis 191/ Book Report 191/ Term Paper 193/ Essay 194/ Resume 195/ Structuring Your Resume (196), Do...Don't... (197), Writing Your Resume (198), Reproducing Your Resume (198), Laying Out Your Resume (199), Customizing Your Resume (202)/ The Cover Letter 203

PART THREE – Using The Skills Of P.P.R.

207 Chapter 13 – You & They... Specifically
Researching Him Or Her Specifically 209/ Write An Essay About Him Or Her 210/ A Research Example 211/ Using Your Him/Her Essays 213/ An Example (214)/ Be Appropriate And Considerate 216

219 Chapter 14 – Planning Your P.P.R. Program
Ten Steps For Planning Your P.P.R. Program 220/ Identification Of Appropriate And Relevant Publics (220), Assessment Of Your Publics (220), Analysis Of All Situations In Which You Are An Integral Part (221), Identification Of Any Problem And Problem Areas (222), Definition Of Needs To Solve Problems (223), Establishment Of Specific Objectives And Goals (224), Development Of A Program To Meet Objectives And Goals (225), Implementation Of Program Using Appropriate Performances (226), Communication Of Performances (228). Evaluation And Refinement Of Performances (229)/ A Review 230/ Be A P.R. Professional Working Just For YOU 232

235 Chapter 15 - Both There And Here

237 Chapter 16 - The Special Event
Getting THE Job 238/ Researching A Company (240), Preparing For A Job Interview (243), Interviewers And Interview Questions (244), Rehearse... Practice... Role-Play (246), After The Interview (247)/ Starting The New Job 248/ About Your Co-workers (249)/ Six Common P.P.R. Stumbling Blocks 253/ Six Common P.P.R. Stepping Stones 254/ Neither Stumbling Blocks Nor Stepping Stones 255/ Networking 256/ You've Got A New Boss 256/ You Are The New Boss 258/ P.P.R. – Minded Bosses 260/ Patients, Clients, Customers 261/ Starting College 262/ Meeting That Very Special Person 263/ Learning About Miss Or Mr. X (265), Meeting Miss Or Mr. X (267), Building A Relationship (268)/ Parents, Spouses, Children, Siblings 270/ An Exercise 271/ The Party... The Wedding... The Funeral... 272

277 Chapter 17 – Your P.P.R. Through Others
   Some one is saying something in your name, doing something for you, saying something about you...

281 Chapter 18 – Good P.P.R. – The "Can - Do" Edge

   288 About the author
   289 Bibliography
   291 Index

Introduction

No matter how much talent, intelligence, or education you have, you will not be as successful as you can be in your career, your practice, your business, your social life, your everyday living - until you know about your P.P.R. - What it is and how you can use it.

Learning to use public relations concepts and techniques in every facet of your life can add up to greater success.

P.R. - Public Relations - does not stand for Publicity and Rhetoric. Ideally, what it stands for is Performance and Response, and the communication of both.

P.R. is not publicity, rhetorical propaganda, or "blowing one's own horn." It is the way an individual or an organization learns about other people - a public - understands these other people, and deals with them.

P.P.R. - Personal Public Relations - will help you do those things. And it will help you become aware of how your performances are perceived by how you communicate. Herein you will find the concept of communication, as well as knowledge that will help you hone your skills for when you communicate - with your looks, your actions, and when you speak or write. When you become aware of these aspects of you and them you can apply this knowledge everyday for success in your career and social life. Then P.P.R. will be a guide for successful living.

More and more during my almost forty years as a P.R. practitioner, the public relations of individuals—corporate officers, college presidents, hospital administrators, and those who aspire to hold public office—in the arena of everyday life, whether that arena is their community or the entire nation, is becoming more and more important. Witness the molding and the projection of the image of

Lee Iacocca in the mid-1980s as the image of Chrysler Corporation.

But Iacocca's image is no more important than yours in your sphere of activity. And the same principles apply: Know your product or service (you); know your customers (people); and define and delineate your publics (those with whom you relate).

Think of P.R. standing for Performance and Response. Each of us can choose from four basic options:

1. We can perform in a certain way so as to elicit a certain response from a certain person or persons - a public;

2. In the face of a negative response to one of our performances we can change or alter it in an effort to turn the negative response into one that is positive, or, at least, neutral;

3. In the face of a negative response to one of our performances that cannot be changed (or one that we don't wish to change) we must educate the particular public to understand the whys and wherefores of the performance, if not to change the negative response to positive, to at least neutralize it;

4. We may say (and some few of us have the luxury to do so) - "This is my performance, like to or not, take it or leave it."

Whichever of the four options we use in any particular circumstances, whatever we do, on purpose or not, we are projecting an image.

Corporations are affected by their performances and responses - their P.R. So are institutions, even governments. And so are individuals. Yes. You are affected by your P.R. - your P.P.R. - in your everyday living. You have it! I have it! They have it!

We all have our publics - clients, customers, patients, bosses, teachers, spouses, children, relatives, employees, parents, neighbors, co-workers, students, classmates, et al. All of them. We all have P.P. R. whether we like it or not.

Who should read P.P.R.?

Most people have potential that is never realized. If you are one of those people, or if you want to avoid becoming one of those people, you should read P.P.R. Once a year. Maybe at the start of a new year; maybe when you start a new job or a new relationship; when you move to a new neighborhood; maybe on the last day of your vacation, the beginning of your new year at work or school; whenever you need renewal of your objectives, goals, ambitions, and direction.

Introduction

If you don't like *your* Personal Public Relations, if you don't know what your public image is, if you're not getting the full benefits of good personal public relations in your job, at school, in your family, in your everyday life - then it will pay you to invest the time in reading about *your* P.P.R.

You and your, we and they, us, them, he and his, she and hers — *P.P.R.* is for *everyone* who wants to better, use, improve, polish, or refine his or her interpersonal relations. Man *or* woman. In my dictionary and in this book, the indefinite pronouns "he," "him," and "his" are equal to, and interchangeable with "she," "her," and "hers." I interspersed "his or her," "he or she," and even "his/her" so many times that some had to be deleted in the editing. I even committed singular-plural error — Everyone has a right to *their* viewpoint — several times, but they were all expunged... I think. What I'm driving at here is I sincerely believe (and intend for you to believe) that every "he" is equal to a "she" and vice-versa, and reading *P.P.R.* can, I believe, make *you* just as happy, wealthy, and successful as you have the potential to become.

Part One

Getting to Know...

1

... In Sheep's Clothing ...

Each of us has an image that we project to other people — to a single person or to groups of people. Some of us consciously project the image we want *them* to see, others do not.

What of the images *we* see? Are they real or do we just perceive them to be what they appear to be? We can only guess at those images projected by our co-workers, classmates, neighbors, relatives, and friends. But we have many examples among those images we can readily learn about — show business personalities.

Easy-going, affable, Mr. Nice Guy — Bing Crosby — if we are to believe his son, should really have had the image of a hard-nosed, unfeeling, cruel parent. Joan Crawford's daughter portrayed "Mommie Dearest" as a heartless, cruel, domineering inhuman being.

How did their positive public images come to be?

A lot of peole take umbrage at the image of brash, tough, seemingly inconsiderate Frank Sinatra. Does his image change in the minds of those who learn that he has done dozens of hospital benefits, and sometimes, in addition to waiving his fees *and* expenses, he picks up the tab for his key musicians?

Everyone knows Bob Hope does hospital benefits each year. Or does he? He does a "limited number of personal appearances on behalf of hospital fundraising activities" and "as he has done before, he will be working for a flat fee and no percentages," his business manager writes, pointing out that is (in 1983) "$45,000 plus expenses; expenses being first-class roundtrip airfare and rooms for three people."

Bob Hope has and does entertain our troops, and that is greatly appreciated. But is even that the altruistic gesture it appears to be? The shows do make profitable televison specials.

Personally, I don't care whether Bing was a good old boy golfing buddy daddy or not, or whether Ole Blue Eyes is a tough hombre or a cream puff. It doesn't matter to me if Joan Crawford was a certifiable bitch, or that Bob Hope may have convinced himself, or you, that he is a 100% altruistic fellow. I like Bing's and Frank's singing, Joan Crawford's acting, and Bob Hope's comedy routines. The point to be made here is one of IMAGE!

The image that Bing Crosby projected to his general public was not the one his son perceived, but the public image brought people to see his movies, while the image perceived by his son may have kept them away. The image perceived by Joan Crawford's daughter, if it was also perceived by the general public, would have kept millions of fans away from Miss Crawford's films. (Remember the mores of those times were such that an extramarital affair resulting in pregnancy almost completely finished Ingrid Bergman's career no matter how fine an actress she was.)

Actor Lee Marvin, in an interview shortly before his death, commented on his violence-loving, tough guy image — an image diametrically different from his charming, thoughtful, gentle real life one.

"I can't destroy my past," he said. "I'm responsible for what I've done. I created that image and now I'm stuck with it. I can't change it."

An image, or course, can be changed. What Marvin really meant was that he didn't want to change it, as he added: "If I did a turn-around now, it might negate my whole career."

In the interview Marvin unknowingly provided insight into the half-dozen important P's that can influence everyone's personal public relations— their public's proclivity, perception, predilection, preconception, predisposition, and prejudice — when he said:

"What you see up on the screen is an actor who brings his film history to new roles. All those action images that spring to mind when you say 'Lee Marvin' help to feed the next characterization.

"The authority of your past performances does half the acting for you. With an unknown actor, it takes up a lot of footage establishing who the guy is, and that deprives you of getting to the plot. When John Wayne rides silently into town, you don't have to say, 'What does he do for a living? You know!"

What do your publics know about you from *your* past roles and performances — your image — that color their expectations and presumptions, and, therefore, their responses?

One of comedian Flip Wilson's characters, Geraldine, says, "What you see is what you get." It seems she's wrong. What you usually get is a perfectly polished public image. Closer to the truth was Carl Jung, the noted psychologist, who believed that each person is judged according to his or her *persona*, the public mask he assumes to meet society's demands.

Image consultants, on the other hand, point out that image-making is not projecting a facade that masks the real you. It is, they say, an attitude and style that comes from within.

Barbara Walters, writing a chapter, "When you meet a famous person," in the Reader's Digest Book, *WRITE better, SPEAK better*, advised:

"Don't expect that his real personality is exactly like his professional one; the confident, zany, or sexy image that the performer projects to the public is often a piece of fiction... ."

But which comes first, the public facade or a change in attitude and style that becomes the real you? *Which* you?

Even if they're not conscious of each of them, people do have many sides — the one their boss sees and the one their co-workers see; the one their teacher and fellow students see; the one their loved ones see; the side their enemies see; and the side that no one (or very few people) see.

Each of these sides is the cumulative effect of how they act, dress, walk, talk, and listen. Is there a proper way? Certainly. For certain circumstances. For certain situations. For certain occasions.

Consultants, for instance, can advise you how to dress. Should you wear light pastel shirts or blouses, or white? A camel-colored sports coat or a navy blue blazer? Wingtip shoes or loafers? Dresses or suits? Bright lively colors or subdued conservative hues? High heels, low heels, or flats?

Yes! To all of the above. Or, No!

Better to look around you. How does *he* dress? The boss. How about his assistant? Your co-workers? You certainly don't want to be (or have to be) a clone. But do you want how you dress to make a statement about how *he* dresses... about how *they* dress?

Information about your boss is valuable information. Potential bosses, too.

If you were going to be interviewed, wouldn't you like to know if he would be wearing a plaid sports coat or a dark blue blazer? Or even a vested suit? Wouldn't that be valuable knowledge?

Wouldn't you like to know a lot more about him before the interview? Is he a Driver...an Amiable...an Expressive...an Analytical? Does he really assert himself? Is he responsive? What turns him on? Turns him off?

Then...

How do I get through to him? Do I know his language? Do I know his goals? What is he trying to accomplish? What are *his* problems?

Can I help him reach his goals...help him accomplish them...help solve his problems?

Of course it doesn't have to be a he or him. It can just as easily be a she or her. And it doesn't have to be an interviewer. It could be your boss. A co-worker. A client. A customer. That special person's father...or mother. Your spouse. A...(whoever is important to you).

We're not talking about subterfuge or trickery, deception or artifice. We're talking about personal public relations. Knowing your publics. Understanding your publics. Dealing with your publics in an honest, forthright, truthful, if polished manner. For probably the first time in your life you can think of P.R. as standing for performance and response — yours *and* theirs; think about your personal public relations — your P.P.R. — and think about how you can use that knowledge for success.

Whether or not you like the idea, you've got P.P.R. You are now prepared to learn about it, understand it, and use it for your own success.

2

Only Marionettes Have Strings

I read a book—*Pulling Your Own Strings*, written by Wayne W. Dyer — and I began to wonder how many lonely, divorced, friendless, unemployed people were that way because they had read it.

To be sure, the concept was appealing. I, too, would like that "special kind of feeling... to wander where you will about life's terrain," just doing everything my way. Like them, I don't particularly enjoy "doing things they really would rather not do." I'd like to be one of the people who "enjoy freedom from role definitions in which they must behave in certain ways because they are parents, employees, Americans, or even adults."

Sure, I'd love to "enjoy freedom to breathe whatever air they (I) choose, in whatever location, without worrying how everyone else feels about my choices."

Who wouldn't?

But really, I am, as most of us are, interdependent on others. It does not matter whether the reason is money, and the food, shelter, clothing, and luxuries it can buy; or altruism and the good feeling it will generate in our souls; or if it is love which will not allow you or me to live life as we choose, just to please ourselves—love for another person, or persons, for your work or your job, for your God, or your country.

There was much in the book with which I could agree. The building of self-confidence — becoming what you expect to become. That's positive. So is the building of your physical, mental, emotional, and social capabilities. And I like standing up for my rights — as long as I remember that *they* have rights, too.

But I can't agree with the unrealistic notion that I can live my life as I please without infringing on your equal right — be you my wife, husband, children, parent, employer, co-worker, neighbor, or a host of others — to live your life as you please. Can I realistically pull my own strings without the vibrations affecting your strings?

Only marionettes have strings. People need to think, act, feel, and love, and respond to that in other people. Each of us has more than just rights—we also have privileges and responsibilities. So, mainly, my quarrel is really with the methodology suggested in the book.

At the end of *Pulling Your Own Strings* there's a test — "Gauging Your Present Victim-Profile." I failed it. Half of my life, it seems, was under the control of other people. The results suggested that I was a "non-string-puller." Am I?

Question No. 3

"The telephone rings while you are making love or otherwise personally engaged." You are a victim, we're told, if "you interrupt your personal activity and answer the phone." The correct, non-victim response — "You let the phone ring and go about your activity without interruption."

I don't know about you, but an incessantly ringing telephone could be tantamount to a bucket of ice water for many people. Wouldn't it be much better to take the phone off the hook before beginning any activity that you didn't want interrupted? Wouldn't that be making the caller the 'victim' (if there was one) without he or she even knowing it?

Question No. 4

This question revolves around an incident where my spouse (partner) unexpectedly changes his/her plans causing a conflict in my plans. I have a choice. I can change my plans and be inconvenienced, and that would make me a victim, or I can carry through with my original plans and not even view the incident as a source of unease. And that would make me a non-victim.

Hah! It seems to be that I'd be a victim following either course of action. It's a question of viewpoint. If I allow my spouse to "inconvenience" me it may very well be that the reward would be greater than the inconvenience warranted. Then who'd be the victim? On the other hand, maybe I decide to win the battle and start a war of attrition. And then who's the victim? Then again, there's always compromise, isn't there.

Question No. 8

This question says that I notice someone (a friend?) is trying to drag me down into his/her own pit of personal gloom. If I'm a victim, I'm told, I listen and eventually I feel just as lousy as he does — the old sourpuss. Ah! But if I'm a non-victim, I'll just excuse myself and leave. Or I'll announce that I'm not interested in discussing his gloom right now.

Now really. A friend would vent his problems and frustrations on me *only* because he considered me a friend. The moment I "announce" that I'm not interested could well be the beginning of the end of that friendship. Then who could I tell my troubles to? Maybe I could just take a few minutes to try and cheer the guy up. Sometimes people just want to talk... all they need is a listener. Sometimes I might just want to talk.

Question No. 11

I loved this question. This is the one where I arrive at a restaurant which advertises a closing time of 10 p.m. I get there at 9:30 and the doors are locked. Should I be a victim and leave, upset because I feel misled by false advertising? Or should I be a non-victim and insist that I'm a paying customer, that it's only 9:30, that I want to be served, or I will inform the management?

I don't know about you but I wouldn't get to a restaurant at 9:30 p.m. if I knew it was closing at 10 p.m. I can't eat that fast (especially with *their* eyes on me). And what gives me the right to make *them* victims by keeping them an hour or so longer than they expected they'd have to work? More importantly, I certainly wouldn't use the tactics advised and insist that I be seated and served. Would you eat the meal they set before you? There are all kinds of victims, aren't there?

Question No. 13

This question is a beauty. "In a job interview you are asked a series of tough questions." If you are a victim "you squirm, excuse yourself, act scared, and apologize for being nervous." If you are a non-victim "you respond confidently and label efforts to intimidate you." You say — "You're asking to get my reaction, not because you are interested in an answer. There is no clear-cut answer."

Let me tell you, my friend, personnel directors do ask some tough questions. And yes, some of them are designed just to get your reaction. That could be just as important to them as your knowledge and experience for filling the position. Following the book's advice, are you really a non-victim? No way. You're the victim. You didn't get the job!

But let's say you played it cool. You didn't squirm, excuse yourself, act scared, or apologize for being nervous. You just answered the questions to the best of your ability. And you got the job. Then maybe Question #19 confronts you.

This question says "you are asked to make arrangements for an office party when you would rather not."

The victim, we read, goes ahead and does it and feels upset, while the non-victim says he or she is "not interested in being an organizer and refuses to do it."

Depending on who did the asking you will probably incur the wrath of a superior, the animosity of your co-workers, or the loss of a few office friends. Once again the non-victim can become the victim. Wouldn't it be better to accept the responsibility with reservations and turn the task into a team effort, getting everyone into the act?

There are other cases described where the non-victim response is basically correct, but the methodology is wrong. As in Question #27.

Question No. 27

Here we have a situation where " a co-worker asks you to complete a chore that you don't want to do and which you are not required to do."

The victim, we learn, will go ahead and do it and feel abused and manipulated. But the non-victim, the test answer says, will say "No!" No excuses. Just No. Wouldn't a simple "Sorry, Charlie. I'd like to help you out, but I'm up to my eyeballs," be a better way? In one easy sentence Charlie would know that you know it isn't your job (I'd like to help *you* out), and that you're too busy (with work that *is* your job) to help him out.

Then there's the question where the boss asks you to stay late and you have a very important personal date. The victim, it reads, will please the boss, break his personal date, and work. The non-victim, however, will tell the boss that his engagement is important, and that working late with such short notice on this occasion is impossible.

I don't know about your boss, but I'd rather mine "owed me one." Chances are your boss also has a boss. And something, it seems, has to get done, maybe by a certain time. I think I'd be able to postpone that important personal date and still keep everyone happy. And I'd be sure that my boss knew what I was doing for him and the dear old company.

An opportunity for the boss to owe you one could be a valuable asset in your career bank.

There's a question and response for you housewives, too. "Everyone in the family is hungry and demanding to be fed, even though you are not hungry and do not feel like cooking."

You, if you are a victim, will "go ahead and cook and feel angry at them."

But you non-victims — "You announce that you are not cooking tonight and you stick by your words, allowing the others to come up with a different alternative for dinner."

Sure! And what will be *your* response, Non-victim, when hubby doesn't feel like going to work and loses a day's pay, or when Junior doesn't feel like putting out the garbage or bathing the dog, or when Sis doesn't feel like going to school or dusting the furniture? That's a great example you've set, Mom. You may be a non-victim tonight, but, hey, they've got a right to be non-victims, too, when they don't feel like doing something you'd like them to do. And when they're a non-victim — Guess who the victim will be?

Question No. 51

One last question.

"You are confronted with the dilemma of sending out greeting cards during the holidays, when you'd rather not do it."

The victim does it, hating every minute of it. The non-victim? He, or she, doesn't send out any cards "nor does he offer explanations." That's what the answer says, folks. Now that is really a great idea. Stop sending out cards to all your friends, co-workers, neighbors, relatives, after doing it for many years. Without any explanations! Do that and they'll think that a) you're angry with them, b) you've gone mad, c) you've lost your job and can't afford the postage, or the cards, or d) you (or someone in the family) died.

There are many questions — 100 in all. But I think you've gotten the idea.

If you follow the advice in *Pulling Your Own Strings* you, too, have an excellent chance of becoming a divorced, unemployed, lonesome, friendless non-victim doing your own thing.

There's a better way. A way to remain married, maybe even more happily married; to stay employed and maybe even climb that career ladder just a little bit faster; to have lots of friends — and still be a non-victim. A way to have their strings and our strings making pretty music together.

We do that by remembering that each of us has rights, privileges, and responsibilities. That means us and them. And since we are, and will remain, interdependent with them, we learn to live within the many environments of our society by using P.P.R. The same public relations methods and techniques used by corporations, hospitals, religious groups, universities, governments, et al, both large and small, can be used by you in your everyday life.

Not publicity, mind you. Publicity is only the tip of the P.R. iceberg. P.P.R. is also concerned with the part below the surface, the part most important to us in our everyday relationships.

Remember, we now think of P.R. as standing for Performance and Response. Your performance right now, as you read these words, could be evoking responses from one or more of your various publics. Yes. Publics. Plural. You have many of them. And they can be quite different from each other. And their responses to the very same performance can be quite different. And if your performance results in a negative response, what then? Is it really your performance, or the perception of that performance that's responsible? The former may require a modification or change, the latter only the proper communication and/or education of that segment of your publics.

Suppose you are planning a new performance — moving to a new neighborhood, taking a new job, attending a new school, trying to meet that lovely young lady or that handsome man, going for a promotion — can you tailor your performance to evoke the kind of response you want? From the people you want? Will one performance be suitable for all your publics? Or will there have to be variations? Can you make each member of each public see your performance as being beneficial to his or her own needs and objectives?

Others have. Why not you?

Consider that public relations deals with the hard facts of behavior, attitudes, and actions that require the ability to evaluate public opinion, how to adjust to gain socially accepted goals, and how to inform and persuade those publics. And, in this context, remember, too, that even one person can be another person's "public."

Denny Griswold, publisher of *Public Relations News*, writes that "public relations is a function generally recognized as essential in just about every area of human activity — business, religion, education, government, and social and civic welfare."

Is it essential to your functioning well in *your* area of human activity? In your everyday life? Do you ever have problems with your interpersonal relationships? Even little flare-ups? Have you ever had a little flare-up mushroom into an out-of-control blaze?

Public relations tries to prevent fires in the first place, preferring to be aware of problem areas, anticipating causes or sources of trouble. But when the inevitable occasional fire does ignite, P.R. is prepared to minimize the blaze long before it builds in size or intensity. One of the ways it does this is by having built goodwill ahead of time so that the cause of the little flare-up, and its consequences, are diminished. (Remember when the boss asked you to work late? When you changed your plans for your spouse? When you did a favor for... ?)

P.R. can also douse a small flame with proper communication before it becomes an inferno of misconception. Of course, proper communication is usually better received by those whose goodwill you have already cultivated. You can't be a bitch, or a bastard, and then change the moment you need somebody. And since you don't really know who you will need sometime in the future, you really can't be pulling your own strings without giving a damn about their strings.

The *American Heritage Dictionary* defines public relations as "the activities undertaken by an organization to promote a favorable relationship with the public."

For you, personally, change that to read "the activities undertaken by *you* to promote a favorable relationship with *your* publics — the many people with whom *you* come into daily contact, especially those who can have an impact on *your* social life, career, education, employment, or standing in the community.

Again from *Public Relations News* (the italics is mine) — "Public relations is the management function which evaluates public attitudes, identifies the policies and procedures *of an individual* or an organization with the public intent, and plans and executes a program of action to earn public understanding and acceptance."

This is in accord with the First World Assembly of Public Relations Associations' definition of public relations as "the art and social science of analyzing trends, predicting their consequences, counselling oranization leaders, and implementing planned programs of action which serve both the organization's and the public interest."

Now you're beginning to learn about the other ninety percent of public relations — the part of the iceberg hidden from sight. Neither of these definitions discuss propaganda or rhetoric. They discuss action to *earn* public understanding and acceptance, action which serves both the organization's (or yours) *and* the public interest. Not one *or* the other, but both.

Remember the key words in both definitions as you read in the following pages how to apply public relations methods and techniques in your everyday life — evaluates... plans ... executes... trends... consequences... understanding...acceptance... adjust... identifies... analyzing — all applied to the basic "planned programs of action" which serve both you *and* your public.

Fortune Magazine called public relations "good performance publicly appreciated because it is adequately communicated."

Communication is the key word here. As someone once said — "A light under a bushel basket illuminates nothing but the inside of the basket." To be useful the light must shine outwardly. To be effective it must shine properly.

Just think. We must communicate our feelings to those we love, our accomplishments to those whose responses we want, and our ideas to those whose approval we seek. And we must do it properly. In language they understand so we are not misunderstood. Would we speak the same language to a seven year old and a 70 year old? To a college professor and a ditch digger? To a nun and to a prostitute? If we did, what would they be hearing? Understanding? Perceiving? Would we be communicating, or just talking?

We must be concerned with communicating effectively; learning the interests and concerns of a public and addressing those concerns and interests in the manner, voice, and language understood by that public. Only then do we create greater understanding between ourselves and that public. And *that's* public relations.

To repeat to remind: Whether you know it or not you already have personal public relations — good, bad, or indifferent. Your public, or publics, thinks well of you...thinks badly of you...or, knowing little or nothing about you, doesn't think of you at all.

Now that is not all bad if it's a public you don't care about; a public that has no bearing on your life. But let's take three of the publics that you, as an employee, *may* care about — your boss, your co-workers, and your subordinates.

Considering that your interpersonal relationships with each of them are different, can you rely on all of them to reach an accurate understanding of your values, objectives, conduct, etc? Not unless you work at it. Otherwise differing and various interpretations are inevitable. Each will have a distinct impression based on and bearing on the other. For instance, your boss' image of you will be predicated on his personal knowledge of your talents, skills, and your work, and how each enhances *his* goals and ambitions. At the same time his perception of your image will be partly formed by what he learns from your other publics — first-, second-. or even third-hand. Each of these perceptions will shade or color his picture of you. You must, therefore, be aware of these influences from your co-workers and subordinates and try to shape them in a positive manner even while you're shaping your performance to elicit a positive response from your boss.

Does this seem like you must play a role? Not exactly true! You must play *many* roles. Every man (and woman) is indeed an actor and the whole world is indeed a stage. But isn't it true that the best actors seem to be the ones who are really playing themselves? In different roles? How about you? Are you really the same person having a beer with Joe at the local tavern as the person lunching with your boss or client? Do you "let your hair down" when you're with Jane in the beauty shop, but not with the cute guy who's taking you out to dinner next Friday? Do you see men in vested suits at the track, in colorful sports clothes at corporate headquarters?

As you will learn, there's more to this than these few examples. We are all playing roles. Government leaders from Washington to Jefferson to our present leaders have had people help them to present their views to their publics, be they groups or individuals. So did the leaders of history — Caesar, Alexander, Luther, and Napoleon. They were their own P.R. person, too. Using various methods. Sermons or tracts, like the Federalist Papers, or Luther, nailing his proclamation to the cathedral door. And just what is that movie star, politician, or author doing on your favorite talk show? Or that preacher in the pulpit? Aren't they filling your needs and communicating it to you in language you understand? Even Ben Franklin knew what he was doing when he entered the French Court dressed in homespun. It was he who spoke of *blowing your own horn* because not many people would do it for you. And it was Abraham Lincoln who said that public opinion in this country was everything.

In the smaller arena of your company, office, home, neighborhood, social or civic organization, school, church, _____, _____, or _____ , public opinion may not be everything to you, but it is certainly important. Public opinion *and* communication.

You may know about you — your values, your talents, your skills, your virtues — but if you don't tell them, and show them — those whose goodwill, acceptance, and favor you need to succeed — how will *you* succeed?

Success can mean winning a promotion or another's affection; a teacher's help or a group's respect; or even_____.
(your goal)

If you don't "show and tell" them, you are keeping *you* a secret. And that presents a danger. Just because someone doesn't know about you, or understand you, it will not necessarily prevent them from making a decision about you. Even if they don't know or understand the situation in which you are a central, or even a peripheral, figure, it will not necessarily prevent them from voicing an opinion, or from initiating an action.

So yes, you do have personal public relations, even at this very moment. The only question is — Is it satisfactory? Can it be improved to further your goals and ambitions? If so, how? How do you create, nurture, and retain goodwill?

How?

By learning the following equation:

Performance and Response + Interpretation and Communication=

Reputation and Image — Your P.P.R.

You must get to know *them* — their goals, objectives, ambitions, needs, and wants. You must know the methods and techniques of serving those needs and wants. You must plan programs of action which serve both you and them. But first you must know your product, your service — YOU!

3

Getting To Know The Product... You

Getting a handle on yourself is a very difficult task. As a person you are a very complex and little understood entity. Especially to yourself. Sure, it's easy to analyze your material components. You can take stock of how you dress, your manners, your looks; things like that. But an analysis of the intrinsic components — your potentialities, capacities, hopes, desires, and the will to work at, and for, success — in any endeavor — is more difficult. This is especially true when coupled with all the aspects of human nature which, for the most part, defy analysis and prediction.

How Do You See Yourself?

It is said that we are, or will become, what we think we are. That as you see yourself can become a self-fulfilling image of how others might see you.

Imagine what it would be like to be anyone...anything you want to be. Twenty years into the future. Ten years. Five. Today.

How you see yourself today is not engraved in stone. You may not have ever *really* looked at yourself before, and, if you have, the *you* you see now, if you don't like it, can be changed. You can shape and project a public image that can, in an evolutionary metamorphosis, become the *real* you.

Take the time now to see the you of today and imagine the you of tomorrow. Look at your accomplishments. Compare yourself with others. In this way you can estimate the you of the future, or the changes needed to fulfill your ambitions. Take pencil to paper. List the assets, the positives of you. Be critical. Which assets can be built upon? Which negatives can be changed to an asset? (Some can, you know. For instance, being impatient may be a negative when your impatience is directed at another, but an asset when directed at yourself.) Which negatives can be neutralized? Keep the list by your side as you read further. Use it for a bookmark. Add to it. Delete. Change it as you read. Be objective as you consider the basic qualities of your product — you.

The Physical You

One of the more important factors is your physical abilities and, if any, your physical limitations. Be realistic. It is obvious that if you are six feet tall and weigh two hundred pounds it would be futile for you to yearn to be a jockey. If you're big-boned and under five feet five inches tall, you have little or no hope of becoming a fashion model. But there are other, more subtle, physical variations you may or may not have considered. Your vision, for instance, and your hearing; your manual dexterity; your response to various strains, tensions, and pressures, all can affect success or failure, or, at least, the degree of each in certain chosen fields of endeavor — a consideration in choosing or changing a career, or its direction.

Do you have the steady hands for surgical work, the strong eyes needed for microscopic work, or the hearing necessary to become a good musician? Do you have a handicap that keeps you less than mobile, or one that prevents you from remaining stationary for long periods of time? On the physical appearance side, are you as pleasant looking as you can be? For instance, would a prospective buyer concentrate too much on the crooked teeth in a salesman's mouth, rather than on the sales talk emanating from it? That may seem facetious, but I know of an insurance salesman who doubled his income after an accident knocked out five of his front teeth —four very crooked, one broken, front teeth.

While these are some of the typical functional differences that can make for adequacy, efficiency, and success; or inadequacy and failure, take heart, in most cases the packaging can be improved.

There was a time when no professional baseball player wore eyeglasses. Neither did any career soldier or sailor. Now many have gone past the eyeglasses stage to contact lenses. Others have even taken to wearing eyeglasses with plain lenses just to look more... whatever it is they think they need to project the image they want others to see.

At one time a hearing aid was an ear-horn instead of the small, wireless, almost invisible unit it is today. A mole on a person's face is easily removed. Teeth can be straightened. We can lose weight, or gain weight. In short, we can do much to improve our physical ability and our physical appearance.

The real question is — Is the 'packaging' right for the product — YOU — that you wish to sell to others?

Most of us have stereotypes of the salesman, the executive, the physician, the farmer, the lawyer, the steelworker, the secretary, the teacher, and a host of others with whom we come into daily contact. Are you trying to break a stereotype? They are being broken more and more, especially on sexual grounds. We are seeing more women physicians, lawyers, accountants, engineers, executives, et al. Even a Supreme Court Justice. And we are seeing more male nurses and, yes, even more male secretaries.

I'm not too sure, however, that we are seeing our stereotypes of appearance broken very much. How often do you see a burly, construction worker type as a physician or banker? The lean, thin type as construction foreman? The heavy, matron-like woman as a secretary, or the dainty, petite miss operating a drill press? They're out there. But not in large numbers...yet.

At any rate, like rules and records, stereotypes are made to be broken. With proper dress, manners, and demeanor, and with a healthy dose of P.P.R., in Pygmalion-like fashion we could turn the burly construction worker into whatever he wished to appear to be. Appear to be, mind you, not be. Being would require the proper aptitude or talent, the education, and the experience. The point is, you *can* fit into your present niche if you want to.

Okay. You have no physical impairment or inadequacy that will prevent you from being successful in your present vocation, or, if you are a student, in your future career. Or, if you have one or more physical impairments, they can be changed in a positive manner. They can even be an asset if you want to work with the physically handicapped. Adjust your list.

The Educated You

The next important factor for you to consider is your formal education. Not your education, mind you, but the education that gives you not only knowledge, but credentials.

Do you have enough to get you where you want to go? How do you stack up against the others who want to go there, too. It is said that the general educational level for a job will determine the standards of that job and the contribution made by those who have chosen that job. How about that next job up the career ladder? Does it require more education. If it does, and you want it, are you prepared to study and work for it? Many firms will finance self-improvement courses that will enhance your value to the company. And large corporations, such as General Electric, have their own training centers because they believe that training, retraining, and multiple career changes are on the horizon for most Americans.

According to Thomas J. Kinney, director of the professional development program at Nelson A. Rockefeller College of Public Affairs and Policy at State University of New York at Albany, American workers can expect up to five career changes over their professional lives including 7 to 10 job changes and up to ten major training, or retraining, programs.

The reasons for the continued career training are (1) 75% of us working today will be working in the year 2000, and (2) with the dramatic advances in technology that are expected to continue, retraining will be essential for keeping up-to-date.

The effect of this pyramiding will probably be fewer positions in top management and an increase in competition for them.

For those not employed by giant corporations, many schools offer courses in the evening or via correspondence. Many may be able to gain experience (informal education) on the job itself that will lead to the next higher position. Others should reevaluate. Is your formal education ideal for the job you're in, or should you consider a side-career-step rather than an upward step? What are your possibilities and potential in other fields? Are you flexible?

There are many stories of career flexibility. I met one woman who earned her bachelor's degree in special education and became a teacher. She then wanted to do more for the learning disabled children she taught so she became a physician. I read of a man who became an engineer, decided he didn't like the nitty-gritty part of his work and became an acountant (another degree). Then, deciding he didn't want to spend his life adding up long columns of figures, he went to law school. He then combined the things he liked best from each discipline — engineering, accounting, and law — and now he's a highly paid consultant for several large engineering firms in the country. Then there's the physician who didn't feel he had the needed "bedside manner" personality to be a good physician, so he became a lawyer. You guessed it. He specializes in medical malpractice cases.

These are extremes, but they show what can be done. They make the point that — YOU'RE NOT STUCK! It may take some doing — time, money, and effort — but you can do what you want to do, what you like to do, and usually, with even more success.

Only you can answer the question of whether or not you are in, or traveling toward, your proper or desired vocational niche in life. If you are, fine. If not, adjust your list. This chapter, which is designed only to make you think about you, may put you on a different road to success.

You And Your Abilities

The next factor you must consider is your mental or general ability level — something which may or may not be indicated by your level of education. In other words, your level of education — bookwork and booklearning — doesn't necessarily determine how far you can go in the field you've chosen. There is no better example of this than Thomas A. Edison who, with very little formal schooling and (for those of you with a physical impairment) deaf in one ear, went exceedingly far in his chosen field, for which we all have benefited greatly. Einstein was a poor student, as was Winston Churchill. And Ray Kroc, McDonald's founder, was a high school dropout and 52 years old when he began the famous burger chain. While his formal education was lacking, his experience and ambition was not.

Your mental ability can also affect your physical health. If you're at a dead-end in your present job, or heading in the wrong direction — whether that's employment or study — it could result in physical problems such as insomnia, indigestion, nervousness, stress, high blood pressure, anxiety attacks, and a host of other ailments. You can do one of two things — change your job or your field of study, or change yourself.

The fact that you're reading this book suggests that you want to know the product that is you; that you're interested in changing the packaging to a new and improved version; and that you want to learn how to promote the new product successfully. That you're reading *P.P.R.* attests to the belief that you have the mental and general ability to do it. You have, in fact, already started to do it, for each time we learn something, no matter how insignificant it may seem, we change; we are not exactly what we were before. As you have read, and evaluated, and assessed your physical qualities, your education, and your abilities, you have become more aware. And awareness is knowledge. In this case, knowledge of you that you didn't, at least consciously, know before. And, as any salesman will tell you, before you can be successful you must know the product, or service, and believe in it.

Now is a good time for you to start believing.

You Are Unique And Special

Look at yet another factor — your uniqueness and your *special* abilities.

First, make a distinction between your aptitude and/or your talent in any given area, and your achievements in that area. For instance, you may never have painted a picture, but you may have the talent to do so. Maybe not as well as Rembrandt, but how many Rembrandts have there been. If you have the raw talent and the desire, and if you receive instruction, you could gradually develop a certain amount of skill as a painter. Or a musician. Or a pilot. Or a business executive, a writer, an accountant, or a teacher.

Make a further distinction between unusual abilities (possessed by a small percentage of people) and the above-average level of abilities that are shared by many people. If a person is tested there will usually be one or two fields in which he or she scores above average for the general group into which his scores have put him. It is these one or two special abilities that sometimes, when coupled with education and experience, can lead you to a special vocation. One which you very much like and enjoy and in which you will be successful.

We have all heard about people in certain fields of employment whose hobbies almost parallel their careers. Or people who have eventually turned a hobby —an interest that he or she was not only proficient in, but enjoyed — into a new career or business.

One youngster I knew had a keen interest in analyzing people and what motivated them, and an equally keen interest in the use of the English language, both written and verbal. For awhile he considered psychiatry as a career, but, upon investigation, found too many aspects of the training distasteful. It required an M.D. degree, of course, and that required, among other things, disecting cadavers. Today, our recalcitrant "amateur psychiatrist" is content in his chosen profession of law. As a lawyer he can combine both of his interests quite nicely and, I might add, quite profitably.

There are many occupations that require a combination of a number of skills and abilities. A sculptor needs both artistic and manual skills; an architect both artisitic and mechanical skills; and an engineeer constructive, mechanical, and mathematical skills, to name just three.

Your talent and abilities, if you think about them, are nothing more than specially directed forms of mental energy that you have used to acquire unusual skill or facility in one or more areas to deal with special types of problems. You can use them in different ways. The young attorney, for instance, could have directed his special interest in motivation and language-use toward sales where an interest in people and communication are useful skills. He could have directed those interests toward journalism which might have led him into public relations, or toward social work or politics. In any case he would have been supplementing his education by using his special interests, which had evolved into special abilities, to earn a living while doing something he enjoyed. And, to repeat, enjoying what you are doing usually leads to success.

Think about *your* special talents and abilities. Those 'extra-curricular' activities or hobbies, or whatever you call them, that you enjoy doing. Adjust and edit your list. Write them down. They are assets. They are the part of the product that is uniquely you. And they are the foundation for that "new and improved" product that you will be promoting. Maybe even in your present job. But as you think about your special talents and abilities, your formal education, and your experiences, remember that what you can do right now, in any certain function, is *only* your level of performance at a particular stage in your development.

What we are interested in now — at this time — are three things about the product or service that we call *you*:

1. What can you do (offer) right now to your consumers;

2. What is your aptitude and desire for potential performance and achievement with additional instruction, training, and/or experience;

3. How can either, or both, be enhanced by using your personal public relations —P.P.R. — effectively.

What you are able to achieve today is a good predictor of your aptitude. Do you have the talent to learn languages? Do you like to solve mathematical problems? How about puzzles? Crosswords? Do you have the talent for the growing computer industry — programming or operation? Would a knowledge of computers be an advantage in your present career, a stepping stone to a promotion?

Let's look at your list of assets — your special talents, abilities, interests, and achievements. Let's adjust them and list them by function in three categories:

1. Your level of performance;

2. Your strengths and weaknesses;

3. Your desire (and opportunity) for improvement.

If you think you require formal testing to determine the answers to these questions, you can get it from any consulting psychologist, or you can spend a few hours in your local library testing yourself. If not, just think about *you* as if you were thinking about another person. Think convergently, and think divergently. (To jog your memory—Convergent thinking requires a specific answer, i.e., there is only one correct solution or answer to a particular question or problem. Divergent thinking considers that there are many possible solutions or answers to a particular question or problem, and that the best of these must eventually be chosen.)

When you've concluded thinking about you (and adjusting your list), and you're satisfied that you know you, it's time to consider how you may be perceived by others. It's time for us to examine the outer wrapping of your product — your personality.

Personality —You Have One

A personnel director I know says that to him personality is the most important contribution anyone can carry into his organization.

The qualities on which potential employees are evaluated may vary from one company to another. In some, emphasis will be placed on such characteristics as neatness, thoroughness, accuracy, carefulness, sense of responsibility, and the capacity for loyalty to the company. In others, the major emphasis might be on flexibility, versatility, leadership, and curiosity. It would seem that these variations are determined by the demands of the situation.

But the bottom line is that most personnel managers recognize that job failures are more often the result of personality inadequacies than of any deficiencies in skill or knowledge. Ask him what he (or she) means by personality and the personnel manager's definition will usually come out as the ability to maintain and sustain interpersonal relationships — getting along with people.

In her book, *Office Politics: Seizing Power/Wielding Clout*, Marilyn Moats Kennedy discovered that out of 100 employees who were fired, or who left because they thought they were going to be fired, only 25% lacked the skills necessary to do their job. The other 75%? Thirty-five percent couldn't get along with the boss, 25% couldn't get along with their co-workers, and 15% had values that conflicted with the organization.

Experts contend that the ordinary worker relies 90% on know-how and 10% on the ability to deal with people. A supervisor relies 75%

on know-how and 25% on the ability to deal with people. A corporate chief executive officer, on the other hand, relies 20% on know-how and 80% on the ability to deal with people. It seems the higher we go on the delegation/supervision ladder, the more the scale swings to the people-orientation side.

We can easily see that an important aspect of doing our job is dealing and getting along with the people with whom we must interact. And, we must realize, our personality is a very important contributor to that interaction. It is the visible and audible you/me/us.

So get busy and assess and evaluate your personality because, like that box of cake mix on the supermarket shelf, if the packaging doesn't sell the product the consumer will never know how good the "cake" is. Coupled with appearance, your personality is your outer wrapping. The part everyone sees first. The first impression. If they like what they see, you might be able to sell the contents. And then you can prove its value. And that leads to success.

How do we assess our own personality? We do it the same way we assess the personalities of others. Stop and think. How often have you made a judgment about the personality of another? Dozens of times a day you form an impression of someone's personality. Consciously or subconciously. It's easy to judge others. Now back away and judge yourself. To help you let's first ask the questions: What is personality? Why are we who we are?

One person is said to have "lots of personality," another has "personality problems," and yet another has "no personality." One definition says that the more effective a person is in pleasing and getting along with others, the better his, or her, personality. Another theory emphasizes the overall impression a person makes on others. Still another says a person's most obvious or outstanding trait is usually labeled his personality.

In biophysical terms, personality is viewed as the qualities within an individual, and that it exists whether or not it is seen by others. In bio-social terms, personality is equated with the social stimulus value of the person — that the reactions of others define personality.

Some theorists define personality in terms of uniqueness — the characteristics and behavior patterns that set one person apart from another. One says that it is important to know in what ways you are like all other persons, like some persons, and like no other person. Another theory concludes that no substantive definition of personality can be applied with any generality.

So, even though most of us use the word freely, there seems to be considerable controversy among psychologists as to what elements make up personality.

People have been trying to put the pieces to the puzzle together for a long time. Centuries ago they pondered the connection between physical appearance and personality. The Greek physician, Hippocrates, classified physiques as short and thick, or long and thin, and then divided these types into four basic temperaments: Choleric (irritable), Melancholic (depressed), Sanguine (optimistic), and Phlegmatic (listless). I don't know about you, but I've run the gamut of these temperaments during the course of a single day. Yet, even today, some think there's a certain amount of truth in this "constitutional psychology"; that a person's build may influence his or her behavior and interaction with others. That's part of the stereotyping that was discussed earlier. It is valuable to be aware of it.

Shaping Your Personality

Can we fashion our personality? There are many who say that personality can be formed according to any desirable pattern; that the only question is the nature of that pattern. Now that's something that I can agree with. With one small change. I'd make the word "pattern" plural.

Is it ever too late to change?

While Freud considered that your personality was completely formed by adolescence, Erik Erikson added three more stages — young adulthood, adulthood, and maturity — in which the adult personality develops the basic virtues of love, care and wisdom.

H.S. Sullivan, a practicing psychiatrist, felt that personality is not fully formed at an early age, but changes with an individual's interpersonal encounters *throughout* his or her lifetime.

The Social Learning theory states that personality is shaped not only by behavior reinforcement, but by the observation and imitation of others.

Humanist Carl Rogers, author of *Counseling and Psychotherapy*, spoke of a general theory of personality known as "self-theory" — the interrelationships among our total person, all of our experiences. Rogers' major concern is the interrelationships among the organism (the total person), the phenomenal field (all of our experiences), and the self (the I or Me that is a result of these experiences). The individual's proper goal, he said, is self-actualization — reaching a point of full function in which the total person's experiences and self-image are in harmony.

To answer the question: Yes, we can change our personality. If you doubt that you certainly cannot doubt this: We certainly can change what is perceived about us by others; that visible outward behavior that reflects various facets of our personality. Sir Laurence Olivier and Bette Davis, and many others, do it to project the personality of each character they portray.

Assessing Your Personality

When we are assessing our personality, or at least its manifestation, part of what we are really doing is assessing behavior —analyzing action and reaction. As we do it with regard to others — "Would he be a nice person to work for? Would she, or he, be someone nice to meet...to know?" — we can stand back and look at ourselves.

Think back to some of those Victim/Non-Victim situations and responses in the second chapter. As you read the responses — How would you have reacted if the Non-victim response was not yours, but targeted at you? How would you have felt or reacted if you had to change plans and your spouse, or partner, didn't have the understanding you needed? Or if you were the one who was "down" and your friend excused himself, or herself, and said, "I'm not interested," and walked away? Or if you were the tired waiter or waitress at that restaurant and someone came in a half-hour before closing and insisted he be seated for dinner?

The Indians had a saying about walking in the other person's moccasins for a few miles. Not a bad idea. There are lots of sayings. Not the least is "Do Unto Others... ." And, as trite as it may seem, it's still a good idea to think about the other person, to consider his viewpoint. To think of his, or her feelings. To realize he has goals, ambitions, and, yes, even problems and worries. Yes, it is a good idea to think about him, to "walk in his moccasins" for a few miles — especially when he, or she, is, or could be, our boss, our spouse, or someone equally important to us.

When Ray Kroc bought his first hamburger stand in California, he set out to make himself rich, by making others rich. He knew the goals of the people who bought his franchises, and he knew he could help them reach those goals. And he communicated his enthusiasm to them.

Some call it humanism — thinking about other people as we would have them think of us. Why not do it on purpose, for a purpose, with personal public relations — P.P.R.

As you assess your personality, how does it fit in to the examples given in these pages? Even if you can't make yourself rich by making others rich, as Ray Kroc did, can you make yourself successful by making others successful? Making yourself liked and loved by liking and loving others? Making others more considerate, by showing consideration? Walking in their moccasins for a few miles?

As we said before there are those who say that personality can be formed to fit any desirable pattern; that the only question is the nature of that pattern.

So, we may be short and fat, strong and athletic, tall and slender; we may be relaxed, sociable, energetic, assertive, adventurous, extroverted, introverted, inhibited, intensely private; we may be shy, aggressive, curious, honest, attractive, pessimistic, unselfish, optimistic, selfish, spontaneous, cautious, wise, foolish... or a few thousand more adjectives that describe us — you and me and them.

Chances are, in various situations and environments, we are all of these, in varying degrees and combinations. And if we learn how, we may even use these "adjectives," and a thousand more, to shape our personality — the personality that best applies, in certain situations, to help us achieve our desired results.

Get out your list and answer some questions. But before you do keep in mind that the answers — the picture you produce — will apply not only to a business situation, but can just as easily apply to a family or a social situation. For instance, "How do you think others see you?" could mean your boss, co-workers, teachers, classmates, parents, siblings, a social or love interest, a relative, and so on. "What can you offer to them?" could mean them, or her, or him. "What is, could be, your role in your marketplace?" could be as a student or teacher, employee or boss, child or parent, friend or spouse, and so forth. There may even be multiple answers, i.e. for Question Number 2 if three (or more) "others" included a boss, a sweetheart, and a friend.

Six Self-Assessment Questions:

1. How do you see yourself?

Come on now, be critical, be honest. The physical you — Appearance? Dress? Grooming? The social you — Do you like people? Do you really enjoy interacting with people? Do you care about people — their welfare, their feelings? Are you understanding? Are you reliable? Do you have the ability to lead? To follow? Are you curious, creative, intelligent, well-educated, interesting, interested, loyal, cooperative? What are your greatest strengths?

(Some real ones are commonsense, maturity, intelligence, the ability to relate and interact with people, drive, dependability.) What are your real weaknesses? Where are you lacking in your list of strengths? (Don't forget, some strengths and weaknesses are interchangeable—patience and impatience, pliability and stubborness, being hard or easy to please, etc.) One very important assessment of yourself — Can you be a friend?

2. How do others see you?

The poet Robert Burns mused about perception, saying what a gift it would be if only we could see ourselves as others see us. How do your friends, your co-workers, relatives, family, etc., see you? Be honest. Critical. Is there a descrepancy? Whose perception is correct — yours or theirs? Do you get comparatively good responses (from your performances) from all of your publics, or are some being neglected? Ask yourself again —"How do others see me?"

3. How do you compare with your peers? Your supervisors?

How do you compare with your peers? Don't say "He's better than I am," or "I'm better than she is." That's too general. Better to compare point by point— the same debits and assets as in Questions 1 and 2. It's hard, of course, to say —"He's a little smarter than I am on that subject," or "She has a knack for dressing that I don't have," but it's more productive. And, if that subject is important to your success, and if dressing better is important for your success —then, if you recognize this shortcoming you can do something about it.

4. Of your talents, which are outstanding?
Good? Average? Fair? Poor?

Really list your talents. All of them. Whether they're career talents, social hobbies, sports, arts, etc. List them and then rate them. If they're purely recreational — golf, bowling, photography, etc. — list them as such. Are any adaptable to your career? Can any of them give you "an advantage?" I know of one executive whose talents included singing with a band in his college days. He had no trouble with public speaking and (volunteered) did so for his company.

5. What can you offer to them?

You offer your talents, skills, and experience to your employer's organization; you offer your social skills and talents to your co-workers; and a combination of both to your supervisors? Now change the nouns to teachers, parents, classmates, siblings, friends, etc. You offer them all of the skills and talents you have that will make them happy... make them successful... make them appreciative...

make them offer you their skills and talents in return. What are they? List them.

6. What is—could be—your role in your (targeted) marketplace?

What makes you valuable to your business, clients, industry, organization, patients, institution, friends, relatives, — *each* of your publics? What, if anything, is unique abut you, what you offer, how you offer it? What could your role be in five years? Ten? Granted, it is very difficult to objectively assess yourself and compare yourself to others. But do it. And do it in writing so you may review it when you finish reading this book. Visualize. Be specific. If you see yourself in five years as a department head, *really* see yourself. Behind your desk... dressed as a department manager today is dressed...doing the work... answering questions...giving advice, orders, making requests. If you see yourself being married to that special person, visualize it. Be specific. What did you do...say... offer... be... that got you there. Delineate your roles. Imagine what you want to be, learn what will get you there, and you will be it, or do it.

If you want, or need, further assessment, go to your local library — in the psychology section, the self-improvement section — and take a half-dozen or so evaluation tests. Your librarian will be happy to help you.

What is important in this entire exercise is that it fosters an awareness in you — of YOU.

After learning a little more about your product and service— YOU — the next step is to research your consumers — THEM.

4

Getting To Know The Consumers... Them

Okay! You've examined yourself — your strengths and your weaknesses — now it's time to examine *them*. All those people out there. Your publics. As you do, do so with an objective attitude, an open mind. Don't be surprised that as you examine them — their style, their motivation, their perception, and their behavior — you're going to learn even more about you.

"We are better able to study our neighbors than ourselves, and their actions than our own," Aristotle said.

And that's true. But while it's easier to examine them than ourselves, that, too, requires some effort. It is not easy to examine them. People don't always let others see them as they really are. They'd rather we see their image. (Even Ben Franklin, we learn in 1987, was not fully the public image he projected as a kindly, congenial, homespun signer of the Constitution and the Declaration of Independence. Not when he could write, cynically, to a physician-friend that "Half the lives you save are not worth saving.")

So, once again, this time as we look at others, we have to first dip into the basics of psychology. Then we can try to combine what we learn of a general nature with what we can learn specifically about *their* behavior by keeping our eyes open and our ears cocked.

Public Relations normally deals with groups, even masses, of people, while recognizing that groups are nothing more than a lot of individuals. P.P.R., on the other hand, normally will deal with individuals, while remaining fully aware that they are also part of a group, an organization, or an institution. As we attempt to get to know them, let us remember two things:

1. We are a part of someone else's public, just as they are a part of ours;

2. Each of us keeps a part of ourselves hidden from public view, and another part of us which is kept (mostly) under control.

This would suggest that what we can learn about *them* — these other individuals — first in a general way — those things we all have in common — and then what we can learn about their "public images" by research and observation, they, too, may be learning about us.

It also suggests that even though we can never predict for certain how another person will act, or react, we can, at least, become aware that these hidden or controlled elements do exist. We can learn, too, that they might just be the "whys" of certain actions or reactions. We will not try to become seers, predicting what he or she *will* do, but we can learn enough about human behavior (and them) to make an educated guess about what he or she, or even they, *will normally* do.

This knowledge of course, can help improve your communication skills. The more you know about how he or she will think, act, and react under certain circumstances, the more effective you will be as a communicator. Each time you — the sender — transmit a message to someone — the receiver — of whom you have knowledge and understanding, the easier it should be to predict an anticipated response. Before we go into more depth regarding communicating (that's a chapter of its own later in the book) let's get on with trying to learn about how he or she will act and react; what makes him, or her tick.

Fundamentals Of Human Behavior

Each of us have had certain qualities or characteristics passed on to us by our parents, as they have had from their parents. Heredity is a basic ingredient of each of us. To that we add the environment in which we were raised and in which we are now living. Throw in age, color, sex, class, religion, living conditions, education, political beliefs, economic status, social class, and whether we are upwardly or downwardly mobile, and we begin to get some idea of what affects people in positive or negative ways, and what causes each of us — normally — to behave in certain ways. That's the key word — normally. Regarding action and reaction — Performance and Response — how will she, or he *normally* perform, hoping for what *normal* response, or how should we perform to elicit, *normally*, what response from him or her?

We begin to learn about them by examining what many believe to be the four fundamentals of human behavior — perception, motivation, emotion, and learning experience.

Getting To Know The Consumers ... Them

Hunger, for instance, is not just a physiological response to being deprived of food, but a psychological response as well. A person can perceive that he is hungry, possibly by the sight or smell of a favorite food, and he is driven (motivated) to eat. He is then emotionally satisfied, and the experience is filed into his memory ledger from which he can draw at another time.

Each of us can and do draw from this memory ledger at will. Or, items from it can surface and intrude upon us at any time.

Your memory, for instance, catalogs foods you prefer, foods you tolerate, and foods you reject. This means that the *smell* of frying bacon, the *sight* of a ball of vanilla ice cream on a slab of blueberry pie, or even the *sound* of a sizzling steak, can trigger the drive of emotion and motivation, and our taste buds will begin to salivate in anticipation. (This reaction may even occur while reading about certain foods, more or less in proportion to the vividness of the description. I have tried to be kind and considerate; the hour could be late, the weather foul.)

This particular simple process under discussion probably started when we were only a few hours old and slowly, but surely, over the following months, we began to categorize tastes, even spitting out those we rejected. Until recent years, when the hue and cry of the health advocate was heard, baby food was generally laced with salt and sugar in an effort to take advantage of this categorization process of human behavior.

Hunger and its satisfaction is a very simple example of the four fundamentals of human behavior in action. Let us examine each of them — perception, motivation, emotion, and learning experience — very briefly. As we do, keep in mind that what applies to *them* also applies to each of us. As we learn what they see and perceive, what motivates them, their emotions — we learn what we see and perceive, what motivates us, our emotions.

Perception

> There was a man who, having taken a bath, stepped upon a wet rope, and he thought it was a snake. Horror overcame him, and he shook from fear, anticipating in his mind all the agonies caused by its venomous bite. What a relief does this man experience when he sees that it is no snake. The cause of his fright lies in error, his ignorance, his illusion. If the true nature of the rope is recognized, his

> tranquility of mind will come back to him; he
> will feel relieved; he will be joyful and happy.
> (From The Gospel of Buddha)

Have you ever had a comparable experience? Physically or mentally? When you were convinced the danger was real, but later discovered it to be an illusion? Sure you have. Because illusions happen due to the nature of the perceptual process — the interpretation we make from the information we receive from one or more of our senses. Did we really see what we saw, hear what we heard, feel what we felt? How about tasting and smelling — why do we hold our noses to take unpleasant-tasting medicine? Does this change the sensation? If you made spaghetti sauce green and meatballs black, would the meal still taste the same?

We receive certain sensations from each of our senses. Combinations of sensations, many times, create new sensations. These sensations, feedback from our senses, are then subjected to our interpretation and understanding — our perception. And that's where our communication problems can start. How *we* see things and how *they* see things may be different because of our differing ideals, values, environment, heredity, expectations, etc.

I remember watching a crime show on television where the viewer had to decide if a crime was indeed committed, and, if so, what were the circumstances and who was the criminal. It was nothing short of amazing how five eyewitnesses could see things so differently. Or was it? How about the way 50,000 baseball fans see a close play at second base — depending on who they're rooting for. And, personally, I always have trouble when I first hear a Democrat and then a Republican — or vice versa — explaining just what the issue really is.

Our minds — their minds — a product of many things — are, to a degree, set, and this may color our view — and theirs — like the man who stepped on a wet rope — turning perception into misperception.

This is dangerous because *what* people *see* as truth or fact is very important, because, to them, (unless we can counter or correct their perception) it is an illusion of truth or fact. And if a person has a mistaken perception, one that does not convey the actual nature of the event, either because of the ambiguous qualities of what was perceived, or the receptiveness of the receiver, or both — the illusion becomes, for all practical public relations purposes, a reality — *the* truth for that person or group of people.

Think for a moment. If he or she *thinks* you've said that derogatory statement about him or her, because you were misinterpreted or misunderstood by someone, either because you did not clearly state what you meant, or because the receiver heard something different from your words, your tone, your inflection, then he or she *believes* it to be the truth, and to him or her, *it is the truth.*

This misinterpretation or misunderstanding need not happen only with a perceived derogative remark. It can be a program you'd like to present; how you feel about your boss' ability or personality; a remark about the company, the school, the teacher, a co-worker, et al. (You imagine a situation.) We must try to prevent this from happening. When it does happen we must correct it.

Perception is also dependent on the fact that different people have different attitudes concerning the same thing—the same old thing really is not the same for different people. Each of us behaves according to a unique you or I or they or them.

From all of this, as you can surmise, a large share of our discernible personal public relations problems are, or will be, traceable to *mis*perception. Suppose, in class, you make a suggestion for the teacher to cover a new aspect of a course, believing it will give you and your classmates a better grasp of the subject. One of your classmates, call him Tom, sees only extra work — thanks to you. In another example, you initiate a new system at the plant which makes a task easier and increases productivity, too. One of your subordinates, call her Mary, sees only a threat to her job.

Some misperceptions and misconceptions are, of course, inevitable. But if you carefully plan, communicate, and execute your action properly, they can be minimized. For instance, if classmate Tom were made an ally *before* your suggestion was made to the teacher, what then? If Mary had input into your new system *before* it was initiated, or had knowledge that it would *not* make her job unnecessary, what then? They may have understood your motivation and you might even have motivated them.

Motivation

Motivation is the *why* of behavior. It comes in two ways. Primary motives are those things and actions that are essential to our well-being and survival — self-preservation; the avoidance of pain, hunger and thirst; sex; and familial instinct. Secondary motives are our needs and desires for success — good health; moral religious conformity; peer approval; the acquisition of things; the need to be informed; hedonism; achievement; recognition; and other learned motives, much, if not all, of which could be defined as self-interests.

Motivation then is the fuel that drives us to constructively use our abilities to gain affection, acceptance, wealth, power, importance, protection, _____, _____, or _____, — whatever *your* motives are.

Most of us are not driven by a single motive, but rather by several, sometimes with a domino effect of one leaning on, or leading to, another. Economic protection, for instance, leading to wealth, and that leading to acceptance, and that leading to affection, etc. Sometimes we even find ourselves caught in the middle, between two peer groups, between two personal attitudes or desires. We must then make a choice. We must decide what would give us the most satisfaction with the least amount of difficulty in attaining it.

Between the pressures of two peer groups, and motivated by self-preservation, Peter denied Christ three times, until his fear of displeasing God became stronger than his fear of pain or death.

Sometimes when a need becomes too great, discomfort, displeasure, and sometimes even pain may result. One of our basic motivations is the avoidance of pain. We have a reflex behavior (we'll pull our hand back from a flame), and we have learned behavior (we'll pick up pieces of broken glass very carefully). But what of mental pain? Suppose we are frustrated by someone, which can, of course, result in physical pain (an ulcer, for instance, or indigestion)? But wait. We're talking about trying to avoid pain. What do we do in the face of an impending confrontation? Do we try to regress, escape, avoid pain? Or do we turn to aggression? Fight back? If we do fight, they then have a decision to make — fight back or run. Normally, people fight back, one way or another. So it behooves us to look for ways to prevent *their* pain, prevent frustrating *them*, so that we will not become a target of *their* aggression. How do we do that? Maybe by using behavior modification or positive reinforcement. Maybe by using incentives — those external factors that act as goals.

Incentives come in two packages: Negative (you're studying for an exam on a subject you think is super dull, you feel the urge to quit and take in a movie); Positive (which incidentally comes also in two styles — psychological and physiological). A Positive incentive can reduce a drive by satisfying you psychologically — your perceived need for good grades to get into the college of your choice, to get into graduate school, to get a degree with honors, to satisfy someone, etc., keeps you at the books even if the subject *is* super dull. A positive incentive can also satisfy a physical need — a Big Mac when your stomach is growling.

Sometimes one incentive can affect another, i.e., the need for food can distract the mind trying to satisfy the need for good grades.

Because incentives interact with drives, and because they can be negative or positive, conflicts can develop. You may have occasion to choose between two attractive alternatives. For instance, a college student may have to choose between two equally interesting courses, even between two equally attractive people to take to a party. The choice may be quite easy as either will be satisfying and acceptable. But suppose it's a toss-up between two alternatives of which neither is acceptable or satisfying? — "Son! Either you're going to summer school this year to improve your grades, or you can come down to work in my factory putting little nuts on little bolts on the assembly line!" Now that's a little harder, but still not a real difficult decision to make because all you're really doing is choosing the lesser of two evils. The real hard decision to make is when there is a balance — where one is attracted and repelled at the same time. For instance, you need money. You can have a job that pays quite well but is extremely boring, or Dad will loan you the money with a few strings attached.

You should be getting the idea about now that your goal-directed behavior depends to a great deal on your needs and drives, and on the different incentives available. Just as important for you to realize — so does *theirs*.

Many psychologists believe that anxiety, affiliation, and achievement — the three A's — are the most significant human motives. Just think of your first day in a new job, in a new class, on your first date. Chances are all three A's were called in. Did you feel anxious? Did you observe others (him or her) trying to conform, hoping to be accepted, liked?

Freud regarded fear, shame, and guilt as different forms of anxiety, produced when we find ourselves in a situation with varying degrees of danger. Is that what we felt in that new situation — fear that we'd foul up, shame if we did, and the aspect of guilt? It's nice to know that this type of thing affects *them* too, isn't it? That they, like us, have the basic needs and drives such as hunger and thirst. That they, as do we, have acquired other motives — achievement, for instance — through conditioning and learning. That each of us have cognitive functions such as thought, memory, and foresight that can enter into our motivation and that, aware of our actions, we actively anticipate and weigh their consequences, and decide and plan what to do that will satisfy our needs and desires most effectively.

Isn't it nice to know that motives involve needs, and needs can be aroused by internal or external factors; and that motives involve drives and incentives to incite action; and because we know this we may be able to provide the factors — incentives for instance — that act as goals to arouse *their* drives, that lead to a goal-directed behavior—*the* goal-directed behavior that *we* would like to see.

Motivation, then, is the force that moves a person to act in certain ways. It is used for gain by advertisers who lure us into buying this or that, going here or there, doing something or not doing something; it is used to coerce us, persuade us, or dissuade us; it is used to arouse our needs, desires, and drives. It is used to move us. Consequently it can be used *by us* — to move *them.*

While motivation — the inner needs and desires that direct much of our behavior — is responsible for a large side of our behavior, there is yet another side we should consider — those bodily changes and "experience" feelings that spur many of our actions — Emotion.

Emotion

What is an emotion? The dictionary says it is a state of mind in which feeling, sentiment, or attitude is predominant over cognition and volition.

The British psychologist, William McDougall (1871-1938) listed seven basic motivating instincts and stated that each gave rise to a corresponding primary emotion, and, further, that all other emotions came from these primary emotions: Flight (fear); Repulsion (disgust); Curiosity (wonder); Pugnacity (anger); Self-abasement (subjection); Self-assertion (elation); and Parental Care (tenderness).

To illustrate the instinct for self-assertion, McDougall cited animals — the peacock fanning its tail, the pigeon puffing its breast — and he noted that children will often perform even before they talk or walk. According to his theory, the emotion generated by that self-assertion is elation. Would that be confirmed by many a politician, the valedictorian or sports jock at your school, or someone else you know?

Emotions can also result in body changes that others may or may not be able to see. Anger, for instance, can increase your pulse and your blood pressure, make you red as the blood nears the skin's surface, put a scowl on your face, sparks in your eye, or beads of sweat on your forehead.

Emotions are often caused by external situations. We have learned that frustration — someone being thwarted in pursuit of a goal — is one of the chief causes of aggression and anger. Then we must also realize that aggression and anger can be directed by our/their goal-directed behavior to overcome, or to at least diminish, the frustration.

If the frustration is caused by a peer, or a subordinate, the recipient may find an outlet for his anger, but if it's caused by a supervisor or superior, he may have to wait until he gets home to shout at the kids, bark at his wife, and kick the dog.

Conflicts may also give rise to emotions when motives clash or goals are wanted, but feared. You may, for instance, *want* to learn scuba-diving, but feel panic at the thought of sharks.

Some emotional stimuli seems to produce similar responses in everyone — the reaction to pain which will make a wounded animal fight harder in a frenzy of fear and rage, will, especially when coupled with self-preservation, do the same for a man or woman.

Keep in mind, too, that emotions, even in their minutest manifestations, are a legitimate source of information. Body language, facial expressions, etc., can tell us much about the real feelings of someone toward us, something we've said, or something we've done. And vice-versa. Always vice-versa. *What we can learn about them, they can learn about us, in the same way.*

It is often difficult to distinguish between emotions and motives, but: Emotions are frequently seen in facial expressions, motives are not; emotions are usually pleasant or unpleasant, motives usually are devoid of either of these feelings; emotions are usually the result of how we perceive a situation, thought, or circumastance, while motives are usually produced wholly in our minds. Sometimes, too, the fourth factor — learning experience — plays a part in the process.

Learning Experience

Interwoven with motivation, perception, and emotions is our (and their) learned experiences from our earliest childhood, and the depositing and recording of these experiences in our personal memory bank. This is the way you have, and will, build your beliefs, values, convictions, cautions, fears, etc., so that you may draw on your memory bank whenever a stimulus stirs up not only a similar experience, but all its emotions as well.

For instance, a mannerism of a stranger in an elevator may trigger a feeling of intense dislike if it resembles one possessed by some teacher you had and hated years before. Or some classmate you detested. Or, you may never realize that a slight resemblance to your strict and overbearing aunt made you feel uncomfortable with a woman you've just met. And, is love at first sight really love at first sight? On any given occasion the stimulus you feel might not even be exactly the same as the one it recalls; a single aspect can arouse a whole complex emotional mood and you may never understand where your feelings came from.

It is only important to your P.P.R. to realize that this *can* happen to you. And it *can* happen to them, the people you have to deal with.

Unfortunately, we cannot see an emotion, but we can see some indicators of emotion — usually facial expressions, voice tones, and body movements. While these will be discussed in the chapter on communications, it is sufficient to realize, at this time, that we can *send* signals to others, or we can *receive* them from others, and *either* can affect our P.P.R.

You should be able to see now that your goal-directed behavior depends on your motivation, your needs, and your drives; its close ally, emotion; your perception of the factors involved; the incentives for success; and your learned experiences. This applies to us *and* to him, or to her, or to them.

Okay, we've skimmed the psychological aspects of what makes us (and them) tick — now what? We are not psychologists. We are just people who are becoming more aware of the importance of our personal public relations. And, like P.R. profesionals, we want to know how to solve problems. We want to know what works.

> "One pound of learning requires 10 pounds
> of common sense to apply it."
> (Persian Proverb)

What we want to do is explore public opinion — our public's opinion of us — what we can do about it, and how. Can we prevent P.P.R. problems? What can we do about the problems that inevitably arise? Patience. Before we can tackle P.P.R. problems we must first determine the make-up of our publics. What are they? Who are they?

5

Your Publics — Who Are They?

Every person you deal with, interact with, or relate to, is a member of one of your publics.

Why must you know who they are as a public? Because each of them, as individuals or as members of a group, large or small, has an opinion about many things, not the least of which is you.

So, before we determine just *who* your publics are, let's think a little about them and public opinion in general.

Public Opinion

It has been said that opinion is truth filtered through what I call a person's Six P's — predilection, predisposition, proclivity, preconception, perception, and prejudice.

You have an opinion. I have an opinion. So does she. And so does he. And that adds up to a collection of individual opinions that, when shared by others, becomes public opinion.

If it's a small group who share a common interest, it is that particular public's opinion. If it is shared by other publics, the public becomes larger and more powerful. An opinion not being shared by another segment of the public can result in opposition, creating conflict. Enter you. Depending with whom your opinion agrees or disagrees, and how it may affect you, an opinion in conflict could be very difficult to deal with — you may not wish to take sides.

Witness the evolution of the publics for and against abortion. You may decide to remain neutral on such an issue, at least publicly — in office, social, or other situations. If you're anti-abortion there is no sense debating it with your pro-abortion boss, is there? Unless you think it's more important to change his or her mind than to get ahead in your career. And what if he, or she, thinks it's important to change *your* mind?

Whether you are pro or con is not important to your P.P.R. What is important is who agrees or disagrees with you. Who, within your spheres of influence must you consider? Whose conflicting opinion, and reaction, could affect you emotionally, physically, financially? Should you, in fact, remain publicly neutral? Can you? Only you can answer, and only after evaluating all the circumstances, options, and possible repercussions of your actions. You must be careful discussing such things as abortion, gun control, environmental problems, capital punishment, and a host of other potentially inflammatory subjects. Be sure you know him first. Is he a zealot or is he openminded? Can he discuss an issue logically or will he let his emotions color his viewpoint? Is he a peer, a subordinate or a superior? Is it really important to convert him to your viewpoint or not? Can you win a battle, but lose an ally? And, if you lose enough allies can you lose a war?

The bottom line? Can *he* or *she* help you or hurt you?

People crave something to love and people crave something to hate. Many think we're happiest when we have *both* cravings — a cause to fight for and a cause to fight against. Do we want to be the object of his or her love, or hate?

Now, no one wants to be a bland, milksop, eager-to-please, afraid-to-offend toady, trying to be everything to everyone, but neither do we have to pick a fight that costs too much to win. It may seem basic, but in every fight there is a winner *and* a loser.

A fight (disagreement or even a heated discussion) need not be on a potentially inflammatory subject. It can be a trivial subject. Pick one. You may just encounter a person who cannot stand to be wrong. He may be a peer, who someday might be important to you, or he may be a superior who is. And, most of the time, the subject matter will not be important. So why belabor a point? What is there to gain? More importantly, what is there to lose? It's not a question of whether you shall be right. It is, rather, will you be the person to prove him wrong? Can he live with being proved wrong without harboring a grudge — consciously or subconsciously?

I've had encounters of this kind. So will you. I've smiled while thinking to myself: "Well, my friend. You are wrong. I am positive you are wrong. But you know something — I don't really care. Someday you'll probably find out you're wrong. So, for now, in your blissful ignorance, think that you're right."

(That's an approximation of my thought language translated for a PG rating. You may, of course, enjoy *your* thoughts as you wish.)

Then there's the straddle, used by many politicos taking their stance, for instance, on abortion: "Personally, I am against abortion, but I must support a woman's right to make her own decision." Actually, that is the only statement that will (they hope) not alienate voters on either side of the issue.

Opinion Can Change

Public opinion, of course, is not cast in stone. It can shift, like the wind, especially if attitudes are shocked by a bold action into changing. An assassination, for instance, can change one particular group, or public, from anti- to pro-capital punishment, from anti- to pro-gun control. But, by-and-large public opinion reverses itself gradually. As information is fed to and acquired by a particular public — whether it feeds that public's interest or not — it will result in a heightening or diminishing of their attitude to the particular issue. This is very evident on a national scale as the American public is subjected to more and more polls, bombarded with varying viewpoints and actions by various spokespeople of varying influence with varying powers of persuasion. This is mainly due to the improvement, over the years, of communication, especially the immediateness, convenience, and broad dissemination powers of television, and the acquisition of knowledge on how to use the medium effectively.

We have only to look at the approval/disapproval percentages of a President from poll to poll to see how the public can vacillate as "news" commentators tell them what the President will say, what he has said, and what he really meant by what he said.

We Have Many Publics

The President of the United States, of course, has many diverse publics — the Congress; state, county, city, and local governments; various special interest groups and their lobbies; the Armed Forces; foreign governments (whether pro- or anti-American, or even neutral); people in or out of his party; but the biggest public is you and I — members of the general public — at least every four years.

Members of large groups, many times, are members of smaller groups as well. A national group, for instance, may be together on one issue and splinter on another. The mass of people in our country is one of the President's largest publics. In lesser numbers, however, parts of them can be members of another of his publics. While agreeing with the President on broad issues, they may be against, be neutral, or be opposed to something at the same time. A farmer, as a member of the larger, general public group, may have an attitude, pro or con, relating to some aspect of foreign relations. At the same time, as a part of the "farm vote" he may be concerned, and in disagreement, with price supports or parity. His vested interest, in fact, could very well color his attitude differently from the general public who may not even know the definition of parity. In the early 1980's, for instance, many farmers were in a quandry, agreeing on the one hand with the foreign policy aspects of the wheat embargo (to the Soviet Union), but not particularly caring for the impact on them.

The same problems arise across other groups of publics. The steel worker may want a restriction on imported steel, but the farmer, fearing a reaction in the form of a retaliatory restriction on imported beef by the steel-exporting nation, may not want such a restriction.

When motivations are involved, conflicts of this nature can occur, either within the attitudes of a single public, or crossing the lines of two or more publics. They will occur in the President's publics, and in our publics. Our job is to try and prevent such conflicts within our publics (regarding our performances), and to avoid the conflicts of *his* (whoever *he* is), publics, or to at least minimize their affects.

It's easy to see that there is an overlapping of interests, self-interests, vested interests — what's best for me, what's best for us, what's best for them. Usually what's best for me... how does it affect me... prevails. We must be carefully aware of this when we're dealing with our publics, whoever they are.

Who are your publics? That's a question that only you can answer precisely. With some guidelines, some thought, and some examples, it's a question you *can* answer.

I can tell you, for instance, who a university's primary publics are — the students, the faculty, the employees, the alumni, prospective students, the board of trustees, governments (officials) who regulate and provide grants, foundations, and corporations for research contracts and grants as well as recruiting, and Town and Gown Relations — the people of the community, be they government or business leaders, merchants, service organizations, or, the great majority, just people.

How about the primary publics of a hospital — inpatients, outpatients, medical staff, nursing staff, employees, board members, friends and relatives of patients, visitors, volunteers, government on a local, state, and federal level (regulations, laws, Medicare, Medicaid), Blue Cross/Blue Shield and other insurers, donors, ambulance services, vendors, and, again, just people.

Who Are Your Publics ?

As we begin identifying your publics, let us remember that all of them will not be equally important to you. Let's remember, too, that some members of your publics may impact upon you differently, in different situations and circumstances.

To begin, let's divide a sheet of paper into two parts or columns. Label the top of the page "Sphere I — These People Can Affect My Happiness." In the left column, write the group name; in the right column break down the group specifically, i.e., names will help you define and delineate each of these people. Label a second sheet of paper "Sphere II — These People Can Affect My Career And Finances." A third sheet will be labeled "Sphere III — Members Of A Public Who Can Influence Sphere I or II."

To begin, let's fill in your Sphere I sheet. Write the name of the most important group in the left-side column and then the names and relationships of that group in the right-hand column. Next will come the second most-important group, then the third, and so on. Your completed sheet will look something like this:

SPHERE I — These People Can Affect My Happiness:

Immediate Family — Blood Relatives	Parents, brothers (John, James), sisters (Mary, Jane), nieces (Linda, June), nephews (Robert, Mark, John).
Immediate Family — In-law	Parents-, brothers-(Al, Lou), sisters-(Alice), nieces-(Mary, Jane), nephews-(James).
Secondary Family — First Line	Aunt Jane, Aunt Mary, Uncle John, Uncle Anthony; their children (my first cousins) that I interact with (Joe, Lou, Teresa, Rita) on a regular basis.
Secondary Family — Second Line	All other relatives that I see and interact with on an occasional ba-

	sis. Mother's brother, Uncle Jack, Father's sister, Aunt Mame, first cousin, Mike.
Close Friends	People I see and interact with on a regular basis. (Name, occupation, age, etc.) *Asterisk those who are both a friend and a co-worker. Even those who may be a client, patient, customer, as well as a friend.
Secondary Friends	People I see and interact with on an occasional basis. *Asterisk those who fall into multiple catagories.
Acquaintances	I may play golf, tennis, or racquetball with them, but they are not really friends. *Asterisk those...
Church Member/Pastor	*Asterick those...
Members — Fraternal, Civic, Social, Club, Lodge, etc.	*Asterick those...
Enemies	*Asterisk those simultaneously fitting into any other categories.

There may be some people who fit into one or more categories (a church member who is also a friend), or into more than one sphere (a church member who is also a friend; who is also a client, patient, co-worker, boss, etc.), who will fit into your Sphere II listing). Fill your list accordingly, including, rather than excluding, a person where questionable.

Your second sheet, labeled "Sphere II — These People Can Affect My Career and Finances" is compiled as an employee, the proprietor of a business or a practice, etc. Once again, name names. It will help you to discover and delineate these people who can affect your career and finances. Your second sheet will look something like this:

SPHERE II — These People Can Affect My Career And Finances:

Top Management / Home Office	Even if this is only by directive (memos, policy statements, etc. from the home office) I want to know who "they" are and what "their" objectives, goals, policies, etc. are, and what they expect from me?
Management Team / Local Office	In smaller companies this may be the same as above. In any case you want to know who they are and what they want— from you, *their* superiors, and the company.
Immediate Supervisor	This is *the* person who can take credit for all the good things you do and who will take part of the blame for your foul-ups...maybe.
Executive Secretaries	Their secretaries...his secretary...my secretary. Important than for no other reason than they have daily contact with *him* or *her* or *them*.
Co-Workers	These are your peers. Someday he or she may be your boss, or vice president...possibly even in a different company. What do they want from you, from others, from the company?

Subordinates	These are the people for whom you can take the credit for the good things they accomplish, and some of the blame for their errors.
Support Service Employees	All departments, to some extent, must rely on other departments for something — the people who manage these departments, the key people, on occasion the workers, may be able to affect your career.
Maintenance/Housekeeping	If he likes you he just might fix your typewriter/ phone/ pencil sharpener, etc., before he fixes someone else's; she may keep your desk area/ office/ etc., just a little bit neater. Remember, too, he and she, talk to them.
Business Associations/ Organizations	Never underestimate the fact that your boss may take an outsider's assessment of you as gospel; as "one of your peers" talking about you. These colleagues are also a part of your career network. Many of them can be an asset or a debit. Who are they?
Business Services	They are the vendors, detail people, sales people, etc., and they

Your Publics — Who Are They?

	know what's going on in your industry, your field. They even know about competition— yours and your companys.
Business Neighbors	These people share a floor, a building, an interest, whatever. Who are they? What do they, can they, mean to your success?
Competitors/Business Enemies	If there is interaction, either direct or through third parties, do more listening than speaking. But above all, know them—who they are?
Customers/ Clients/ Patients	If you deal with them, know as much as you can about them. Why? Maybe that disgruntled / satisfied client just happens to be a second cousin to the judge you'll be pleading a case before next month. Maybe that satisfied customer just happens to be the assessor who'll be evaluating your tax liability. Maybe that unhappy patient's son-in-law is a reporter, a policeman, a mailman, whatever. If you can't know each of them at least treat them as if they could have some affect on your success. Just in case.

Friends / Enemies	Some of those listed in other categories will also fit the category of friend or enemy. Who are they? Mark accordingly.

In delineating the Sphere II people who can affect your career and finances, you must tailor your list to your circumstances. If you happen to be a student instead of an employee, your SPHERE II columns might look like this:

School Board / Trustees	Most colleges and many small school districts have boards that get involved in everything from complaints, to teachers' raises, to line-by-line budgets.
Dean/ Principal/ Assistants	These people are your authority figures when you're in school, and they could be your boss someday if you enter the education field. In school or afterward they may be used as references, as allies, as mentors, as advocates, etc.
Professors/ Teachers	They can make school life pleasant... easier... more rewarding. A student that does well is a credit to their teaching. So do well... or try to do well. They'll help.
Classmate(s)	Just like fellow employees, they have their objectives; they have their allies in both the student body

Your Publics — Who Are They?

	and teacher / professor ranks. Some can be friends. Some can be enemies. Who are they?
Student Body As A Group	There's safety and power in numbers. Who are the leaders?
School Employees	Like corporate support staff they can make life harder or easier. Know them.
Student Clubs / Organizations	When you belong you have all the prestige and power of the group. Who are the principals?
Friends/Enemies	You probably have both...Who are they?

If you were a professor or a teacher you may have used Principal, President, or Dean, as boss; Professor or Teacher as co-worker; Students or Assistants as subordinates, etc. in your SPHERE II listing.

If you are in business for yourself, or a professional, you would have a SPHERE II list of clients, patients, customers, vendors, suppliers, associates, competitors, et al.

We now come to Sphere III. Are they important to everyday living for the average person? They are members of the public who could possibly — now or in the future — influence those you listed in either Sphere I or Sphere II. They themselves can, first-hand or second-hand, even affect your happiness or your finances. They may even make it into Sphere I or II at some future time.

Sphere III might contain such names as members of the police and fire departments; the post office; officials — both minor and major — of your local government; your bank or banker; the local garageman or mechanic; the repairman of your appliances, systems, etc.; shopkeepers and merchants; those who provide such services as utilities, fuel, gardening, snow removal, rubbish removal, odd jobs, etc.; an attorney, your clergyman, dentist, physician, accountant, and, of course, those that might know or be known by your enemies.

These people are seemingly unimportant, might by your initial reaction. But...Is the girl who checks you out at the local supermarket your husband's boss' niece? Did you know the chief of police's nephew mowed your lawn last summer? You didn't know that the Town Assessor's brother-in-law emptied your trash cans each week? Can you get to see your dentist at three o'clock in the morning if you had to? These are, of course, hypothetical examples, but I'm sure you get the idea — it pays to treat everybody just as nice as you would like to be treated yourself.

List them on your SPHERE III list. If you don't know a name, give one. One by one, we, in my family, started to go to a certain gas station, and now the four of us go once a week to "the little man" in our neighborhood. He treats us very nice, always has a greeting and a smile, and even gave me credit one day when I forgot my credit card.

Your SPHERE III list could look something like this:

SPHERE III — Members Of A Public Who Can Influence Sphere I or II:

Supermarket Manager(s);	If he or she tells you about Mrs. Jones.
Checkout People	Does he or she tell Mrs. Jones about you? If so, what?
Gas Station Little Man	Does anyone from the office come here too? From the P.T.A.? From the lodge?
Garageman	Gordie (Roger and Russ). He's not only the guy who keeps your car running, he might be a member of the volunteer fire department and emergency squad, your lodge, etc.
Mailman	Hi! He knows everybody in this neighborhood.
Paperboy Johnny Doe.	His dad may work for the county, his uncle for the town.

You've finished your three lists and now you know who *they* are — your publics. What about them? Especially those on your Sphere II list. It will contribute greatly to your success — career or otherwise — if you learn all you can about each of them — attitude in general, and their attitude toward you and your objectives in particular. Even if you find that an attitude toward you is basically non-existent or neutral — that, too, is important information to know.

If an attitude toward you is not favorable — Why? Must you overcome a prejudice, jealousy, misunderstanding, a predisposition, bias, et al? Can the attitude be changed? Is there a common interest to build on?

These questions are most important and hardest to answer about those on your Sphere II list — people who can affect your career and finances. We already know much about those on our Sphere I list (many are relatives) and in most cases we have built a solid relationship with them (or at least we know where we stand). Those on our Sphere III list can usually be handled with a pleasant smile, a kind word, appreciation, and consideration — tactics that are beneficial in dealing with any and all of our publics.

So let us now concentrate on those listed on your Sphere II list; those people who can affect your career and your finances. People in your everyday work-a-day world.

My Fellow-Workers Public

When it comes to your fellow workers — and that is *anybody* who works for the company — get to know all of them. The amount of knowledge you want is directly proportional to the importance to your career that you place upon any individual. All will have *some* bearing, so you want to know *something* about all of them.

Years ago I went to work for a medium-sized university's public relations department. The director was reorganizing the department on an advertising agency account executive concept. Under his plan one P.R. individual would oversee and administer *all* of an "account's" public relations needs — writing, editing, and producing printed promotional material, newsletters, news releases, posters, public service announcements; dissemination of information; media selection and media relations. An "account" would be a school, a department, a unit, or a program.

I began my new job taking responsibilty for two schools, three programs, three ROTC units, and the Graduate School. Surprisingly, one of my new accounts evoked a common comment from several secretaries, the head of the print shop, and the graphic designer:

"Good God. They've given you Doctor X!!!"

Dr. X, the head of a program closely tied to industrial needs for his students, was old, renowned, European, and an iron-handed conservative. Industry wanted his students because of their practical training. So much so, in fact, that they would offer higher than average starting salaries for his graduates, as well as financial contributions to the program itself. All of this made his program financially valuable to the university, prestigious for both the university and its students, and popular to potential students interested in the discipline and in working in the industry.

One of the stories I heard told of a young student, standing before Dr. X's desk, wanting to transfer into the program. This in the late 1960's. Dr. X looked up and suggested matter-of-factly that they might discuss such a transfer as soon as the young man returned from the barber shop.

My new co-workers briefed me about other accounts. Dean Y and Dean Z were easier to get along with than Dr. X (everybody was), but "they expected too much, were short on patience, and thought that our department considered them *the smaller schools* (which they were) and that the department treated them accordingly (which they didn't? I wouldn't!). The three ROTC units? They weren't very popular during those, the Vietnam War years. In addition to on-campus (internal) P.R. problems, and town and gown relations problems, there were inter-service rivalries.

This was the picture in which I was a central figure. The situation I began thinking about. I remembered a story my father told me about two travelers in the midwest:

The first traveler, Tom, stopped in a small town and, after checking into the small hotel, sat on the porch next to one of the natives.

"What kind of folks do you have around these parts?" Tom asked.

"Well, what kind of folks live back in your hometown?" The native answered, with a question of his own.

"Selfish people." Tom answered. "Loners, not very friendly. Some are even downright nasty."

"Same kind we got around here," the native answered, shaking his head.

A few days later the second traveler, Bob, stopped by and he checked into the small hotel. He, too, sat on the porch next to the very same native.

"What kind of folks do you have around these parts?" Bob asked.

"Well, what kind of folks live back in your hometown?" The native answered.

"Wonderful people." Bob answered. "Friendly and kind. Really great people."

"Same kind we got around here," the native answered, smiling.

Learning About Specific Them

First I got the bio out of the file on each of them — Dr. X, Dean Y and Dean Z, the three ROTC commandants, and the two program chairmen. I made a little notebook from those small pads that fit into your suit pocket. On each page I put their name and title and a small photo — a head shot. I put down all pertinent information — how long they were at the university, whether they were married, had children, names, hobbies — especially hobbies — and anything I thought was important of a trivial nature, e.g., one was an avid woodworker and had a complete workshop in his basement, another was a model train enthusiast, one would rather play golf than eat.

Can you picture his surprise and delight when I introduced myself to one of them as he walked across campus? Can you imagine the rapport I built when I casually mentioned my collection of American Flyer model trains to another while we were discussing a school project in his office? Would you believe that a scheduled 30-minute initial meeting with one of the deans (the avid woodworker) lasted for one hour and thirty minutes? And we hardly explored the fact that my father was a professional furniture maker. Would you be surprised to learn that when I left some five years later I received more than 25 letters I can still use as letters of recommendation?

Yes. Get to know as much as you can about everyone you will be dealing with in your career life. How much? To repeat: Proportionate to the importance of that person to your success (especially true for number one — your boss!), and the magnitude of your present and future interaction.

Learning About Your Boss

In addition to learning as much as you can about him or her on a personal level — married, divorced, widowed; children (their ages, schools, names, etc.); likes and dislikes; hobbies; important trivia; ambitions, goals, objectives — you must, of course, learn as much as you can on a business level — when did he or she start with the company and what was his progression throught the ranks; were there previous companies, titles, responsibilities and achievements; what schools did he attend and what degrees were earned; what organizations, clubs, societies, or associations does he belong to and, then, through observation, WHAT KIND OF A PERSON IS HE/SHE, REALLY?

We will learn how to track down the nitty-gritty information we need to know specifically about *your* boss (or anyone else for that matter) as we go along, especially in Chapter 13. For now, let's become acquainted once again with the psychological profiles that can help us to know him, or her, in general way.

Professional consultants talk about a person being a Driver, an Analytical, an Amiable, or an Expressive. We will, of course, only scratch the surface in our examination of these types of personalities. Most people — your boss included — will probably be a combination of two or more of these —BUT— USUALLY — ONE QUALITY *WILL BE* DOMINANT. That's the one you will concentrate on. (In addition to your boss, these styles or qualities may be assessed in your spouse or future spouse, your mother-in-law, your teacher, your neighbor, a sibling, a co-worker, et al. Anyone *you* consider important to your happiness and/or *your* career.)

The Driver

A Driver is usually autocratic, is efficient, wants to know options and probabilities before making decisions. He measures values by results. He is interested in "what" rather than who, why or how. He wants control and he wants support. He wants to build a kingdom he can call his own.

If your boss (spouse, friend, brother, etc.) is a Driver, remember that he will be measuring *you* by results. He likes time-saving ideas, especially if they save *him* time. He requires time to be used efficiently. He wants you to tell him "what" something is all about, not how or why it will happen. He wants *you* to give him options based on probabilities if he has to make a decision. He must have control. He doesn't really like to listen and should probably do it better. He's probably too autocratic. The Driver is characterized as one who *tells* you what to do. He's very assertive and self-controlled. He makes an effort to control people while he controls himself. He doesn't show his emotions and feelings too easily or readily. He is task-oriented, knows what he wants, where he's going, and how he plans to get there.

He's determined, decisive, and dominating; tough-minded, pushy, and harsh; thorough and efficient. He will handle problems or tensions by asserting himself and maintaining control over himself. Actually, he is a control specialist.

The Expressive

An Expressive is usually action-oriented. He wants support for his dreams and wants incentives or testimony before having to make a decision. He will measure results or personal values by "applause." He's interested in the "who" of something rather than the what, why, or how. He craves social acceptance. He wants to stimulate others.

If your boss is an Expressive he will meausure *your* performance by the quantity and quality of *your* applause for *his efforts* — especially the quality of your applause. He likes effort-saving ideas, especially if they save *him* effort. He requires time to be stimulating. He wants to know "who" is involved in something, not what, why, or how. He wants *you* to give *him* an incentive and testimonial evidence if *he* has to make a decision. He wants to be sociable. He needs support for his dreams... *from you.*

The Expressive is a person who is highly assertive (like the Driver), but is also responsive. He will, indeed make his feelings known, but instead of trying to control his emotions he will react, even impulsively, either in a positive or negative way. He puts more value on relationships than on tasks. He is highly intuitive and will trust his instincts rather than objective data.

He is gregarious, enthusiastic, personable, and stimulating; can be dramatic and reactive, manipulative and excitable. He is a social specialist. He handles problems and tensions by asserting himself while relaxing the control over his emotions.

The Amiable

An Amiable usually agrees with people. He takes the time to be agreeable. He needs guarantees and assurances to make decisions. He is usually supportive, is interested in the "why" of things rather than the who, what, or how. He measures personal values by attention received.

If your boss is an Amiable he is an acquiescer, an agree-minded person, and he probably is not *really* your boss, or anyone's boss. He is interested in preserving relationships, measures his personal values by the attention he receives from others. He will take the time to be agreeable and he requires guarantees and assurances *from you* if he is to make a decision. He is supportive and he is more interested in "why" something will or is happening. He is, above all, amiable.

The Amiable is a person who doesn't tell — he asks. He will display his feelings quite openly. He is agreeable, less aggressive and assertive than the Driver or Expressive. He is probably a very nice person. Maybe too nice to be a boss.

He, or she, is the support specialist. He is conforming, dependent, ingratiating, respectful, willing, agreeable, and supportive. He handles tension and problems, not by asserting himself, but by sharing his emotions. As a support person he could be your immediate boss, but it is unlikely that he's in a position to run *the* show.

The Analytical

An Analytical needs a climate that provides details. He wants evidence and statistics for making his decision. He is interested in the "how" of anything rather than the who, what, or why. Accuracy is his big virtue and he seeks that kind of support for the espousal of anyone's principles or thoughts.

If your boss (spouse, friend, sibling, neighbor) is an Analytical he needs an environment that provides him with lots of details. He wants *you* to take the time to be accurate, and then give him plenty of evidence that he can use to make a decision. He appreciates and needs support for *his* thinking and principles and he expects *you* to support *yours*. He is more interested in the "how" it's going to be and expects you to have the answer when he asks — How?

He asks, and he controls. He may not seem to assert himself because he can also control his emotions. But he'll be the kind of boss that will ask questions, gather facts, and examine all sides of every question or problem.

The Analytical is a technical specialist. He is exacting, persistent, orderly, serious, and vigilant. He is also critical, indecisive, can be stuffy and moralistic. He can maintain his emotional control when confronted with a tense problem or situation and will not *have* to assert himself. He is, in short, analytical.

Many consultants feel that for someone to have reached a position of power—real power—the president of a small corporation, the executive vice president of a medium-sized company, or the vice president, or higher, of a large corporation—that your boss probably is a driver with one or more of the other three qualilities as a sub-quality.

To help you recognize *your* boss (or spouse, sibling, co-worker, etc.), consultants talk also about how responsive or how assertive a person is.

Assertive And Responsive Traits

A person is considered *highly-assertive* when he or she makes statements more often than he asks questions; leans forward to make a point; emphasizes ideas by changing the tone of his voice;

more often than not uses dominant or aggressive expressions; clearly lets you know what it is he wants; and has a firm handshake.

A person is considered *low-assertive* when he asks questions more times than he makes statements; tends to lean backwards when he speaks; speaks in deliberate, slow, or studied manner; seldom uses his voice, his expressions, or posture to emphasize ideas; is vague, almost unclear about what he wants from you; and has an indifferent handshake.

A person is considered *highly-responsive* when he is attentive; makes frequent eye contact, often in a friendly gaze; smiles or nods or frowns; uses animated facial expressions; does little asking about facts; makes friendly gestures, and shares personal feelings.

A person is considered *low-responsive* when he is poker-faced, reserved, and vigilant; is cautious and careful about his actions; makes infrequent eye contact while listening; makes limited use of his hands and, when he does, they are clenched, folded, or pointed; presses for facts and details; and limits small talk, or talk about his personal feelings.

Once again it is important to remind you that most people — boss, your spouse, your neighbor — will not fit neatly into one category. There is another way of analyzing his or her personality that has been around since the 1940's and has been used to match up college roommates, analyze human differences, and improve management techniques.

The Myers-Briggs Type Indicator

The Myers-Briggs Type Indicator, named after creator Isabel Briggs Myers and her mother, is based on a theory of Swiss psychologist Carl Jung, who hypothesized that what seemed to be random behavioral differences did indeed make sense if you considered the various ways that people gather information, make decisions, and relate to other people.

The Myers-Briggs system delineates "people types." They can be identified by using a questionnaire or, if knowledgeable about the person, by astute observation.

A person's type is determined by selecting the naturally occurring dominant trait in a person in each of four categories of opposites:

1. Extroverts (E) direct their energy outwardly. They like to talk and to act. Introverts (I), on the other hand, like to think before they act. They prefer jobs that involve quiet, mental activity.

2. Type (S) is a person who uses his eyes, ears, and other

senses to gather and absorb information. He is realistic and adept at handling details. Intuitive Types (N), on the other hand, see deep meanings and far-ranging possibilities as they value and use their imagination.

3. Thinkers (T) make rational, logical decisions. They can easily see what's right or wrong. They analyze. Feelers (F) on the other hand, make decisions based on feelings (and feelings are based on their values). They are also tactful, compassionate, and can be *the* diplomat.

4. Judges (J) live an orderly life and the more they can control life's events the better. Perceptive types (P) on the other hand are spontaneous, welcoming new experiences.

People are, of course, combinations even though one trait may be dominating. Therefore a person could be an ENFJ (Extrovert, Intuitive, Feeling, and Judging). Or people may have built on a trait or be under stress which can bring out an unnatural quality, i.e., an I (introvert) might act like an E (extrovert) in a situation or circumstance where he or she has great confidence and feels completely at ease.

The Myers-Briggs Type method can help opposites learn to know and respect each other, experts contend. Understanding type, they say, can help improve relationships and careers.

A related theory developed by California psychologist David Kiersey, classifies people as having one of four tempernents: NF (romantic, gentle); NT (curious, logical); SJ (organized, caring); and SP (playful, free).

Kiersy is campaigning (1987) to change school curriculum to satisfy students that are often drop-outs — SPs. While many of them are talented, he contends, they dislike the structured atmosphere of school.

As you go about observing and learning about them, don't let this alphabet soup confuse or disconcert you. Rather, as a detective would do, use them as clues to know and understand what may or may not make *them* tick.

We are...they are... made up of many component parts. The material presented in this book was designed to make you think — about them, about yourself — so that you will better understand them — and you.

We must especially understand them and develop awareness so that we can relate to them, and with them. We must understand them so that we can work for them, and with them. When we know them, and understand them, we gain a greater means of predicting what they will do or say in a given circumstance. And, when the circumstance has a bearing on us — our career, our finances, our happiness — that knowledge will make it easier for us to cope with them, and will enable us to manage and control our relationships for our ultimate benefit and success.

Not only will that knowledge enable us to cope with them, but it will help us to motivate them, to push *their* buttons.

6

Motivation — Are There Buttons To Push?

In 1985, businesses across the United States spent more than $10 billion (twice the amount spent in 1980) in their effort to motivate workers with profit-sharing, luxury vacations, elaborate parties, and bonuses. That's a far cry from the days when the anomalous Henry Ford walked the production lines with his checkbook in hand, ready to reward any and all he thought was giving more than expected for the company.

You could do that, too. Your "checkbook" could be praise. Everyone wants to feel good about themselves. Your praise can help them feel that way. A bonus? It can rebound, and make you feel good about yourself.

Lots of managers know that praise goes a long way toward satisfying employees' (people's) needs to feel that their effort is being noted, is pleasing, and is being appreciated. And, lo and behold!, it even increases productivity in many cases.

Try a little praise. On your co-workers. Your employees. On your spouse. Your children. Especially on your children. Kids have a way of delivering the kind of behavior they think you expect. Tell them the kind you expect by praising that kind.

In a survey done by Knight-Ridder newspaper staff, in 1987, employees identified the most powerful non-financial motivators. The top motivator of the "top 4" was personal appreciation (congratulations) from managers. The next three, in order of rank, were promotions based on performance, public recognition of performance, and (any kind) of performance recognition.

We do things because we are motivated by a mental force that induces us to act. They do things for the same reason. If we can learn what motivates him, or her — what mental forces (emotions) or needs induce him to act, or react, in a certain way — then we can push the proper buttons that will induce him to act, if not exactly as we wish, at least, in general the way we wish.

We are already doing this — pressing their motivation buttons — by our performances. We do it mostly unconsciously, haphazardly, without knowledge, without thought, without purpose. And because we do we may not get the specific response we hoped for. Many times, in fact, we may get a response that is completely opposite to the one we desired. One that is totally uncharitable, sometimes even malevolent.

It behooves us, therefore, to learn what motivates them, what makes them tick, what concerns them, what they need or want. Then we can use that knowledge to motivate him, or her, or them.

Is this manipulation? No! Not if *you* are properly motivated. Not if *you* are genuinely concerned about his needs, his concerns, his goals.

Manipulate, in my dictionary, means to handle with skill, to influence, to adapt or change, to manage.

Is there anything wrong with dealing with people skillfully if that means knowing their needs, desires, goals, etc., and trying to help them attain their objectives in such a way as to further *your* objectives?

Is it wrong to try to influence people if it's accomplished honestly, with logic and reason — the art of gentle persuasion?

Is there anything wrong with adapting or changing one's self, tailoring one's performance, to fit into a certain pattern, situation, or circumstance?

Is there anything wrong with managing one's affairs, life, career, even circumstances where possible?

Can you really manage people? You can manage your employees' time, a subordinate's production, etc., but you can't really manage people. You can try to understand another person, be aware of his wants, needs, desires, and try to mesh them with your own so that helping him attain his, attains yours. You can, and you should.

Some may even call the concept hypocrisy. Others would answer that our society would perish without that kind of hypocrisy. They'd ask how often each of us has said "I really love that hat!" or "Your party was a lovely affair!" or "What a lovely child!" or "The roast was delicious!" when none of the statements even flirted with the truth. That, they would say, is nothing more than good manners.

The bottom line? If we are indeed now motivating him — to smile or to scowl, to be pleasant or disagreeable, to be good or bad — wouldn't it be better to know how to motivate him to smile, be pleasant, be good?

What then are the forces that motivate people?

What Motivates Them?

Simply put, we — or they — are exposed to a strong (performance) stimulus — a need that produces a drive that wants to impel us to act (respond). We then receive a cue that tells us when we will respond, where we will respond, and how. We respond. Our response, normally, is the product of our storehouse of knowledge — solutions to recurring problems or situations. Our behavior (response) is then reinforced — we are rewarded.

As a simple example — Let's say we are driving on the highway. We are hungry. Our stomach contracts, our blood sugar decreases. We feel hunger pain. Two innate primary needs — hunger and pain — have combined into one strong drive — the need to escape or alleviate. The strong drive impels us to act. We look for a diner. We receive a cue — a sign. The "Golden Arches." The thought of food increases the stimulus, the pain, and consequently the drive. We stop. We eat. We are rewarded with cessation of pain. A feeling of contentment and satisfaction follows.

Incentives, of course, interact with drives. If the only food available was liver and onions, and you could not tolerate even the thought of it, the sight and smell of liver and onions may actually reduce your hunger drive.

Another example. Our acquired need for money as a means of gratifying many of our other needs and wants, creates a drive that impels us to act to further our career. We note the differences between our behavior, dress, speech, etc., and that of our colleagues, especially our superiors. That notation becomes the cue that ignites our emotion, our motivation. We adapt. We change our behavior, our dress, our speech — whatever — to imitate or to conform to our peers, our superiors. We are rewarded with acceptance. We have climbed the first rung on our career ladder.

How do we motivate them? In addition to special "buttons" there are those we all share. Here are a dozen of them.

A Dozen Motivational Buttons

1. Security
We all want to be safe. Safe in our relationships — business or

personal, and safe in an economic sense. We are concerned with our security now and for our future. Some of us even crave guarantees (social security, pensions, insurance, etc.).

2. Good Health
More and more people are coming to the realization that good health is more than not being sick... it is being well, attaining a sense of well-being.

3. Prestige
Most of us want a good reputation, even esteem. We crave a desire for consideration and importance. We believe we can get it by having something valuable — an object, a talent, a title, etc.

4. Possession
People get a great deal of satisfaction from ownership. The more valuable the possession the more satisfaction... even prestige.

5. Status
We all need to have a definitive standing or rank among our peers. (Peers in the broadest sense — we are all equal.) And it has to be visible among our peers, whether in our family, neighborhood, company, society, etc.

6. Recognition
Each of us wants to be accepted as an individual and, as a progression from that desire, we want to receive special notice or attention when we feel we deserve it... publicly.

7. Approval
Closely allied with recognition is approval by others. We want others to like us and accept us into their/our world.

8. Responsibility
People seek additional obligations — on the job, at home, in the community — in order to achieve a greater sense of importance, as well as a heightened feeling of making a significant contribution.

9. Belonging
We are, mainly, group-oriented. We desire to associate with others for the sake of pleasure, comradeship, even security. We like sharing our experiences with them and vice-versa.

10. Understanding
Each of us needs close, sympathetic, empathetic relationships with others.

11. Accomplishment
People want to exercise their capabilities and their capacities to the fullest to achieve a sense of satisfaction from doing a job well.

12. Independence
People have a need for self-expression and self-assertion. They crave to be recognized as an individual.

Multiple Motivational Drives

There is rarely a single motivational drive. It usually takes a combination of multiple drives to motivate any of us. For instance, our innate primary need, hunger—the satisfaction of our basic need for sustenance — broadens to become an acquired drive, even a need, for particular foods. Thirst may broaden to becoming a thirst for particular beverages. As hot dogs and lemonade become steak and beer, it requires more money; champagne and caviar even more. If our primary need for protection from the elements — clothing and shelter—progresses so that it can only be satisfied by a mansion and designer clothes, it then strengthens the drive to earn money. This can combine with ambition, even rivalry, with its symbols of approval, i.e., awards or prizes in the form of money, promotion, prestige. It becomes a need (really a want) that produces a powerful drive that can motivate a person to act to satisfy, even gratify, the perceived need for furs and gowns, expensive cars and houses, gourmet food and drink. And thus a millionaire is made.

Another motivational factor is the various strengths of the individual needs or drives that make up the whole. Is his (or her) drive for prestige stronger than his drive to compete? Is his desire for approval (gratification of many different primary and acquired drives) stronger still? Is money more important than pride, or vice-versa?

A person may be predominantly motivated — at any particular time or in any particular circumstance — by a desire to avoid (the negative aspects of) failure, (low motivation), while another person may be predominantly motivated by the hope (and rewards) of success, (high motivation). It will be beneficial for you to be aware of *which* will motivate him, or her, in any given situation.

What we must try to accomplish in our lives — at work or at play — is to become aware of his or her needs and drives. How? Review the 12 motivational buttons. Which ones fit? Then write the person's name down along with each of his or her perceived needs or drives. Next, rank each in the order you perceive to be the strongest, second strongest, etc. You will then have, for each of these persons, a "panel of buttons" to push.

Once your list is complete and ranked you can adapt, adjust, or change a performance to stimulate him to act with a desired response as your objective. When your objective is met you can then apply liberal doses of positive reinforcement, or reward, from a simple "Thanks, I appreciate that," to a formal acknowledgement and public recognition (a certificate, a press release), to something more valuable, i.e., a promotion, a gift.

A reminder: People can be motivated. People are not only your boss, co-workers, teachers, students, but spouses, children, siblings, neighbors — everyone with whom you relate.

Entire books have been written on motivation. This is not one of them. If you want to get deeply into the subject, your local library can provide them. The interest here is not in concepts and theories as such, but rather why people do the things they do — why they act or react in certain ways. So, as they pertain to your P.P.R., let's look at the emotions, the needs, and the drives under some of the more common motivation buttons.

Why People Do What They Do

As an extension of our primal aversion to pain, we not only want to avoid it, but even the thought of its possibility causes us to experience anxiety and fear. This can lead to psychological pain as well as the more basic physical pain. As we matured, our fear of physical pain lessened — we no longer fear spankings, slaps, or the class bully — but our fear of psychological pain —embarrassment, rejection, ridicule — probably increased. He, or she — you and I — normally will not inflict physical pain on another — a teacher, a boss, a fellow student, a co-worker, a friend, a relative, etc. — in order to get him to behave in a certain way. But he, or she — you and I — does not want to be wronged, or chastised, or ridiculed, or embarrassed. Each of us will attempt to avoid the psychological pain to more or less degree depending on the thickness of our skin or our personal sense of security.

Our performance can, legitimately, present a danger that kindles his or her or their fears. It can allay their fears. It can do both. For instance, if I communicate (even hint) to a peer that my performance is a response to Mr. Important's request for something, and that his cooperation is essential if I am to satisfy Mr. Important's need or want, I can make him realize that he must cooperate. He can hope that I give him credit for doing so. (If he does not cooperate and, consequently, becomes a stumbling block in my effort to satisfy Mr. Important's need or want, he provides me with an excuse for not satisfying Mr. Important's order or request.) Presuming he cooperates, and *my* P.P.R. is enhanced with Mr. Important, I can, if I consider it advantageous, enhance my P.P.R. with my peer by giving him recognition and credit for his cooperation — from a thank you to actually telling Mr. Important of his contribution.

A performance of this kind requires tact and diplomacy. You could have matter-of-factly given Peer the word — "I've got to do this for the boss; for me to do it you must do this." That, of course, would have motivated his cooperation (fear, not of you, but of the boss). Being cognizant of your P.P.R., I'm sure you would have delineated the boss' request (demand actually) of you, shown him (Peer) how you and he (we can) could satisfy the boss' need or want — "Here's what we have to do..." and, putting Peer in the boat with you, you would have rowed together. And, when you have several Peers upon whom the successful conclusion of your project depends — no problem, Cap'n, you'll have a whole crew in the boat with you.

Peer, of course, could be a fellow student, a co-worker, a lodge brother (or sister), a neighbor, etc. Mr. — or Ms. — Important could be a professor, a boss, the lodge master, an authority, etc. The names and faces may change, the premise is always the same.

Hunger, thirst, and protection (from cold, heat, etc., clothing, shelter, etc.) are also primal needs which have progressed from a satisfaction of basic needs to forms of gratification. Money (income or perks) then becomes the requirement as the means of gratifying these many different needs, the lack of which equals unsatisfied desires. That usually requires ambition.

Ambition

To satisfy ambition (even as you allayed Peer's fears) you could have dangled the carrot of approval (by Mr. Important if not yourself). In this way you would have fueled (1) Achievement — the need to succeed, excel, accomplish; (2) Affiliation — the need to interact with others; (3) Approval — a means of gratifying many different primary needs and desires. (Disapproval, on the other hand, can mean pain, hunger, etc. when disapproval equals termination equals no income.) All three — achievement, affiliation, approval — could have reinforced any and all ambition drives that Peer possessed.

Another facet to ambition, with ties to achievement, affiliation, and approval, is rivalry and competition. Its symbols of approval are awards, prizes, and recognition — a medal, a promotion, a trophy, a salary increase, the prestige of a title, or, when we were young, a gold star. And although people get a certain amount of inner reward and satisfaction, public is better. Being lauded or honored or commended or rewarded is best when *they* know about it.

There's a joke that illustrates this very well. It's about a priest, an avid golfer, driving down a highway that paralleled a beautiful golf course.

It was a lovely Spring day. He's tempted. But it's Good Friday. The temptation became too great. He gave in. Taking off his coat and collar he was soon teeing off on the first tee. That's when St. Peter, looking down, first noticed him. He brought the problem to the Lord. A few minutes later the Lord nodded his head. The priest was just teeing off on the Par 3 third hole. The Lord smiled as the priest swung the club. The ball made a graceful arc toward the right, guarded by woods. It hit a tree, bounced high into the air and landed on a hill next to the green. It rolled down the hill, deflected off a stone, skidded across the green nudged slightly left by a tuft of grass, and dropped into the cup. A HOLE IN ONE! St. Peter was aghast. "Lord," he exclaimed. "He's playing golf on Good Friday. He's a priest. And you reward him with a hole in one?" The Lord looked at St. Peter and, with a twinkle in his eye, said: "Who's he going to tell!"

Emotions Motivate People

There are emotions that motivate people to do the things they do: Hope (somebody or something has to promise something to somebody); Love (we want to please someone, make someone happy); Hate (we want to displease someone or make someone unhappy); Religion (it shapes our beliefs and our values); Curiosity (we can explore new things, new ideas, new feelings, etc.); Control (of situations, circumstances, others); Aesthetic Needs (what makes us, or them, "feel" good).

And then there's sex.

Sex, a primal need, but one whose pursuit can make people irrational on the one hand, overpower or distort their other motivations on the other.

We've all heard stories about indiscretions by residents of the White House, even, in the case of President Warren Harding, in a White House cloak room. We've heard about congressmen and women (one such couple reportedly dallied in the outdoor Tidal Basin, another on the Senate steps). And, the story of a couple of congressmen who took up with young men — congressional pages — made the front pages of newspapers across the country. There are stories aplenty of corporate sex at the water cooler, in the stockroom, and in the boardroom. And the casting director's couch, we read, still exists.

If men and women can jeopardize lifetime careers, sex must indeed be a strong motive, one that can easily conflict with other motives.

Motives In Conflict

Most motives can conflict with other motives. A single motive can, but rarely operates by itself. Psychology texts point out that motives can interfere or conflict in several ways. Most common of these conflicts are termed approach-approach, avoidance-avoidance, and approach-avoidance.

An approach-approach conflict occurs when there are two goals, equally attractive, competing with each other. For example. Do you buy that new dress or have a night out on the town? Or, two mini-series are on television opposite each other and your VCR is broken — which do you watch? Do you do graduate work in college or take that great job you've been offered? It can even be as simple as choosing between two mouth-watering entrees on a restaurant's menu.

You can say that all of your problems — conflicts — should be so simple. The bottom line is you must make a decision as your needs, desires and drives want to go in two equally pleasant directions. Which of your motives (which of *their* motives) are stronger? Should you dangle the reward of a raise or a promotion, money or prestige? Will he do it for love, or his religious beliefs? Will she do it for recognition, or approval? Can you offer both so no matter how he resolves his motivational conflict you will get the response you desire?

An avoidance-avoidance conflict happens when there are also two goals, but neither is desirable. And one must be chosen. A good example of this happens every couple of years when you'll hear from more than one person — "I voted for the lesser of two evils!" This conflict is also personified by the "damned if I do, damned if I don't" problem. When it happens to you, you can only make the best of the situation. Accentuate the positive, as one song says. Look for the silver lining, says another song.

In those cases where you must give this conflict to someone else — the government gave millions of young men a choice of being drafted or going to prison — then you should explain the necessity. Educate. Stress the need for the task instead of the task itself. And do it only when absolutely necessary, when other motivations will not work, i.e., not enough young men were being motivated to volunteer for the Army, hence the draft.

The approach-avoidance conflict happens when there is one goal, but conflicting motives. The recovering alcoholic who wants a drink, but doesn't want a drink. The dieter who wants the chocolate eclair, but doesn't want it. The young man at a party who sees an attractive woman, wants to approach her, but fears rejection. If it happens to us we can resolve the conflict when we know it exists. We can make a decision. On the other hand we don't want to present such a conflict to another whose response we want because often this will keep him (or her) from actually responding. We are better off presenting situations whereby we motivate him or her in a positive manner that will not present a conflict of either his emotions or drives, will not make him feel guilty or anxious for doing the act.

The bottom line? Do not put his or her motives into conflict if you can avoid it. Now that you are aware that such motivational conflicts are a possibility, you can avoid placing him or her in such a situation — unless you want to.

Self-Actualization

As you are observing and studying your peers, your subordinates, and your superiors — learning about their motivational buttons — be aware of the person that psychologists refer to as the self-actualized person. He or she accepts himself/herself and other people for what they are. He enjoys working, and playing. He's spontaneous and creative, appreciates just about all the arts, has developed (or is developing) all of his or her potential.

Who is he? Abraham Maslow, the humanistic psychologist, studied people he thought were self-actualized — Lincoln, Eleanor Roosevelt, Einstein, and others who had the need to fulfill their potential to the greatest possible degree.

Maslow proposed, in his self-actualization theory, that the basic needs were satisfied before a person could begin to do anything about his or her safety needs; then his love needs — acceptance, affiliation, etc., became his concern; then his self-esteem needs (achievement, approval, recognition) became paramount; followed by his need to explore, learn, and understand. Then followed his aesthetic needs. Impelling all of these is his (or her) overriding need for self-actualization.

Why should you be aware of the self-actualized person? What do you do with him or her? What would you do with a Lincoln, an Eleanor Roosevelt, an Einstein?

You get them to work for you, or with you. You make them a friend, an ally, and possibly (if your ambition, like Mary Todd's, could be vicariously satisfied, or because love was one of her needs, or both) your spouse. Above all, you learn from them. You learn about them. Because knowledge about people, is, after all, important to understanding and using your P.P.R.

Needs, Drives, Incentives

When we concern ourselves with our P.P.R. — our performance and their response, in particular — we must remember that motives involve needs, drives, and incentives that can incite him, or her, or them, to action.

Needs are internal states of him or her or them that must be met or relieved; Drives are aroused needs that lead to goal-directed behavior; and Incentives are external factors that act as goals.

According to Anthony Davids and Trygg Engen in their text, *Introductory Psychology*, the three main theories of the function of motivation strongly suggest that (1) it leads to organisms (and that includes people) selecting appropriate responses, (2) it arouses them to make appropriate responses, and (3) it reinforces those responses which are conducive to homeostasis (keeping things in balance).

Our performances right now —today — this minute — are provoking responses from them. Wouldn't it be prudent of us to tailor our performances to motivate them, persuade them, influence them so that those responses are indeed favorable to our objectives? Of course it is. It's called the art of gentle persuasion.

It goes without saying that before we can persuade someone we must know about him and his interests, his concerns, and his goals. Many times the best way to satisfy our needs is to try to help him satisfy his needs. That's what Mrs. Norman Vincent Peale did a long time ago.

The Art Of Gentle Persuasion

In *Plus, The Magazine of Positive Thinking*, Vol. 37, No. 7 (Part II), September, 1986, a publication of the Foundation for Christian Living, Ruth Stafford Peale writes of using the art of gentle persuasion. She tells of a time, many years ago, of persuading her husband, Norman, (the renowned Dr. Norman Vincent Peale), to buy the family's first home, "an eighteenth-century farmhouse set in about twenty acres of lovely, rolling countryside."

Mrs. Peale wrote that the four important rules in successful persuasion are timing, the other person's self-interest, a climate of acquiescence, and patience. Not necessarily in that order.

Norman, she wrote, was against the purchase. "We can't afford it, and I'm all against it, so you'd better forget about it," he said.

Mrs. Peale decided to wait until the timing was right. While she waited she applied Rule No. 2 — interest in the other person's self-interest. She reminded her husband from time to time about "his need for a quiet, restful place to think, to write, to plan his speeches and sermons." She created, she wrote, a climate of acquiescence. "In a lot of small things I made myself as agreeable and thoughtful as possible. I consciously put Norman's needs ahead of my own.'

And, she was patient.

Six months later the timing was right. That's when Mrs. Peale's performance got her the response she wanted when, out of the blue, Dr. Peale said to her, "Ruth. I know how much you loved that old farmhouse up in Pawling. I've been thinking. Maybe we could get a mortgage and somehow borrow the rest of the money... ."

Abraham Lincoln would applaud Mrs. Peale's success. He said you won people to your side through "kind, unassuming persuasion," making friends with them, appealing to their reason, "that a drop of honey catches more flies than a gallon of gall."

Positive Reinforcement

If we get Peer to cooperate with us and thus are able to complete our task — a work project, a school paper, a date, or even fixing a leaking faucet — to the satisfaction of our superior, our teacher, our spouse, our friend — and we give credit to Peer — a co-worker, a friend, our child, a classmate, etc. — for his or her response (cooperation), we then increase the probability of the same response, under the same circumstance, occurring again.

We have used positive reinforcement.

And, if we give more credit than is actually due, that could result in an even more positive future response.

Positive reinforcement is a valuable public relations tool. It's the investment now (our response to his response) which could pay off later with a similar or even greater response.

There are many forms of positive reinforcement —a word of praise for a job well done, the thank-you note for a dinner attended, the certificate of service or achievement, the plaque, public recognition. Each is a reward. Each preferred — even a simple thank you — enhances your personal public relations — your P.P.R.

Positive reinforcement is one positive way to motivate people. Here are a dozen more.

12 Positive Ways To Motivate

1. Let your boss, your spouse, your co-workers, your children, know what your standards and values are, and consistently show them.

2. Recognize your own biases as well as prejudices, predispositions, and the other four important P's (to communication). Be aware of them, in yourself and others, and allow for them. Consideration begets consideration.

3. Be sure that they — your spouse, children, classmates, co-workers, et al — know where they stand, what you expect from them, what they can expect from you. Make it easy for them to please you.

4. Praise. Whenever it is appropriate. Publicly whenever possible. Lavishly if you can. Praise, as your response to their good performance, will usually result in even better performances.

5. Keep them informed of changes that could affect them in any way. If a change could affect them in a major way bring them "into the boat" with you.

6. Care about them. This may seem simplistic, but listen to the lament of many a son or daughter, spouse, co-worker — nobody cared about me! Care about them and let them know you do. And they may care about you.

7. Make an effort to help. Be there when you're needed. It could motivate them to be there when they're needed.

8. Give, and take, responsibility. They'll usually respond in kind.

9. Be tactful as you deal with them. A little consideration, a little diplomacy, goes a long way. Treat them the way you'd like them to treat you. And they may.

10. Be more than willing to learn from them. First, you probably will learn something, and secondly they'll feel great for having been able to teach you something. And they *may* teach by showing.

11. Give them the freedom to express themselves. From the youngest child to the oldest parent; the student to the teacher; the janitor to the company president — we all like people to know what we think and feel.

12. Encourage them to use their creativity. We are all artists, musicians, inventors, architects, designers and artisans. Some of us just aren't very good. (In whose eyes?) Some of us are!

We all know there are ways to turn people on — motivate them. There are also ways to turn people off. Here are a half-dozen of them.

6 Ways To Turn People Off

1. Dont ever—ever—belittle anyone. Especially in public. No one likes to see their importance lowered in the eyes of anyone else. If

you must discredit someone, or someone's ideas, do it in private, tactfully.

2. A close second in the "turn-off derby" is criticism. Never do it in front of others. If you must criticize, do it constructively, tactfully, and privately.

3. Always give him or her — your child, spouse, co-worker, boss (of course), teacher, et al, your undivided attention. Do not even seem preoccupied with your own interests while they are discussing something of obvious (to them) importance.

4. Never, ever, show favoritism. Show is the operative word. No one wants to know that someone else (especially a rival) is preferred in any way. Showing favoritism can even foster rivalry where it is not wanted, needed, or desirable.

5. Do not be insensitive, especially, believe it or not, to the "small things." Human nature, being what it is, can make small things into very important big things.

6. Be resolute in opinion, sentiment, and determination (but openminded) in your actions and decisions. Vacillation produces perplexity, confusion, uncertainty, and disorder.

Now you Know... Now What?

You have come to the end of Part I. You have a better idea of what public relations is, and isn't, and how the concept relates to P.P.R. — your personal public relations. You have done the research of learning about you, the product — and them — who they are, what they are, and how they are. The next thing we've got to learn is to use that knowledge. And one of the ways to use it is to communicate more effectively.

Whether you realize it or not you are already communicating with them. And they are communicating with you. In the four different ways people learn about you and you learn about them as you communicate to each other:

1. *How you look.*

How you dress; how you groom yourself; personal hygiene; the choice, upkeep, and maintenance of your clothes. The style of your hair, the design of your glasses, the jewelry you wear or don't wear.

2. *How you act.*

How you act at work — at lunch, walking down the hall, at the water cooler, at a meeting; with those with whom you socialize; your

Motivation — Are There Buttons To Push?   93

manners, your poise, your savoir-fare. And how you react to the actions of others.

3. *How you speak.*

How you speak person-to-person, one-on-one, over the telephone, in group conversation. How you speak addressing a group of people — small or large — in a meeting, at an event.

4. *How you write.*

How you write memos, letters, notes, reports, essays—even resumes.

You have given, and you are going to continue to give, little bits of information about yourself by the kinds of clothes you wear and how you wear them, and how you care for your nails, and how you comb your hair; by how you act in the office, in the supermarket, at church, in the cafeteria, even at the company picnic or the family reunion dinner; by the words you speak and how you speak them, to him, to her, to them; and by the words you write and how you write them. Let's determine now that you will give those little bits of information about yourself to them consciously. And let's give them those little bits of information in a way that they will perceive us in the way we want to be perceived.

What we need to do if we are to accomplish that which we are striving for — good P.P.R. — is learn to communicate effectively. Let's begin now by honing our communication skills.

Part Two

Honing Your Communication Skills

7

Communicating with Them

You cannot blame someone for not knowing what you haven't told them, and you cannot blame someone for perceiving what you have told them in a way that you did not mean to convey.

We acquire information designed to persuade, to modify or accept, to educate; we integrate attitudes, consider predilections, predispositions, perceptions, prejudices, proclivities, and preconceptions, and, using proper communication methods, we transmit the information we have acquired — to increase understanding and gain support.

If he, or she gets all the information, but doesn't get the message, who is at fault?

Communication, contrary to popular belief, is not an easy accomplishment, using easily acquired common skills. We don't really know very much about what happens to an idea as it travels from one's lips to another's ears, from one's actions to another's eyes, and from one's pen to another's senses. Yet we all have the need and the urge to communicate. We are, in fact, always communicating whether we want to or not, like it or not, good or bad.

Your friendliness, your attitude, your understanding and intelligence, are usually apparent to others — at least, apparently apparent — whether your commmunication is written or spoken, unwritten or unspoken. People will get to know you. They will discover you in four basic ways:

1. How you look — the way you dress and comb your hair; how you keep your nails; your personal hygiene; how you dress and how you maintain your wardrobe; your personal grooming in general and, as an extension of *how* you look, how your work place or space looks — neat and orderly, sloppy and disorganized, or a little bit of each.

2. How you act — the way you respond to various people in various situations and circumstances, i.e., your superiors, your peers, your subordinates, your friends, your relatives, acquaintances, the butcher, the baker, et al; your actions, your attitudes, your habits, and even your manners; how you eat, how you sit, how you stand, and even how you walk.

3. How you speak — what you say and how you say it and, more important what they *think* you're saying and how they *think* you're saying it and what they *think* you mean; one-on-one, within or to a group, at a meeting, over the telephone; your voice — tone, inflection, pronunciation, — and the words you choose, spell Y-O-U.

4. How you write — letters, notes, memos, essays, compositions, reports. How you write is perhaps the most important of the four ways that people get to know about you. Unlike how you look or act or speak, the written word is a record, evidence, in someone's else's file. It can be read and reread. It can be studied. It can be, factually, thrown back in your face.

If you change your looks, like the man in the Grecian Formula television commercial — You look great! Lose some weight? — your old look will soon be forgotten. If you improve your manners, your social graces, or the tone of your voice, it will soon be accepted as having always been what is now perceived as that new, improved you. But your writing stays on and on — in that letter file, memo book, or as a bundle of letters tied together with ribbon — as testimony to your writing ability be it for style, grammar, or content. How you write is just about as important as what you write. It's the benchmark of your intelligence.

The way we write and talk to each other — how we sound, the words we use, the tenor of our written communications — can make or break our careers and our interactions and interrelationships with *them* — our peers, superiors, and subordinates; our clients, patients, customers; our suppliers, merchants, service people... our publics.

If each of us could communicate perfectly; If we could understand each other perfectly; If each of us were in the perfect mindset to accept each message as we receive it; If each of us were free of prejudices, predispositions, proclivities, and predilections, there would be few problems in our world. Unfortunately, that is not the case. Consequently, we must continually try to understand the various aspects and nuances of communication, the basic process of communicating, and the inherent dangers in the transmission and reception of messages.

Before we tackle the four areas of your communication — looks, actions, speaking, and writing — all of which impact forcefully upon your P.P.R., let us think about communications in general.

As we do it may seem that there are what appear to be inconsistencies. There really are not. Usually it has to do with a point of focus and the fact that all of the functions of public relations (and your P.P.R.) are interdependent. The principles and techniques of communication are relatively constant, but their application changes depending on the focus and the targeted recipient.

Just about every minute of every day we are communicating in one way or another. We are speaking or listening. We read and we write. We are seeing or being seen. We are acting or reacting. We are sending or receiving messages. One to another. From me to you. You to me. We to them. They to us. Even when we do not overtly communicate — we *are* communicating.

The person who storms out of the office because his appointment was at two o'clock and it's now 2:45 may have remained contentedly patient if he knew that the person he was waiting to see was held up for a very good reason. But if no one tells him — and we can act unreasonably when we are not told about something that is affecting us — then he can assume the worst. He is ready to believe that he was being cruelly slighted by some uncaring, inconsiderate oaf. That probably wasn't the case. There was probably good reason. But if we are not told the reason for some happening that is inconveniencing or frustrating us, we will imagine our own reason. Our blood pressure will rise, our stomach may knot, and our nerves can fray. If we cannot leave, as might be the case if we are waiting to see a physician, we will suffer and seethe silently.

Communication is a powerful tool that can stimulate emotions. Even silence or inaction is communicating. They are forms of communication we can easily avoid. The kin of silence, "no comment," can also be avoided. "No comment" is indeed a comment. A very dangerous comment. Like giving someone a blank check. He or she will speculate or imply or generate doubt. You should have no one sully your ideas or thoughts because they did not know them, or because they misunderstood them, or misinterpreted them. We must strive to transfer the picture in our head to their head effectively.

The Transmission Of Ideas

Communication is the transmission of an idea from one person or group to another person or group by various means of transmission.

How do we transfer an idea, a thought, an emotion, a feeling, from one head into another? Let me see of I can get this idea from my head into yours in such a way that the result will be an indentical picture in each of our minds.

The originator of the idea, or his/her agent, wants to communicate the information to others. The idea can take the form of a new dress or hairdo, the acquisition of a new skill, the formulation of a new method, the explanation of an actual or perceived error, or thousands of other ideas, concepts, beliefs, thoughts, attitudes, opinions, impressions, notions, vagaries, or fantasies.

How will the idea be communicated? Will the sender wear the new outfit, describe it vocally, or write about it? She, or he, might do all three. Wear it so that friends and co-workers might see it, describe it to a close friend who lives in an adjoining city over the telephone, or describe it in a letter to a friend who lives across the country.

Hopefully, she already knows her target audience, be it one (a friend) or many (the gang at the office). She already knows the receiver's(s') interests and goals and concerns and how her message will probably be received and perceived by him or her or them. (She did her work well as she read Part I.) Now she must package her message so that it will be received and perceived as she wishes it to be. In the case of a new outfit, which will reflect her taste, her personality, even, to some degree, her economic status, the package *is* the outfit, as is how she wears it, and what image it projects. In the case of a new method for doing something, or the acquisition of a new skill, the package may be composed of symbols, or language, or pictures, or sounds, as determined from research, i.e., what appeals to your target's senses and intelligence.

"This is a cow. The cow says mooooo," says a mother to her year-old son as she points a finger at a picture of a cow. (Words, sound, pictures.)

"This is a cow. The cow says moo," reads a five-year-old girl looking at a cow's picture. (Words and pictures.)

"Cow. (kow) n. the female of various large animals, esp. of domestic cattle," reads the 12-year-old boy. (Words.)

"Put this item in the company newspaper," says the young executive, handing a paper to his secretary as he prepares to hang his new diploma on the office wall. (Words and symbol.)

"They're going to love this new method," thought the young executive as he clipped the charts and graphs to his neatly typewritten paper of a new, money-saving method. (Words and symbols, possibly pictures.)

Once he has determined — if only by educated guess — what his target's personality and P-factor is (predisposition and the other five Ps) he must encode his message. He chooses the language or symbols that best fit his chosen method of transmission and one that the receiver will understand. He now has a message package. He then transmits the message. The receiver gets it and decodes it. If all is done to perfection — carefully prepared, properly packaged, and competently transmitted — the receiver gets the identical image of the message that the sender wished to convey.

Or does he?

Whether it is by memo, letter, or other written missive; a telephone call, personal visit, or shouting across a backyard fence; a newspaper story or an advertisement, a brochure, a slide presentation, or a video cassette; the sender is sending his message to the receiver so that the receiver will interpret what he has seen, heard, or read, in such a way that the picture formed in *his* head is a precise duplicate of the picture formed in the sender's head.

That is easier said than done.

Multiple receivers of the same message may get slightly different or radically different perceptions of the same message, depending on the state of the receiver's P-factor, and on the relationship of the sender and the receiver. If the sender and receiver share a common experience, a common background, or friendship, it becomes easier to communicate, and communication gets closer to, but still doesn't reach, perfection.

For instance, regarding our example of a new outfit, one person at the office may perceive her new outfit as a testimony to her good taste, another as an enviable extravagance, and still another as a sign of her economic well-being or success. How and whether you should communicate *this image or that* to such a diverse group of receivers is a question of knowing your relationships with members of that audience, and how they will probably respond to your performance.

No matter what medium you choose to communicate your ideas, thoughts, or concepts; no matter to which of your receiver's senses you want to appeal, there are three things you must know and consider *before* you draft and package your message for transmission.

1. Know The Other Person

A food processing company, many years ago, had a product which was field tested and found to be overwhelmingly desirable by a large sample group of ethnically related people. Based on this researched acceptance the company decided on an all-out marketing program for the product in the county of origin of the sample group. Sales were more than disappointing, They were almost nonexistent. Company officials were bewildered. They had tested the foodstuff and the recipe with the ethnic group who had accepted it wholeheartedly. They had priced it affordably. They had packaged it beautifully to command attention on a small section of market shelving — What was wrong? What was wrong, indeed! Color! Color was wrong. The color of the box, they learned, had bad connotations to the inhabitants of this particular Asian country — people did not want to *touch* the box, let alone eat its contents. A new package, with new colors, plus renewed advertising, and, Voila!, success.

2. Know The Other Person's Language

If you wanted to convey your ideas to one whose language was other than American, the steps you would take would be quite obvious. What is not so obvious is the language differences, not only with regard to vernacular, or slang, or jargon, but with regard to ethnic, regional, and even age differences between what comes out of one's mouth and what goes into another's ear.

Have you ever heard two physicians, or two scientists, or two lawyers talking? Chances are you didn't know what they were talking about as they discussed edemas and ischemias, quantum theories, or torts.

And then there is, once again, the matter of the P-factor — he is predisposed to... she has the proclivity for... his perception is... they have a predilection for... his preconceived notion is that... they are prejudiced... — when people *try* to hear what they *want* to hear.

I remember an incident at a mid-sized upstate New York university, in 1969, when students were not adverse to taking over college buildings to protest our country's "military-industrial complex." It was at this time, that the university's on-campus SDA group — Students for Democratic Action — numbering some 300 students, were threatening to take over the administration building,

The university president decided to talk to them from the steps of the building. He also decided that he required no counsel from members of the university's public affairs staff, of which I was a member. He *knew* what their concerns were...what their interests were... and what they wanted to hear from him. He stood on the steps looking down at them. I was in the audience. I wasn't dressed in my P.R. suit-uniform, but in slacks, a sports shirt, and a winter mackinaw. What the president had to say about the war in Vietnam, and the research that was going on in the university, was cogent, informative, and meaningful. Unfortunately, what the students *heard* was not. From the undercurrent of remarks I heard, as well as the occasional shout that everyone heard, his words didn't have the same meaning. The president's mouth and the students' ears never made contact. At least not until two days later *after* the students had occupied the adminstration building for a day and a half.

3. Know The Other Person's Concerns, Goals, Interests, Expectations

That story, relating to choice of words and language, could also have been used to illustrate this conception. It applies here as well.

Ordinarily we use words as our communicating means, even if we buttress their meaning with photos or pictures or graphics or gestures. Television news, for instance, uses words implemented by moving pictures or, in the case of weather reports, voting results, et al, by graphics.

But none of this is as important as to know what our receiver, our listener, our viewer — is concerned about or interested in.

A newscaster in Cincinnati, for instance, won't be spending as much time on a ten-car accident in Boise, Idaho, as he would on a two-car accident in downtown Cincinnati. The weatherman in New York City may spend a few seconds on the weather in Montana, usually just to tell New Yorkers how it is going to affect the weather in the east, unless the weather out west is so devastating that it is news in itself and, as such, is interesting to those who live in the east.

Whether we are talking to one person who's fidgiting, or a group of people who are stifling yawns (in neither case are they paying enough attention to fully receive or properly perceive the message that is being sent) what we are communicating must be of interest to those with whom we are attemptimg to communicate.

I remember coming home to a wife filled with consternation about our young (two-year's old, plus) son's hearing, or lack of it. It seems that throughout the day she had asked him questions, or spoke to him, and he didn't answer, didn't even look up toward the sound of her voice. Even when she spoke louder. Surely, he couldn't be that preoccupied with other things each time, could he? She asked. I shrugged. Let's try a simple test, I suggested. In a stage whisper from about fifteen feet away, I said: "Hey John-Boy! Want some candy?" His ears perked up, his eyes darted in my direction, and his hand stopped moving a toy truck and reached out, palm side up. His hearing was fine. You just had to know how to make contact between your mouth and his ears. You had to know what *really* interested him.

And you've got to know what really interests *them*. And if it's something that *you* want them to know that's not of particular interest to them, you have to put it into a form that *is* interesting.

You have now considered these three points: 1) you know about the other person including any idiosyncracies, taboos, quirks, and P-factor influences; 2) you know the other person's language so you can speak to him and; 3) you know the other persons concerns, goals, interests and expectations. You know, too, what problem you are trying to solve, your objective, or on what performance you want to educate. You are ready to determine your medium, prepare your message, and choose your method of transmission. You are ready to "package" your message and send it.

Packaging Your Message

Whether we write our message or say our message we are using words. In that way we are limited by *what* the words mean to others. So we must choose words that mean the same to both us — the message sender— and them — the message receiver. We must be on guard against misinterpretation of words, faulty presentation, or meaning-changing punctuation.

Does the word "home" mean the same to you and to him? Possibly. Physically? A Cape Cod with a white picket fence aroud it, a mansion with a circular drive, or a ghetto apartment, are all called home by somebody. Emotionally? A home can be remembered as a place of pleasure, love, and harmony, or a gladly forgotten prison of misery and pain.

What does the word "inexpensive" mean to you? Does it mean what you say, or what she hears?

When you present the message, "Do Not Administer..." should you underline "Not?" Print it in a different color? Red? In bold face type? Any of these attention-getting devices may have prevented a young patient's death when a resident in an upstate New York medical center said he did not see the word "Not."

How important is correct punctuation?

"Have your people moved to the new building" means one thing with a "?" and another with an "!" doesn't it?

"Harry's daughter Mary was with him" implies that Harry has other daughters, "Harry's daughter, Mary, was with him" does not.

Clarity is one of the most important ingredients of communication. Unless the message is clearly communicating the proper meaning — the meaning you want to convey — it has failed, and you have failed to communicate.

Our relationship with the receiver or receivers is also very important. It will have a great bearing on the way our message is received and perceived, accepted or rejected.

When the President's message is heard it can be received in one of several ways. If you think you know what motivates him, if you like him, if you trust him, even admire him — or *anyone* sending *you* a message — his message is more likely to change your mind, move you emotionally, or reinforce your beliefs.

So, when the President delivers a speech — or you send a message — it is "heard" differently by those who voted for him and those who didn't; by conservatives, moderates, and liberals; by those who are directly affected by what he is saying, and those who are not; by those who agree with him and those who do not. Based on that knowledge, he and his staff must determine what will be said, if it will be said, and how it will be said to produce, if not in its entirety, most of the desired response.

People, too, and that includes your co-workers, friends, and relatives, are usually amiable to ideas, opinions, and other information that is congenial to their personal values and beliefs. They will usually search for information that reinforces their opinions or decisions. While we no longer have a tendency to cluster and interact with "our own kind" — political party affiliation with political party affiliation, religious denomination with religious denomination, nationality with nationality — it is still probable that if Liberals read William Buckley's newspaper column at all, they do so with a different predisposition and for a different reason than do Conservatives.

John E. Cook, writing for *Public Relations Quarterly*, said "the program message must be positioned and expressed in the language, goals, and interests of the intended audience, rather than those of the message sender." He gave, among others, the following example of perception, understanding, and interpretation:

"When it was first offered only four girls enrolled in a special female weight lifting class at the University of California. The following term the instructor changed the name from 'Weight Lifting' to 'Weight Training for Figure Control', spread the word about how his students were shaping up, and thereby enrolled 200 coeds."

It cannot be stressed too often or too strongly that predisposition (and the other five Ps) must be considered as you deal with him or her or them in your everyday relationships. You, the communicator, must give every consideration — not always easily determined — to the predisposition of the receivers of your message. Are you trying to change his or her made-up mind, or overcome a preference, a prejudice, or a bias?

Another consideration: *When* people are, or may be, or are not, amiable to your message is also important. How was *he* feeling *when* he received your message? Did it affect *how* he received it? Was his response affected by it? In what frame of mind was he for *what* kind of message?

On the occasion of our first space tragedy, in January, 1986, President Ronald Reagan cancelled the delivery of the annual State of Union address scheduled for some nine hours later, in deference to the national mood and grieving of the nation.

Even when you try to consider every aspect of communicating, if you work less than diligently, or get lax and careless, your message may go askew. Consider these road blocks to effective communicating.

Twelve "Roadblocks" To Communication

While Director of Developemnt and Public Relations for Baylor College of Medicine, Houston, Texas, Ralph E. Frede delineated twelve "roadblocks" to communication:

1. Censorship;
2. Absence of a clear purpose;
3. Audience not clearly defined;
4. Faulty language selection;
5. Conflict of message and action;
6. Lack of semantic knowledge;
7. Faulty arrangement;
8. Choosing the wrong channel;
9. Unattractive packaging;

10. Bad timing;

11. Lack of useful information;

12. Incorrect premises or assumptions.

While the twelve "roadblocks" were developed for institutional public relations, let us examine my viewpoint of each as they might pertain to your *personal public relations*, both as a sender and as a receiver of information.

1. Censorship

Natural censorship exists when distance, language barriers, or mental capacity isolate you from *their* information, or *they* from your messages. This can be a physical distance, from the second floor to the penthouse, or across the country to the home office; a language barrier that is merely a result of scientific or "insider" jargon; a mental capacity that may be just an inability to read a financial statement or a technical report; or a combination of one or more of these obstacles. Each can be surmounted by education — yours or theirs.

Artificial censorship occurs when someone stops or alters someone else's message. Regarding one's personal communications this could occur when one's actions are controlled (you will not partake of alcoholic beverages with lunch and return to the office), or one's looks are regulated (required dress is a dark blue suit, white shirt, and subbued color/patterned tie), or one's words are restrained (if you cannot say good things about this company you should not be working here). These three examples might seem to be exceptions, but they are the rule in three American corporations.

If you cannot send the message you wish to send; if you cannot modify your message to conform to authority while still transmitting your thoughts; you have to reconcile yourself to the situation, or move to another school, neighborood, company, etc., which will afford you the total freedom you desire.

Surely, if you had suddenly developed a pechant for loud, showy, uninhibited clothes, after wearing conservative three-piece suits for many years, it might not be unexpected or unreasonable for your employer, a staid investment banking firm, to exert censorship of *your* message.

2. Absence of a clear purpose

Whether your message is being sent in writing, or by your actions, or appearance, or your voice, you should have a clear purpose for sending it.

Are you performing to get a positive response? Are you changing your performance to change a neutral or negative response into one that is positive? Are you attempting to educate — explaining, clarifying, justifying your performance — to neutralize or make positive a negative response?

The purpose of your message might involve a facet of your job performance, a business/workplace relationship, a personal relationship, or a combination of several of these purposes.

Your purpose may be as simple as showing your genuine concern for another (better communicated than kept to yourself), as normal as letting others know you have a master's degree (by hanging it on your office wall), or as complex as explaining to a group of friends that you can only get two complimentary tickets to a production that your school is staging.

The important thing to remember — If the purpose of your message is not clear in *your* mind, chances are it won't be clear to *them* either.

3. Audience not clearly defined

You had better know, even picture, your receiver or receivers correctly, because this obstacle can get larger and larger, almost insurmountable, in direct proportion to that knowledge. The less you know about your receiver's personality, character, likes and dislikes, interests, needs wants, concerns, the more trouble you can get into.

A simple example: It was once said that if, after dinner, in a home in China, a guest was to belch loud and long, it would be a delightful show of praise for the host and hostess, as well as the cook who prepared the meal. I don't know if that is still true in today's China, but I'm certain it would not be interpreted that way in today's America.

Another example: It would be obvious that you could probably get away with telling your youngsters to "shut up" and your wife to "stifle it," but it would be wiser to tell an acquaintance, or peer, or co-worker, or superior (especially a superior), to "please be quiet," if you could tell him or her or them at all.

The bottom line — Define him or her or them *before* you compose, package, or send your message.

4. Faulty language selection

If, after clearly defining our audience we choose the wrong words or looks or actions to transmit our message, we have failed. Not the obvious — speaking English to a foreigner who doesn't, wearing loud sports clothes to the office, or being the life of the party when there is no party — but the subtle, almost imperceptible misses, such as words, images, and sounds that put different pictures in the receiver's head than the one in the sender's head.

Think carefully about your receiver's ability to understand words, or actions, and *what* words and *what* actions. Would you deliver the same worded message about nuclear energy to a group of fourth graders as you would to high school seniors? Would you engage a rock group for a senior citizens' dance? I remember reading about a kindergarten teacher's method for reminding herself everyday about her charges. She had a small sign on her desk — "Think Small."

These are simple examples. Most of yours are more complex and require more thought before you speak or write or act. Do it!

5. Conflict of message and action

If your message *says* you are a kind, considerate, feeling, human being, but you kick the dog as you leave the building, and burn rubber getting out of the parking lot, then your message, it goes without saying, will not be credible or believed when received by the same audience.

"Actions speak louder than words," may be a bromidic saying or an old adage, but action is a strong means of communication, and does indeed carry more weight than words when there is a conflict between them. If you don't believe that, try to convince your boss you're working hard when he can see you're hardly working.

In any case, you cannot transmit different messages, in different mediums of communication, to the same receivers. It is inconsistent, unbelievable, and confusing. You wouldn't do it on purpose. No one would do it on purpose. Don't do it without thinking. Guard against it.

6. Lack of semantic language

Carefully... carefully... select the right word so the meaning, connotation, or shading can not be misunderstood. Some argue that there are really no exact synonyms; that there can be no exact equivalence of meanings in the total range of contents in which a word may be used, i.e., we *accompany* our peers, *follow* our leader, *escort* someone who needs protection, and *chaperone* those who require supervision. When in doubt consult a dictionary, or better yet, a thesaurus. If you can't find a substitute for a questionable word that may possibly transmit the wrong picture, be misinterpreted or misperceived, use a substitute term or phrase. Spell it out if you have to, but do transmit your message as close as possible to the original — the one in *your* head. You want to communicate with the receivers of your message; you do not want to offend, confuse, disturb, or rile them.

7. Faulty arrangement

When you do not arrange words, or sentences, or phrases in the proper sequence, you can create problems. Don't bury your idea in a torrent of verbosity (unless that *is* the purpose of your message). Don't place the emphasis in the wrong place. Don't make your thoughts difficult to follow logically from one premise to another. Be careful of such juxtapositions as: "Are you fully aware of the boredom prevalent in our organization? I'll be stopping by next week to talk to you."

8. Choosing the wrong channel

Each means of communication at your disposal has strengths and weaknesses. At any given time, in any given circumstance, one may be more appropriate than another. Only you can decide, in any given situation, which method will be more effective for the delivery of your message. Is a letter more appropriate or effective than a short note? If you would rather not have a written record of your thoughts or opinions, would a telephone call suffice? How about one-on-one conversation? I remember at the university where I worked, how the professors would run into the university's president "by chance," and they could, as one said, "bounce an idea off the old man." It wasn't only that he would not be sticking his neck out formally, on the record, in writing, he said, but he could tell by the old man's reaction, especially a look in his eyes, an expression, whether to even pursue the idea further. It became, he explained, a screening process — a message, immediate feedback, evaluation, decision to drop or pursue — all within minutes, without laying oneself open to a colleague's views, comments, or criticism.

On the other hand you may *want* your idea, opinion, decision, etc., recorded and you may choose to transmit your message in writing. Or at a meeting where minutes are taken. Or for public dissemination by a news medium. Only you can decide how and when and what channel will best serve your purpose. And, hopefully, when you conclude this section of P.P.R. on communications, you will be able to make that decision more wisely and more purposefully.

9. Unattractive packaging

If a corporate public relations person had no expertise about paper stock, color selection and inks, typography, art, photography, or layout, he'd be a fool to try to design and produce an expensive brochure. Instead of winning respect he'd be jeopardizing and losing his reputation. Knowing his shortcomings, he'd get an expert to help him. You can do the same. To write a better letter, essay, report, or memo; to improve your manners and social graces; to dress and groom yourself for success; and to speak more effectively — get yourself an exprt. There are many available at your local public library. P.P.R. will help you in the following chapters, but you have many more experts, for specific problems, available to you.

10. Bad timing

You can cover all the bases. You know your receiver or receivers, what you want to transmit to him or her or them — and why. You have prepared and packaged your message carefully. You've checked it and rechecked it and rewrote it, or rehearsed it, until it is perfect. You have chosen your channel or medium carefully and skillfully. But your message falls flat on its face. It could be bad timing.

P.R. people know enough not to send promotional pieces out during the Christmas mail rush, not to hold a phonathon on Superbowl Sunday, and not to introduce a new line of skis in July. How about you? You know enough to not telephone him or her at midnight, but how about during the evening television news, during a favorite program? Not because it would make him angry, but because he could be preoccupied, distracted. Is her dinner hour from six to seven p.m., or later? Would it be better for him to get your letter on Monday (his first day back to work), on Friday (does he leave early for the weekend), or another day? Does he have any special projects, meetings, or conferences on another day? What is the best time, the best day, to discuss that matter with your teacher... your boss... your fiance... your...? Is there a good time, a better time, a best time? Whenever possible consider the timing of your message.

And still, there will always be the danger of some unforeseen occurance that could turn good timing into bad timing. A dented fender on your boss' way to the office only an hour before he gets your memo... a mishap in the kitchen just minutes before you call your mother-in-law... or ringing the doorbell just as your best friends are having their first domestic squabble in months — all add up to bad timing. Learning about these unforseen happenings after the fact will, at least, put an adverse response into proper perspective when you attempt to determine future strategy.

When it comes to timing *you* do the best you can. After that you take your chances along with the rest of us.

11. Lack of useful information

We are bombarded with messages every day — by mail, telephone, in person, television, radio, and newspapers — so much so that we become selective, sometimes overly selective. We learn to tune out, in our heads, tv and radio commercials; scan newspaper stories and advertisements; speed read our mail (especially what many call "junk mail"); and we can listen on the telephone with half an ear— UNLESS something in the message grabs our attention almost immediately because it addresses our interests, says it will help us attain our goals, or promises us a benefit if we just listen to and assimilate the message.

Just because you are excited and enthusiastic about your idea, you cannot assume that they will be, too. It is safer to assume that they will lack the same excitement or enthusiasm unless you can win the contest for their attention.

Experienced and skilled advertising copywriters address themselves to their consumers and communicate with them by providing useful information. Successful P.R. practitioners do the same. So should you.

12. Incorrect premises or assumptions

A friend of a friend of mine was hospitalized several years ago for appendicitis. The prognosis called for the surgical removal of the appendix — an appendectomy. His family physician made arrangements for the surgeon, a Dr. Leslie Something-or-other, who did the surgery at several hospitals in the multi-city area. My friend said his friend was totally surprised when the woman surgeon removed his appendix. He had assumed that doctors, especially surgeons, were men.

True. Today this assumption may have lessened somewhat — maybe. Another friend of mine went up to the counter of one of those "department store" pharmacies and asked the young woman if the pharmacist was in. She assured him that yes, *she* was.

You must try to keep your receiver from making assumptions. You must try to keep the viewer from forming a negative opinion when he or she first meets you... when he hears you speak. When he reads your writing you try to keep him from scanning the first paragraph or two, forming a negative impression, and then reading the rest (if he reads it at all) with prejudice permeating his mind. This will be easier to do if you've done your homework so you can act from strength — knowledge is strength — instead of having to react solely by intuition. Mind you, acting intuitively is fine. If you are blessed with comprehension without the effort of reasoning — and much of intuition is a result of our inner *computer* spitting out the experiences, mistakes, successes, goofs, failures, gems, and errors that we have programmed into it. Just think of the potential of your P.P.R. when you have to interact with that *special* person if you can combine your intuition with adequate research and good communication skills.

Ah! If communicating with *them* were so simple! You can avoid each of the twelve "roadblocks" to communication, even having the luck to avoid "bad timing." And then you only have to contend with psychological factors. Here are ten of them.

Ten Psychological Considerations

In his book, *Public Relations In Action*, Robert T. Reilly refers to provocative statements (ital) by Berelson And Steiner, in their book, *Human Behavior* to which Reilly sometimes adds his observations (in parenthesis) and to which I have added some thoughts on P.P.R. Let's just call them ten psychological considerations involved in commnications:

1. *The spread of rumors is directly related to audience predispositions; rumors tend to be heard by people to whom they are congenial; they are changed into more personally satisfactory forms; and they are best countered by the circulation of objective information that is not explicitly tied to the rumor itself.*

This would suggest that if a rumor is going around your office that the boss is sweet on Miss Goody in the typing pool, it may be changed into an affair by those who dislike the boss and by those who think Miss Goody is too good for words. This may be countered, not with denial, but by the circulation of objective information — the truth with, if necessary, a coat of varnish — that is not explicitly tied to the rumor itself, i.e., the boss' devotion to his wife and children, Miss Goody's impending engagement to a minister, etc.

2. *People are especially likely to seek out congenial information on a controversial matter just after coming to a decision on that matter.*

(Religious converts experience this; so do those who switch political parties. Even in noncontroversial matters, that can be true.

The best readers of Ford ads, for example, are those who have just purchased a new Ford. The ads provide positive reinforcement for their decision.)

We are people, and people like to reinforce their beliefs. If you can agree with his or her decision on a controversial matter, do so. If you cannot, it may pay you to keep quiet, or, at least, know what you are getting into. In noncontroversial matters you have the opportunity to engage in a little friendly debate, a way for you to project your personality and learn a little more about his. If you must disagree in the course of your work performance, a little tact and diplomacy can go a long way. The point is, if you are fully aware of this psychological aspect, you can use it to your advantage.

3. *People interested in a topic tend to follow it in the medium that gives it the fullest and most faithful treatment.*

If *you* are the topic, and the medium is small talk around the water cooler or in the company cafeteria, that is where it will be nurtured or quashed, depending on your response. If it's a rumor, again you can use the truth of objective information that indirectly refutes it. If it is the truth, and negative, you have the option of educating to neutralize the negative, or even turn it into a positive response, or you have the option of changing the performance (even if it is only changing the visible aspect) so that it is no longer the subject of negative talk.

4. *Anticipating subsequent use increases retention, even of uncongenial material.*

(Students who anticipate a certain question in an upcoming exam will pay more attention to that part of the lecture. If you hear a good argument for or against a position you take, and foresee a future debate with a colleague, you will remember these bits of data.)

You may want to buttress what you are saying with a statistic or two that could be valuable for your receiver to remember along with what you have been saying. This approach can strengthen your position and is good P.P.R.

5. *Strong appeals to fear are less effective than minimal appeals to fear.*

(What the authors are saying here is that a strong threat may cause you to balk, or to submit without changing your attitude. A mild threat may cause you to rethink your whole situation and decide to change your opinion or conduct of your own accord.)

What Reilly says is applicable to your P.P.R. Now reread his statement and change *you* to *them* and *your* to *their* and make it twice as applicable. It works both ways — a strong threat *by* you, or *to* you.

6. *Presenting only the favored side of an argument is more effective than presenting both sides in persuading less educated audiences and in reinforcing the already persuaded. Presenting both sides is more effective with the better educated and the opposition and is more effective as innoculation against subsequent propaganda.*

Simply put, it is again knowing your receiver or recievers. That will tell you whether to present both sides or only the favored side of an argument. The reverse of this coin is — what is being presented to you? The answer in either case is important to your P.P.R.

7. *The higher the education, the greater the reliance on print; the lower the education, the greater the reliance on radio and television.*

While the authors were referring to media for the masses, it is probably true with regard to the need for *more* information in *greater* detail. Many people prefer to "get it in writing." If it's an important message for an important target, research will reveal the best way to package your message. If it is not important to get every "edge" you can get, then you can trust your intuitive judgment.

8. *People tend to misperceive and misinterpret persuasive communications in accordance with their own predispositions, by evading the message or by distorting it in a favorable direction.*

(Witness the stated skepticism of intelligent smokers against the findings of cancer specialists. Note how grade-school children will misquote their teacher if they can turn this teacher's remark into a more favorable suggestion. The teacher tells the children: "Don't do your homework at all if you are going to turn it in this messy!" The children tell their parents that the teacher says they don't have to do any homework. Note also that when the first news of Watergate began to filter out, those who supported Richard Nixon were slow to accept the facts. The whole issue "impacted" very slowly. Until the evidence became overwhelming, Nixon sympathizers tried to ignore the details or tried to explain them in more palatable terms.)

Predisposition again! The tendency or inclination for people to... believe or not believe, understand or not understand, agree or disagree... *in advance to hearing arguments for or against*. Why? Research it in *them*... use it... or guard against it... but, above all, be aware of predisposition (or the other five P's) in any person who can affect your welfare... *your* P.P.R.

9. *In cases where the audience approves of the communicator, but disapproves of his conclusions, it tends to disassociate the source from the content.*

(Voters in normally conservative South Dakota support Senator George McGovern even though they would disagree with many of his liberal policies. They value his work in other areas, such as agriculture and Indian Affairs.)

Anytime you can get him or her to like you (first) you get a break on those occasions when they don't particularly like what you're saying. In addition, if they like you first it may be easier for them to accept what you're saying, and maybe even like it. The other side is when they like and approve of *him*, and you are debating him, formally or informally. You must always be careful in "it's your word against mine" situations. Do your homework if you are to be an adversary... if you want an edge. Or if you just want to be careful in building and maintaining your P.P.R.

10. *Arousing audience predispositions in favor of the intended message early in a communication will increase the likelihood that the message will be accepted and decrease the chances of later attrition.*

(This explains why speeches, letters, and articles should get off to a good start. If you alienate an audience at the outset, or leave them with the impression that you don't know the topic, it is virtually impossible to reroute their thinking.)

Hear ye! Hear ye! Hear ye! Even an audience of one!

Superstar Lee Marvin said that an actor brought his film history to each next role. The audience has an image of that person which sharpens and adds to the character the actor (or actress) is portraying. It gives the audience a mindset.

None of your audiences — the receiver(s) of your message — has a perfectly clear, objective mind. Rather, it is cluttered with the sum of all his or her or their experiences. This clutter can present stumbling blocks to our effectively communicating with them.

And there are other factors which can hinder the seemingly simple processes of transmitting your messages to them — the six P's.

Consider The Six P's

In addition to Frede's twelve roadblocks to communication; Berlson and Steiner's (and Reilly's comments) ten psychological considerations involved in communications; please consider what I call the Six P's that will impact on the reception of your messages as they enter the minds of your receiver(s).

1. *Predisposition* is the tendency or inclination to draw conclusions, to be influenced by previous experience, knowledge, or familiarity, even to the point of prejudice or bias for or against something or someone, *before* the facts are known. It is a tendency to hear what we want to hear, see what we want to see, believe what we want to believe. Many times, in fact, people will make up their minds and then look for evidence to support their position or beliefs. *His experience with the legal profession predisposed him to endorse (or not endorse) the candidate.*

2. *Proclivity* is the natural inclination of people for some thing, some one, or some performance, While it is a natural inclination, it can be nurtured or used. *She has a proclivity for....* Wouldn't you like to know?

3. *Perception* is a tendency to see what we would like to see. It is therefore what people *think* they see, hear, understand, conclude, recognize, distinguish and discern. More important to be aware of — *What he or she perecives to be your image is your image to him or her.*

4. *Predilection* is a person's preference, partiality, fondness, or desire for some thing, or some one, or some performance or action. *He had a prediliction for tall, blond women*—which you should know if you're a petite brunette.

5. *Preconception* is an idea or opinion formed or conceived in advance of acquiring full information. *All Italians eat pasta, therefore if you're Italian you must eat pasta.*

6. *Prejudice* is a judgment or opinion, often unfavorable, formed without good reason, often on insufficient and subjective knowledge, of people, situations, or issues. *No examples are necessary.*

The response to your performance — your message — by any one of your publics, can be influenced by any or all of the Six P's. What can you do about it? If the public is an important one, seek the knowledge. You can use a person's natural inclinations, correct a misconception, provide a better example, educate, even change a perception.

Perception could be the most important "P" of all. I remember when "Made in Japan" meant cheap, shoddy copies of products originated elsewhere. The Japanese changed that perception (and therefore predispositions) with their performance, and by communicating (advertising) that improved performance.

Perception is defined in my *Funk & Wagnall's* dictionary as (1) The act, power, process, or product of perceiving; knowledge through the senses of the existence and properties of matter and the external world; (2) The faculty or power of acquiring immediate and fundamental knowledge through the senses; (3) Any insight or intuitive judgment that implies unusual discernment of fact or truth.

Perception, as defined above, can impact greatly on our communications, on the reception of our messages, on our P.P.R. Awareness is the key. The following fundamentals may help you to understand how and why others perceive your messages as they do; they may help you to understand others just a little bit better.

Fifteen Fundamentals Of Perception

1. Your perception is a highly subjective matter. So is his.

2. Your perception is highly selective. So is hers.

3. Perception is the characteristic that accounts for individual differences. And individuals add up to *them*.

4. Neither you nor he will see things exactly in the same way, or in the same exact way.

5. Your or his or her perception is your or his or her interpretation of some excitation of one of your senses — a stimulus.

6. People (we and they) tend to fill in the gaps to complete something that appears to be incomplete.

7. Each person thinks, feels, and sees something based on each of their individual experiences.

8. People gain new perceptions only through new experiences.

9. How he or she perceives another person depends in large part by what he or she *expects* to see in that person.

10. You or he will see things differently at different times and in different situations and circumstances.

11. His or her or your self-image will depend a lot on what he or she or you see/sees.

12. You — people — will tend to simplify things you do not understand.

13. Your (his or her) emotional reaction to the actions of

others are often barriers to effectively communicating with each other.

14. People, many times, see things, not the way they are, but as they want them to be.

15. You have *learned* to see things as you do. So did they.

All of the standards, rules, and principles, and the like, laid out in this chapter, are merely guides whose prime purpose is to make you aware of the difficulties we encounter as we try to communicate. And *awareness is the foundation of effective communication.*

Communication is basic to our everyday existence. Recognition of the power of effective communication is power in itself. It has been so since even before Plato wrote in his Dialogs:

> " ... What is there greater than the word which persuades the judges on the courts, or the Senators in the Council, or the citizens in the assembly, or at any other political meeting? If you have the power of uttering this word, you will have the physician your slave, and the trainer your slave, and the money maker of whom you talk will be found to gather treasures, not for himself, but for you who are able to speak and to persuade the multitude."

At the beginning of this chapter we listed four ways that you are communicating with others whether you wanted to or not — how you look... how you act... how you speak... and how you write.

Let's take a look at just how *you* look.

8

Here's Looking At You

"For thousands of years human beings have communicated with one another first in the language of dress. Long before I am near enough to talk to you on the street, in a meeeting, or at a party, you announce your sex, age, and class to me through what you are wearing — and very possibly give me important information (or misinformation) as to your occupation, origin, personality, opinions, tastes, sexual desires and current mood. I may not be able to put what I observe into words, but I register the information unconsciously; and you simultaneously do the same for me. By the time we meet and converse we have already spoken to each other in an older and more universal tongue."

So begins a book, *The Language of Clothes*, by Alison Lurie.

It's not only clothes. Add hairdo, makeup, jewelry, and grooming, and you have the complete uniform or costume for your role as business executive, golfer, laborer, housewife, secretary, mother, priest, hiker, skiier, nun, physician, merchant, lawyer, father, mother, merchant, banker, salesman, nurse, stockbroker, reporter, teacher, student — you. It is *your* visual image and — along with your posture, how you walk and how you sit — an important element of your whole image.

"Clothing is 90 percent of what people see of you," Debra Gae Cox, an image-consultant, told a group of first-year MBA students at New York University's Graduate School of Business Administration (according to a Knight-Ridder Newspapers feature story). "People judge us — decide who we are and where we're going and where we've been — based on one glance at our clothing," Ms. Cox said.

"Most American women dress for *failure*. I have said that before about men, and research shows that it applies equally to women," writes John T. Molloy, in his book, *The Woman's Dress For Success Book*.

"You may object to the idea that clothes can make or break a woman, but the conclusions in this book are the results of years of research," according to the blurb on the book's jacket.

That seems to be Molloy's opinion about men, too. His book, *Dress For Success*, is about men, and his article in *Success* magazine, February, 1986, states that even so seemingly a small symbol as the tie you wear carries an important message from, and about, you to them. Molloy calls ties the "heraldic shields of 20th-century corporate America." The correct tie, he writes, is the diagonally striped "rep" tie. It heads his list of recommended ties and is followed by dotted ties, the foulards (with small, repeated geometric shapes in a regular pattern), the "club" tie (a regular pattern of animals, insignias, etc.), and last, but not least, the always appropriate solid tie.

To the most sophisticated executives, according to Molloy, the diagonally striped tie or patterned "club" tie, "announce that you are a member of his club."

More and more, it seems, *how* you look is occupying more and more attention from people concerned about what I refer to as your P.P.R. I've read (and clipped and filed) such newspaper articles as "Proper Dress As Important As Contacts, Consultant Says," "Fashion Writer Knocks Bow Ties," "Do's and Don'ts Of Updating The Vest," "'Image' Opens Doors For Clients In '80s," "Dressing For Success," and others. And then there are the books.

"Today," Lurie writes in her book, "...sociologists tell us that fashion... is a language of signs, a nonverbal system of communication." She writes of the vocabulary of dress which includes not only clothes, but hair styles, jewelry, and make-up. "Theoretically, at least," according to Lurie, "this vocabulary is as large or larger than that of the spoken tongue, since it includes every garment, hair style, and type of body decoration ever invented."

What do *you* do? Since you are communicating, whether you want to or not, saying, in effect, "Hey! Look me over!" or "I don't care what I look like today!," describing and defining yourself to others — What *do* you do?

First, you consider that there are different images of you for different people or groups of people. If clothes communicate like words — which they can do — then remember that words can be common or they can be unusual. They can be foreign or native, acceptable or vulgar. And, as with all forms of communication, you must be concerned not only with the message you are sending to them, but the message that they are receiving. Once again, if *they* are important to your welfare, you must know, if at all possible, *how* they will decode your message, *how* they will interpret it, as well as their predisposition (and some of the other P's) toward the contents of your message.

As it is with what you say or write, the meaning of any particular uniform or costume you are wearing depends on circumstances — the specific place and time, the situation, the P's of your receiver or receivers, and any variation which may alter your message's meaning.

Bright, splash-colored golfing slacks topped with a red sports shirt, could create quite a stir if worn to a board meeting or a wake. And you certainly wouldn't play golf in a three-piece suit (although they did so many years ago). Those would be obvious no-nos, as would wearing a halter and short-shorts, or ragged jeans and tie-dyed T-shirts to church. A kerchief over a head full of curlers probably wouldn't cause a head to turn in most supermarkets, but you've never seen a receptionist that way. As the old adage proclaims — there *is* a time and place for everything.

How we wear the clothes we choose can have the same important connotation as how we write or speak the words we choose. People judge us not only by the words we use, but how we write them or speak them. They will likewise judge us not only by the clothes we wear, but on how we wear them and how we maintain them. Do your clothes fit properly? A $500 suit or a designer dress a couple of sizes too big... or too small, can send many messages. You gain a few pounds... you lose a few pounds, but why tell them? Are your clothes (if not new or old) in new or old condition, wrinkled or pressed, soiled or clean? Does anything look worse than a wrinkled neck overlapping a wrinkled shirt collar, unless it also suffers from "ring around the collar?" How about a dress belt that disappears when you sit down? Or trousers that have multiple creases going in the wrong direction?

Yes, people judge us by how we look. And if we're honest we will admit that we judge them by how they look. Let a well-dressed, well-groomed businessman-type, carrying an attache case, stop us on the street and ask for directions, we are at ease. Not so if the same man were in ragged clothes, sporting an unkempt beard and long hair, and carrying a plain brown paper bag which may contain a bottle.

Then there is the circumstance and the situation. We expect the automobile mechanic to be less than sparkling clean, but we recoil from the filthy tramp, and we wouldn't tolerate a waitress with soiled clothes or dirty hands. We have come to expect certain standards, and any deviation from those standards disturbs us. We might even suspect that the automobile mechanic wearing clean, crisp workclothes, and having clean hands with clean fingernails, couldn't possibly have worked on our car (other then turning a screw or adjusting a wire) so why should we be charged so much.

We have this tendency or inclination to draw conclusions based on previous experience, knowledge, or familiarity. We are predisposed to believe what we are accustomed to believing. We want our mechanics to look like mechanics, our waitresses, our doctors, our lawyers, etc., to look like what they are supposed to look like.

Theatrical costumers call this fashion characterization or the signature look of a character. The Lone Ranger's mask and costume, black hats/white hats on good guys, bad guys, Superman's uniform, a policeman, et al are simple examples. More complex character uniforms are evident in the mid-1980's Dynasty, Miami Vice, Dallas, and L.A. Law television programs. In real life many people in rural America still have a smalltown suspicion of that neat, well-dressed city slicker; a farmer dressed in bib overalls might be looked at with some skepticism if he walked into a Wall Street brokerage office;and an attorney dressed in slacks and sports shirt might have trouble impressing a jury.

Many people could have a tendency based on previous experience to believe that a 6-year-old girl would look adorable in shorts and halter, a 26-year-old would look sexy, and a 56-year-old would look ridiculous. Each of these predispositions could be absolutely wrong. The 6-year-old could be grossly overweight, the 26-year-old could be skin and bones thin, and the 56-year-old could be any one of a half-dozen actresses that would look anything but ridiculous in shorts and halter. In each of these cases, however, most people would have to be shown.

These examples, of course, are generalizations. You have to be more concerned with the specific predispositions (and other P's) of your receivers — in your office, at school, even at play. If one of five, for instance, was jealous of you, the message sender, or harbored resentment over a real or imagined affront, then you can be assured that one of five will not receive your message as favorably as you might have wished. Moreover, one of the five may even attempt to convert one or more of the remaining four to his or her way of thinking. What to do? You may flinch at the idea of seemingly giving up your independence and individuality and wish to continue to "do your own thing." Consequently, living with the consequences may be the direction for you. You may want to forget about the "one in five" and be satisfied with your four-in-five success rate. Or you may want to compromise — Do your own thing with your friends, and in your social life, while you play a role in your business life.

Lurie writes: "Perhaps the most difficult aspect of sartorial communication is the fact that any language that is able to convey information can also be used to convey misinformation. You can lie in the language of dress just as you can in English, French, or Latin, and this sort of deception has the advantage that one cannot usually be accused of doing it deliberately. The costume that suggests youth or wealth, unlike the statement that one is twenty-nine years old and has a six-figure income, cannot be directly challenged or disproved."

Under the subheading of "Dressing for 'Success'," Lurie writes, "A more ambiguous sort of disguise is the costume that is deliberately chosen on the advice of others in order to deceive the beholder. For over a hundred years books and magazines have been busy translating the correct language of fashion, telling men and women what they should wear to seem genteel, rich, sophisticated, and attractive to the other sex. Journals addressed to what used to be called 'the career girl' advised her how to dress to attract 'the right kind of man' — successful, marriage-minded."

As Lurie writes: "In dress as in language there is a possible range of expression from the most eccentric statement to the most conventional."

Under the subheading of "Eloquence and Bad Taste," Lurie writes, "Between cliche and madness in the language of dress are all the known varieties of speech; eloquence, wit, information, irony, propaganda, humor, pathos, and even (though rarely) true poetry."

You, as do I, and most of our friends, can and do use a variety of language. But we usually keep our tongues under control. We are careful how and where we may use slang or vulgarities, foreign words, taboo words, modern words, professional jargon, and the like. So, too, must we control our dress and our looks.

While dress is some 80 to 90 percent of our looks, there is more. Do we (men) wear a mustache or beard and, if so, what kind? Do we (men and women) wear our hair short, medium, or long? Styled how? What type and style of make-up do we (women) wear? What kind and how much jewelry do we (men and women) wear? How about eyeglasses? Are yours in style? Some people wear them when they don't have to — to look more mature, more intelligent. Some have as many as four pairs to coordinate with different outfits in their wardrobes. "Lawyers generally go for classic, preppy, tortoiseshell frames such as those in the Ralph Lauren 'Polo' line. Women lawyers might go for Liz Claiborne frames in such colors as navy blue, forest green, or bright red. They want to look both stylish and highly professional," said an optician at a local shop.

How about hair styles?

Much has been written about women's hair styles and most salons can advise on what's in and what's out for what occasions or functions. Men's styles have been moving (1988) toward closer cropped hairstyles with ears showing. Your barber (or unisex salon) can give advice. In any case, men or women, just look around — at your fellow workers, executives, bosses, professionals, etc. How the same, how different, do you want to be?

Then there is grooming. Commented on very well by the late Andy Warhol:

"Well-groomed people are the real beauties. It doesn't matter what they're wearing or who they're with or how much their jewelry costs or how much their clothes cost or how perfect their makeup is: If they're not clean, they're not beautiful. The most plain or unfashionable person in the world can still be beautiful if they're very well groomed."

The two books by Molloy, quoted by Lurie, teach businessmen and businesswomen "how to select their clothes so that they will look efficient, authoratative, and reliable, even when they are incompetent, weak, and shifty."

In his books, Molloy will advise you, man or woman, every step of the way, in words and drawings.

You may not want to go that far, but if you want to climb the ladder in your company you *will* dress for success in *that* company. How? By dressing, in general, *as* the already successful in your company dress. How does your supervisor dress? His boss? You become — not exactly, but almost — a copycat. You do not become a clone. You maintain your individuality, but within the dress code — written or unwritten — of your company ... your circle of friends ... your school ... your business ... your profession. Then, all things being equal — talent, attitude, competency, initiative — you'll be a copycat for success. And when you are successful *they* will dress like you. And in your social life, at the country club, it can begin again as you dress as they dress for tennis, for golf, for dinner and dancing.

But you may be a professional. Great! Then you have lots of bosses — your clients, patients, or customers. And you have a role to dress for.

Would *you* feel confident of your attorney if he wore jeans, beard stubble, and sneakers in the courtroom? Could you go the optician whose nails were dirty or whose breath smelled bad? How about your doctor? A survey of 200 patients was published in the Journal of the American Medical Association. It showed that patients wanted their doctors to look like doctors. More like Marcus Welby than Hawkeye Pierce.

Thirty-seven percent wanted their physicians to wear ties; 34% thought female M.D.s should wear dresses or skirts; 65% thought doctors on duty should wear white coats or jackets; 52% said blue jeans were a no-no.

One of the investigators, Dr. Thomas H. Lee, a cardiologist at Harvard Medical School's Brigham and Women's Hospital in Boston, said that doctors should dress better to convey confidence, not fashion sense.

"I don't think the patient needs to feel like the doctor just walked off the set of 'Miami Vice'," Lee said in a newspaper interview.

Lois Fenton, a consultant to many of the Fortune 500 companies, and co-author (with Edward Olcott) of *Dress For Excellence*, has spent more than ten years telling business executives how to dress to climb the career ladder. Fenton, who knows the power of dressing, says look in the mirror when you dress and you can avoid most dressing mistakes.

Top executives, she says, know that appearance translates into power. Think of the executive world as an exclusive club, she says. Club members generally dress similarly. And if you want to join the club, you should dress as other club members do.

"Dress for the job you're aspiring to, not the job you have." Fenton says.

Some general rules:

From Molloy (for men) —

— Wear suits in the workplace (unless you work in a profession — advertising, entertainment, etc. — where it is acceptable to dress down. Your suits should be wool, or look like wool. In blues and grays.

— Shirts should be cotton or look like cotton. Solid colors preferable to patterns although subtle pinstripes and plaids are acceptable. And long sleeves. No matter what manufacturers say about the popularity of short-sleeved dress shirts, Molloy, in *Dress For Success*, wrote: "If you intend to take anything I've said in this book at all seriously... you will never, ever, as long as you live, wear a short-sleeve shirt for any business purpose, no matter whether you're the office boy or the president of the company. Short-sleeve shirts are symbols of the lower-middle class, and therefore pack no psychological authority or power."

— Ties should be silk or look like silk. Solid is safest, but acceptable patterns include club, rep, paisley.

Socks, executive length (calf), color matching suit.

Shoes, conservative. Wing-tip or lace-up styles are best. In black, brown, or cordovan.

In his updated edition (1988) Molloy says brown suits are now acceptable in business. Contrasting shirt collars and cuffs are okay. And suspenders are popular and acceptable.

From Molloy (for women) —

— Look professional, organized, and neat; never sexy or artfully dressed. Makeup minimal, hair shoulder length or shorter.

— Suits should be wool or look like wool. Skirt-and-jacket combinations can work, but the look is not quite as professional as the suit.

— Blouses can be just about anything that "looks expensive."

— Shoes should be pumps, closed heel and toe.

— Stockings should be nylons.

— Accessories should be the highest quality you can afford.

Molloy says the color of your suit can increase or decrease your aura of power or likability. To add to your power wear solid navy, solid dark gray, dark gray pinstripe, or best, dark blue pinstripe. Also good is medium blue solid, medium gray pinstripe, or medium blue pinstripe. To project a neutral power image wear medium gray solid. To decrease your power image, wear light blue or light gray solids.

From Fenton (for men)

— Give priority to quality over quantity. One (or two) very well-tailored suits plus a variety of shirts and ties that will give even one classic suit a different look each time it is worn. Three basic suit colors: blue, gray, and tan. Acceptable suits are blue, from dark navy to medium; gray, from medium to dark charcoal; tan, from camel to beige.

— Shirts should fit properly. White, blue, hairline stripes.

— Ties. Avoid the polyester or polyblend ties. Wear silk. Tie it properly, not too short.

— Shoes. Black, dark brown, or cordovan.

— Socks. Dark, over the calf, color of your suit.

The overall effect, Fenton advises, should be one of careful coordination.

The P.P.R. Way (for men and women) —

— Study how *they* dress and, *in general*, follow suit. I stress, *in general*. If top management *reserves* some "dress code" for themselves — french cuffs, pink shirts, whatever — and absolutely no middle-management person dares encroach... don't. If you're middle-management, that's your domain — at this time. Study how *they* dress and follow suit.

— Peruse Lurie's, Molloy's, and Fenton's books. Each is expert help. Each is probably available in your bookstore or library.

"The name of the science I practice is wardrobe engineering, says Molloy. "The idea is to use research data to manipulate the dress of an individual to draw favorable response from the people he or she meets... .

"The term manipulate may strike you as sinister. It's not. Wardrobe engineering, like all sciences, is really amoral. In our money-oriented, status-conscious society, most people want to succeed. And you stand a much better chance of succeeding if you know what research has determined to be the look of success."

Looking right for success is only part of being successful. You have also to act right, for many times actions do indeed speak louder than words about your P.P.R.

9

Actions Can Speak Louder...

Nothing else affects our P.P.R. more than our actions and reactions. Every day, in every way, we can make some situation better or worse. We may be affectionate, kind, or compassionate; hateful, malicious, or pitiless. Conversely, so can *they*. We can be cheerful, courteous, and smiling; gloomy, impolite, or frowning — as *they* can.

Our actions or reactions can be deliberate, conscious behavior, or a product — good or bad — of our attitudes, habits, or manners. So can theirs — our business associates, subordinates, peers, and superiors; friends, enemies, and acquaintances; family members and relatives; classmates and teachers; the butcher, the baker, et al. Sometimes we are the *they* and *they* are our clients, customers, students, patrons, or patients.

Why do we act as we do?

Four Basic Reasons For Our Actions

We act, or react, in a certain way — good, bad, neutral, or indifferent for four basic reasons:

1. *Subconsciously* — from attitude, habit, or instinct;

2. *Ignorantly* — because we do not know the standards or mores of conduct; we don't know we should act differently;

3. *Unconsciously* — Using non-verbal communication we are acting without knowing we are acting at all;

4. *Planned* — we are communicating by design; communicating exactly what we want to communicate.

There are fine lines separating the first three reasons. So fine, in fact, that the lines of one may often be crossed by, or combined with, another.

Our attitudes, habits, or instincts, for instance, may result in bad manners being perceived by another, while we may not even realize we have committed a breach of propriety. Then, again, we may act properly just from attitude or habit, because those attitudes and habits were instilled in us in our formative "growing up" years by our parents and teachers.

If we have little or no knowledge of how to act within a certain group, or in a certain situation or circumstance, we may very easily offend, or, at the least, be made to feel foolish.

We can feel foolish, too, if we communicate non-verbally and the only clue we have is a negative response.

Getting past the generalities (of 1, 2, and 3) we must attempt to communicate with an awareness of ourselves, and of the basic reasons for our actions.

Let's examine the four basic ways we act:

1. Acting Subconsciously

Are you acting subconsciously? Assess *your* attitudes, habits, and instincts. Ask yourself:

1. Which of your attitudes... your habits... your instincts... contribute to negative or undesirable actions or reactions on your part that result in unfavorable performances?

2. Which attitudes, habits, and instincts result in favorable performances?

3. Which of those attitudes, habits, and instincts in your answer to Question #1 can be eliminated? Which can be modified? Changed?

4. Which of those attitudes, habits, and instincts, in your answer to Question #2, can be cultivated and nurtured.

How do I really know which attitudes or habits are negative, you might ask. Some are plainly evident.

If you are the only smoker (habit) at a table full of people (socially dining, business meeting, etc.), and you light up without concern for others because you feel you have the right to do so (attitude), that could be termed negative behavior. If you have a habit of interrupting during conversation (business or social), which many consider an attitude that says what you have to say is more important (others consider it a bad habit), then that is a negative performance.

The best answer to the question of what attitudes or habits are negative would seem to be another question: Does an action (habit or attitude) impinge on another, project an image of inconsideration or selfishness, or is it simply a breach of good manners? If it is, chances are good that it's a negative action that will elicit a negative response from the receiver of your message.

This is not to say the same action will be negative (or positive) in all situations and circumstances, and with all message receivers. An action may be inconsiderate and bad manners to one receiver and not to another, i.e., you may give a favorite uncle a hearty slap on the back, along with a raucous "Hello you ole S.O.B.," but you wouldn't greet your pastor that way. Then again, maybe you favorite uncle wouldn't appreciate that friendly, if rowdy, greeting under certain circumstances.

So, we must consider who, what, when, and where of each of our performances if we wish to elicit positive responses. The key word to remember is — appropriateness.

In assessing our performances, we must always be careful to consider the perception and interpretation of our message recievers, as well as the number of receivers. You will not, usually, change a performance, for instance, based on a minority of unfavorable perceptions or interpretations of your message. Usually, that is. If a dozen co-workers do not seem to mind your habit of (whatever), but it drives one—your boss— up the wall, you may want to exercise controlled awareness when you interact with him or her. Be aware, too, that your dozen co-workers may be (consciously or subconsciously) overlooking your (annoying) habit because they know you and like you. If you eliminate that habit it may be (consciously or subconsciously) that they will like you even more.

Do not, however, endeavor to change a performance just because a *he* or *she* is predisposed to be anti-you for one reason or another. You may, if he is, or may become, important to your success, make an effort to win him over with your overall performance (consideration, friendliness, helpfulness, cheerfulness, etc.), so that his predisposition toward your smaller, individual performances will be favorably receptive.

2. Acting From Ignorance

To combat our acting inappropriately from ignorance of *their* standards or mores, we must assess our knowledge and understanding of the standards of conduct approved by the society in which we function, and by society as a whole. In this way we will know how to act differently if and when we want to.

Assess too (review) your knowledge of *them* so you will know how your actions or reactions are being interpreted or perceived.

If you know your alternatives of action you can, when you want to, behave with imaginative courtesy and friendliness to improve the quality of any interaction or relationship.

(Any good book on manners will give you the knowledge of *their* standards of conduct. But don't stop reading this chapter to get one. The basics will be covered when we tackle the fourth reason for our actions — planned communication.)

3. Acting Unconsciously / Nonverbal Communication

To understand how you may be communicating without even knowing you are, you must first assess your knowledge of the unconscious or subtle actions of nonverbal communication. Much has been written in recent years about such communication as eye contact and movement, and body language.

Whenever we talk to another person, we not only send a verbal message, but we express nonverbally our attitudes and feelings about the message or the person. You've probably heard someone say, "I'm *not* angry" or "That doesn't bother *me*," when, in fact, it's easy for you to see that the opposite is true. How? You picked up another kind of communication that was more obvious than the words — the speaker's fists were clenched, or his body was rigid and tense. He may have glared as he spoke. In other words, he was sending a double message — a verbal message of peace, and a non-verbal message of anger. If you don't perceive this dual message (words and physical actions), you may miss the real meaning. You must therefore be aware of the physical signals being sent as well as *what* is being said.

Response to nonverbal communication is important if you are to be an effective communicator. To stay in tune note the words *and* the nonverbal expressions and your chances of open, two-way communication with employees, classmates, customers, clients, friends, patients, relatives, et al, will be increased greatly. Be aware that nonverbal messages exist and learn how to read them.

Of course, you know *he* is bored when he yawns or looks at his watch, or he develops *heavy eyelids*, instead of leaning forward, eyes alert, interest on his face. Too obvioius? How about crossing one's legs, folding arms, head movement, hand movement, and other theories of body language? How about posture and the theory that different positions of different limbs relate to different inner emotions?

Everything must, of course, be put into context. Generalizations are always dangerous. Nonverbal messages should be taken *only* as clues, not as absolutes. Besides, with knowledge, a person could lie nonverbally, couldn't he?

Nonverbal messages usually come in four general forms: body action, body position, eye contact, and facial expressions:

Body Action — the substitution of a physical movement for words. These nonverbal clues and cues range from nodding or shaking the head to signal *yes* or *no*, to shrugging the shoulders to indicate "I don't know," or waving the hand to say "goodbye."

You are probably familiar with these signs and most people can agree on their meaning. But others are generally less understood. Foot and finger tapping, nail biting, loud sighs, rapid eye-blinking, pacing, knuckle-cracking, are not easily interpreted. Your first reaction may be — he seemed a little nervous.

A better explanation might be *blocked* communication — unspoken feelings seeking expression. If you respond to the nervous person by trying to make him feel relaxed, when in fact the actions are caused by anger, he may become alienated, convinced you are not aware of just how important the anger provocation is to him.

Be aware, therefore, of his *complete* performance — actions and words — so you may respond to his performance with your own — one that can have a positive impact on your P.P.R.

Body Position — the nonverbal expression that can be seen in such body positions as posture (how far he leans forward, toward you, or backward, away from you), openness of arms and legs, the distance maintained between two people who are communicating. Many believe that a relaxed, forward, leaning position by a speaker indicates a more positive attitude toward the listener, than does a backward leaning position.

When you are talking with someone note whether their arms and legs are in an open or closed positon. Arms in an open, unfolded position is supposed to indicate a positive feeling. (They might be feeling: I'm finding this meeting to be pleasant, helpful, etc.) Arms folded in front is normally thought to indicate negative feelings. (I'm not too comfortable with this person or the discussion.)

Once again, be aware of the possible messages of body language. When they are in agreement with the words, it is safe to respond to a complete message. When they conflict, be aware that there may indeed be a conflict.

Eye Contact — Studies indicate that there seems to be greater eye contact with a person who is liked or trusted than with one who is disliked or mistrusted. This behavior trait reverses itself with extreme anger or hostility where a continuous glaring type of eye contact is maintained. Notice, too, the distance a person chooses to put between you and himself — his eyes and yours — in conversation. Generally, it is thought, the closer he stands, the closer he is, the more positive he is.

The nonverbal messages of eye contact have become so common — if he doesn't look you in the eye he must be lying — that one wonders if people who lie can purposely look directly into your eyes, while people who are telling the truth may not be able to do so.

At any rate, knowledge is power, and awareness is knowledge. And now you know.

Facial Expression — the nonverbal communication which includes such common facial expressions as frowning, smiling, clamping down one's teeth, wrinkling one's nose, or positioning one's eyebrows. Most of us note these emotional signals as we communicate, although we probably should be more watchful for those that are very subtle. Too often we fail to respond properly to them. We surmise, for example — You're frowning. Are you confused or troubled? You're scowling. Are you angry? Your scrunching your eyebrows. Are you confused or bewildered? Usually we just continue to respond only to the verbal message. "You *say* you understand. Good. Go ahead. Finish the plan... project... whatever." The result could be poor communication and its consequences.

There are many gestures that *could* mean something, *could be* a message or part of a message, in conjunction with words, or not. Here are twenty-five to be aware of and think about:

25 Nonverbal Communications Gestures

1. Tapping of fingers	could mean	impatience, boredom, nervousness.
2. Shrugging of shoulders	" "	disinterest, ambivalence.

3.	Wringing of hands	" "	despair, hopelessness.
4.	Clenched fist(s)	" "	aggressiveness, controlled anger.
5.	Open hands, palms up, in front of body	" "	puzzlement, perplexed.
6.	Unbuttoning coat	" "	getting ready for action.
7.	Arms crossed on chest	" "	defiance, judgmental.
8.	Walking rapidly, arms swinging freely, chin held high	" "	confidence, assertiveness.
9.	Shuffling walk, hands in pocket, head held low	" "	despondence, dejection, depression.
10.	Palm of hand held to cheek	" "	surprise, wonderment.
11.	Stroking chin	" "	conjecture, thoughtfulness.
12.	Touching, rubbing nose	" "	thinking.
13.	Hands on hips	" "	superiority, defiance.
14.	Steepling of hands	" "	interest, thinking.
15.	Head tilted to side	" "	quizzical.
16.	Dropping eye glasses (not Ben Franklins) to lower bridge of nose, peering over rims	" "	wants more... especially facts.
17.	Pacing	" "	anxiety, nervousness.
18.	Pinching bridge of nose	" "	fatigue (if eyeglasses aren't ill fitting).
19.	Sitting on edge of chair	" "	anticipation, interest.

20.	Moved crossed leg in slight kicking motion	" "	boredom.
21.	Pointing of index finger	" "	making a point.
22.	Feet crossed on desk	" "	attempt to impress, uncouth.
23.	Leaning back with both hands behind and supporting neck	" "	relaxed, attempting to impress.
24.	Hands covering mouth while speaking	" "	doesn't want to be clear.
25.	Holding an arm behind back and clenching its hand, while the other hand grips the wrist	" "	restraint, tension, or he, or she, is a contortionist.

As you can see, if we are aware, we may be able to learn more about *what* he is saying by his nonverbal language.

Many people believe that body language is a subconscious indication of how you *really* feel; what your message is *really* saying.

We can learn much when we are the receiver of these messages, whether or not they are combined with verbal messages. Conversely, *they* can learn much about *us* and our messages when we are the message sender. Now that we are fully aware of the possibilities, we will send only those messages that we want to send.

There are many experts in your public library that can provide you with just a little more insight into what people may really mean when they say what; how to perceive attitudes from impressions. Don't take every theory or concept as gospel, but with a little patience and practice you just may be able to read, at least, the mood of others—when to broach that *delicate* subject to the boss, how *she* is reacting to your suggestion, *when* to end a conversation or a meeting, or what he *really* thinks about your idea.

4. Planned Communication

What each of us should really be concerned with is acting or reacting by design — communicating exactly what we really want to communicate, to whom we want to communicate, when we want to communicate, and how. This is something we can only do on purpose. We can only fully tailor our behavior to suit a particular person or circumstance when we are fully aware of, and know how to build on or change, our options and alternatives. The key words here are *fully aware* and *change*.

We now have assessed our attitudes, habits, and instincts, and we can cultivate those that are positive, and modify, or eliminate, those that are negative; we have assessed our understanding of society's mores and *their* interpretations and perceptions; we have learned that there are ways — a look, a tilt of the head, the movement of a hand—that can sometimes communicate our *true* opinion or feeling; we now should become aware of what are considered proper or improper actions, or reactions, so that we may use either to communicate exactly what we want to communicate.

Action, in my dictionary, is simply defined as "behavior; conduct;" as is the word, deportment. Mores is defined as "customs of behavior." Manners is defined as "polite, courteous deportment." It would seem, then, that manners is *customary, polite, courteous action.*

Consider Manners

Just about everyone has some idea or concept of manners, but very few of us have given much, if any, thought to using the knowledge to improve our relationships; to improve the quality of our business or social lives by behaving with creative and imaginative courtesy toward others. It is not that difficult. Once we have given some thought to manners we will probably become more mannerly. Or, if we consciously desire to, on occasion, we can become downright unmannerly. Our knowledge and awareness provides us with this choice. Knowledge (and awareness) is, indeed, power. Power we can use every day, in many ways, to enhance our P.P.R.

Good manners, it is said, requires that we know and understand enough about other people and their behavior, so that we may avoid treating them badly, or being treated badly. A friend, for instance, may be hurt, and remain silent, by our curt remark under one circumstance, or laugh it off with a light "go to hell" on another occasion. Or *we* could. Our boss (or professor/teacher or parent or a police officer or...) could produce a different result if we don't know enough about him, or he doesn't know enough about us.

"Manners are the happy way of doing things," accordng to Ralph Waldo Emerson.

So let's get on with our brief study of manners.

If you had a reference library that contained *McCalls Book of Everyday Etiquette, A Guide to Modern Manners*, you could learn the correct silverware, where you put it when you set a table, and how you use each of the utensils. You could learn who to tip, how to tip, and how much to tip. You would learn how to introduce him to her, her to him, they to them, or you to whomever.

In *Amy Vanderbilt's Everyday Etiquette*, in Q and A form, you could get the answers to such questions as "...can you eat it (bacon) with your fingers... how do you address a sympathy card to..." and "when you are a week-end guest, are you supposed to take a gift to the hostess, to the family as a whole, to the children if any?"

From books (available in your local library) you can learn how to eat artichokes, not to tip a hospital nurse (they are professionals), and if you write to the President on a business matter you close with "Respectfully," but if it is a social letter with "Very Respectfully."

One book you may want to refer to is *Letitia Baldridge's Complete Guide To Executive Manners*. As is written on the book's jacket: "This is a new kind of guide to business success in America. Every company, every executive or executive-to-be needs it. The first *complete* guide to manners that smooth life at work, it shows people and companies how to perform flawlessly, with poise and confidence, in every business-related situation."

This book not only discusses manners, but dressing and grooming for business; business card etiquette (when and how to offer your card); calling, organizing, and running one of the more than 750,000 corporate meetings held each year in the United States; business entertaining from lunch for two, to thousands; and executive communications. It offers help for you to act properly in the boardroom, at the water cooler, in the boss' home, and even, among other countries, in India, France, and Japan. Its more than 500 pages can help you with your business relationships, visual communication, and even greeting others.

This is not a commercial for the book, but rather an attempt to show you the broad coverage it gives for the business executive. I have no personal interest in this book other than I own a copy. I refer to it time after time. It is, in my opinion, the ultimate guide to business manners. Everything I need to know to do the right thing, at the right time, in every business situation, is there for me to know and use. When you need such advice this expert is as near as your local library.

If, as Emerson wrote, manners are the happy way of doing things, let's read a few of the words written by an authority on manners.

Manners — by an authority

"To rebuke someone presupposes that we are above him in some way."

"A courteous silence is more effective in keeping the peace than whole days of explanation, followed by whole weeks of explaining one's explanations."

"Egos make people behave badly to one another... ."

"...the lie as a form of manners. Most people would rather be treated courteously than be told the truth, and if you can add an imaginative flourish to your courtesy so much the better."

"It is the style with which anything is said or done that matters most."

"...we generally accomplish far more in social relations when we disarm an opponent through charm rather than... boxing his ears with verbal crudities."

Any of these quotations would be good rules to remember as you build your personal public relations image. If you think they are just as apropos to the improvement of the quality of your life, you might want to read *Manners from Heaven*, written by Quentin Crisp, a "brilliant reprobate (who) now directs the mischevious glare of his wit to create a guide on good behavior for the '80s."

The 75-year-old-plus Crisp is, as he says, "...not merely a self-confessed homosexual, but a self-evident one." Why did he become an authority on manners? "If you feel that you cannot comply with the morality of the world," he wrote, "you must do everything else you can to be agreeable."

In his foreword, Crisp begins, "Nothing more rapidly inclines a person to go into a monastery than reading a book on etiquette. There are so many trivial ways in which it is possible to commit some social sin. This book endeavours to circumnavigate this. It tells you neither how to eat artichokes nor how to address an archbishop. You can avoid both these hazardous experiences and yet enjoy a rich, full life."

In the remainder of the book, "With deadly accurate insights into human foibles ('manners are a means of getting what we want without appearing to be absolute swine'), Crisp covers all the bases of day-to-day life: how to be polite in an impolite society; why charity begins at home ('in some families manners went out the window, and haven't been seen since'); getting rid of unwanted guests and unwanted hosts; how to weed your social garden and, perhaps the trickiest arena of all, how to steer through the rocky trails and whitewater rapids of sex."

Your nearby library no doubt has a copy of this serious, but lighthearted book. If you like delightfully caustic commentaries, biting satire, and unrelenting humor, you might want to read it just for fun. If you do, keep a corner of your mind tuned in to your P.P.R. — it could be profitable. As it could be if you read any of the other books, especially Baldridge's ...Executive Manners. I emphasize the word *could* because overriding every single rule or theory or concept regarding your action or reaction is the interpretation and perception of your message's receiver(s).

The Message Must Fit The Receiver

If your boss is a coarse, earthy person you may act *too* proper for his liking (consciously or subconsciously), and you may or may not want to be perceived that way. To a potential customer you may look and act like a banker, and he or she may, consciously or subconsciously, have no respect for bankers. It may not be advantageous for your teacher to envy your *too* fashionable clothes, your *too* expensive jewelry, or if you're a teacher, for you to dress that way.

Crisp writes (and I've added the word *sometimes* in parentheses so I could agree with him):

"(Sometimes) To say what we think to our superiors would be inexpedient; (sometimes) to say what we think to our equals would be ill-mannered; and (sometimes) to say what we think to our inferiors is unkind. Good manners (sometimes) occupy the terrain between fear and pity."

Sometimes, depending on *what* we think and *what* we say and *how* we say it.

Our actions, too, must be consistent with the image we are trying to project. We cannot say one thing and contradict it with our actions. Possibly more important, we cannot have an action that is perceived or interpreted as one that contradicts what we have said was our principle or philosophy.

We must not contradict, either, when we are using two or more mediums. Crisp, for instance, writes of "...the lie as a form of manners." True, we may not want to unfavorably comment on her new hairdo or his new jacket or their children. Crisp writes: "Whenever someone says to me, 'But what do you *really* think about me (him, her, it)? What I *really* think is that it's time to go."

But, alas, we cannot always go. And we may have to lie. "Yes, I like your new hairdo!" That gentle kind of hypocricy to spare another's feelings. *This can be dangerous if our eyes are going to be telling the truth.* Better to use the circumventive "Your new hairdo suits you perfectly?" "Your hairdresser really did it this time!" "That's really a very complimentary (complementary) hairdo!" You *are* telling the truth so that your actions, even involuntarily, should not betray you.

In all of our actions we must remember the basic meaning of P.R. — performance and response. If you *look* confident and authoritative; if you *act* with confidence and authority; you will be perceived as being confident and having authority. (Change the adjectives and nouns to fit your specific objectives.) In that way you use how you look and how you act to accomplish those objectives that are important to you.

How you look communicates the first impression of who and what you are, even from a distance. How you act not only adds detail, but confirms or contradicts that impression.

What you say, and how you say it, adds color to the image.

10

Say It Better ...

Just as you would find it difficult to communicate if people were distracted or disturbed by your looks or actions, you will not easily arouse their interest by *what* you say if they are distracted or disturbed by the *way* you are saying it. The medium — your voice — becomes *the* message and the message is negative.

Now, reverse that supposition. You may convince people by *what* you say if they are pleased by the *way* you are saying it. The medium — your voice — becomes *the* message and the message is positive.

Now, if you can combine the two — people are pleased by the way you are saying it *and* are finding that what you are saying is interesting, factual, informative, entertaining, intelligent, or exciting, one complementing the other, both complementing your looks and your actions — you have a combination that can spell good P.P.R. and success.

What you say and how you say it will, no doubt, not shake the world, but it can have a tremendous effect on your business, social life, and family life relationships.

To repeat what was written in the last chapter: If you act with confidence and authority, you will be perceived as *being* confident and *having* authority. Now add: If you speak with confidence and authority, you will be perceived as *being* confident and *having* authority. Combine all three — looking, acting, and speaking confidently and authoritatively — and the perception will be increased many-fold.

Whether it's a formal speech or address; expressing your thoughts and ideas in a meeting; a telephone conversation; an interview; making a sale; small talk at the water cooler or the cocktail party; lunch or dinner conversation; conversing with your boss; talking to your students, your clients, your patients, your customers —

whatever to whomever — the ability to speak, not only confidently, concisely, and convincingly, but properly and pleasantly, is essential to anyone's career. In addition to your looks and your actions, your speech completes an image that "sells" you before you can "sell" your ideas and talents. This is equally true if you are to enjoy a successful social life. The picture that is *you* is an animated "eye" picture and "ear" picture. A deficiency in any one aspect of your image — how you look, how you act, or how you sound — can have a deleterious effect on each of the others.

In the Nixon-Kennedy debate (1960) it was widely concluded that Nixon lost the debate (and, consequently, an extremely close election) because of his looks (five o'clock shadow, posture), his actions (eyes, nervous perspiration), and the sound of his voice (nervousness), and not because of argumentative substance. The television camera, experts said, was relentless in exposing Nixon's shortcomings. Kennedy, they said, had more skilled advisors and make-up people to take advantage of the then fledgling political medium. Indeed, while radio listeners gave the edge to Nixon, deficiencies in all three areas — looks, actions, and voice — made it difficult for TV viewers to concentrate on substance, and remain objective.

Sounds, words, delivery — together they create your speech image; an image that can help make or break a meeting or conference, a relationship, a sale, or a career. It can help people decide if they'll buy a used car from you, go to dinner with you, have you run their business, invest their money, design their insurance program, or just decide if they want to get to know you better. Even if you're an expert on a particular subject, they may never get to know it if they are concentrating on your nasal twang or your nervous, fidgity delivery. These types of distractions can make you ineffective by distorting your verbal message or by diverting their attention.

The Sound Of Our Voice, The Choosing Of Words, And The Skills To Use Both

Assuming that what we have to say is interesting, important, or, at least, relevant to them, our first concerns with our speech image are (1) the sound of our voice, and (2) the words we choose to express our thoughts.

Our next concern is how we use this combination of skills in dozens of business and social situations — public speaking (to a public that might number in the hundreds, thousands, or just be those few attending a staff meeting), talking on the telephone for business or pleasure, small talk or dinner conversation, as well as one-on-one conversations, discussions, and debates.

Each of us speaks in many ways, at different times, in different circumstances. We change our vocabulary, as well as the tone of our voice, to fit the varied and different situations in which we find ourselves. Sometimes it's friendly, sometimes not; now gentle, now harsh; asking, telling, ordering, entreating, even commanding. It is in this one medium of the four (looks, actions, speech, and writing) where we are virtually on our own. We can copy how they dress, how they act, or how they write; we even can be guided by them in choosing our words; but when we deliver those words, transmit our message, we are primarily on our own.

Choosing Our Words

In choosing our words we must be careful (as we must be with the written words we use) that they convey the precise meaning that we wish to convey.

"The difference between the right word and the almost right word," according to Mark Twain, "is the difference between lightning and the lightning bug."

In her book, *Speech Can Change Your Life*, Dorothy Sarnoff says " a well-stocked wordrobe is a big part of colorful speech."

Many people have said or written, in one form or another, that it's not *what* you say that's important, but *how* you say it. I would add — what is *really* important is what they *think* you have said and what they *think* you meant.

> "I know what I have given you. I do not know what you have received."
>
> — Antonio Porchia

Probably the easier of the two factors to change, modify, or control, is your choice of words.

The Right Words

Words do not mean what *you* choose them to mean — not what *you* decide they should mean, or hope they mean, or guess they mean. They mean what *they* want them to mean. And if you want people to understand your ideas, you should understand how words work, and how they combine with other words to project images from your mind to his/her mind.

One of the reference books on my shelf is *How To Increase Your*

Word Power, by the editors of Reader's Digest. Such chapters as "Three Keys to Greater Word Power," which can help you increase your vocabulary by families of words; "Spell It Right," which brings you the most frequently misspelled words used in the business world (and school); "Spelling Demons," a collection of words that give students trouble from grammar school through high school and into college; and "Say It Right," which will help anyone to get the right accent in the right place — can be invaluable in climbing the first rungs of your career ladder.

If you don't want it as a reference book, consult it when necessary (or give it a read) in your local library.

Assuming that your vocabulary is such that you don't have to search for the right word to convey the precise meaning you want to transmit, you must be aware they you cannot always use the same word, or group of words, for both your written and your verbal communications.

When people use writing as their medium they tend to be formal; in speaking they try for informality and, especially, simplicity.

When speaking is the medium we choose to transmit our message, we must first remember that choosing the right words — those words that describe the precise meaning of our ideas and thoughts — is only part of our task. We must also remember that the written word and the spoken word can be comprehended differently: The eye can dwell, the ear cannot; the eye can study a phrase or a word that to the ear is a fleeting sound. When speaking, we must try to choose and use words that are simple and easily transmitted through the ears to the brain of our receiver(s).

Secondly, you, the speaker, must be concerned with your pronunciation, the physical ability of the receiver to hear, and the intelligence of the receiver to comprehend your message.

Third, you must be concerned with how you sound — not only your pronunciation, but your tone, pitch and delivery.

These second and third concerns, many times, will determine your choice of words. If a word's pronunciation presents a problem — you have trouble pronouncing it or cannot pronounce it correctly — you must, unlike when you compose a written message, find a suitable substitute. One that will still transmit your message precisely as you wish; one that will still make you sound as you wish to sound.

The bottom line, however, is always the *right* word. Choose your words to convey the exact idea or concept you wish to communicate.

If the right word or phrase is difficult for you to deliver clearly, then choose a substitute. (If the situation requires a certain amount of vagueness, don't hesitate to choose a word or phrase of varying interpretation.) At the same time you are choosing your key words, you are also constructing your sentences. Keep them short, clear, and simple. Remember that your main objective is not to show your audience that you can use long, difficult-to-pronounce words (unless the purpose of your talk *is* to illustrate how intelligent you are), but to have your audience acquire complete comprehension of your message. In many cases a pre-written text is important *before* you deliver your words. But the final test is not how the words appear to the eye, but how they sound to the ear.

Pronunciation

When in doubt, check it out, is good advice when it comes to the pronunciation of the words you've chosen to speak. You know, of course, how to pronounce most of the words you use, but there are times... .

Actually, there is no such thing as *correct* pronunciation. There is no single, correct way to say most of the words we use. It is better, therefore, to think of pronunciation as being acceptable or unacceptable, popular or unpopular, in good usage or not — in your geographic area, your situation, your societal circle, your culture, your sphere of action.

The best way to find and select the acceptable pronunciation is by using your dictionary. It will give you good usage, choices in pronunciation, and, in many cases, indicate regional variations.

Should you say (women) WIMM-in or WOH-men, (culinary) KYOO-li-ner-ee or KULL-i-ner-ee, (comfort) KUMM-fort or KOMM-fort, (forehead) FORR-id, FOHR-id, or FOHR-HEDD, (raspberry) RAZZ-berr-ee or RASP-berr-ee, (says) SEZZ or SAYZ, (chiropodist) ki-ROPP-o-dist or tchi-ROPP-o-dist? Look them up. Some may surprise you.

Many times our pronunciation is the victim of laziness or carelessness. A few examples are saying El-em for ELM, or FIL-em for film, RAS-el (wrestle) for RES-el, or myoo-ne-SIP-el for myoo-NIS-e-pal. There are many others.

However, be careful in another way, too. You don't want to be so "correct" that you'll be perceived as being too ostentatious or affected by using ultra elegant pronunciation. Saying sho-FUR, for instance, instead of the more popular SHO-fer, is one example. Saying AHNT, instead of ANT, eh-GAYNST instead of eh-GENST, or AV-en-you, instead of the more populare AV-e-noo, are several others.

Above all else, remember that effective pronunciation is popular pronunciation. *Listen to them!*

The Sound Of Your Image

While you should listen to them it would be wise to be very aware that they listen to you. They decipher and assimilate *your* words with *only* their ears. It would be fine for you to write "Peter Piper picked a peck of pickled peppers," but it might be better for you to say (assuming that people have never before heard either statement), "Peter Piper gathered a quarter-bushel of brine-preserved peppers"; it would be perfectly all right to write "polish it in the corner," but it would be dangerous to say it.

If our message is carefully constructed, and our message is worth communicating, then we must be careful to communicate it (in whatever medium we choose) in a way that it is comprehended as closely as possible to that which is in our mind. After choosing our words carefully, knowing their correct pronunciation, we are next concerned with the sound of our voice, and (always) what predispositions, predilections, etc., will be stirred in the minds of our receivers when they see us, as well as hear us, or when they can only hear us. People make judgements.

Does the sound of *his* voice match his looks? If people couldn't see him would they imagine that he's small, medium or tall? Lean or large? Does he sound whiney, or forceful? Is the pitch of his voice low, medium, or high? How about when he's angry or sad or afraid — does he sound that way? Do his words come out s-l-o-w-l-y so you feel you'd like to help him, or in machinegun rapidity so your brain can't keep up with your ears? Do you have to strain to hear his whisper or mumble, or do you recoil at the loudness of his voice? Does the sound of his voice keep you alert, or lull you to sleep? Does his voice convey a warm, kind, considerate, caring person, or a cold, mean, haughty, selfish person.

Answer these questions as if *his* was you. Does *your* voice convey a warm, kind, considerate, caring person, or a cold, mean, haughty, selfish person?

It can do all of those things, and more.

People tend to perceive images in accordance with their predispositions. If you sound like a banker (especially if you look like a banker and act like a banker) you'll have a difficult time convincing people that you're an auto mechanic; if you speak with a southern drawl, they won't believe you're a Yankee from Boston (even if you are); and if you speak coarsely they'll think you're coarse. So when we use the medium of speech we must be concerned, not only with our words, sentences, and pronunciation, but the very sound — tone, pitch and inflection — and how it delivers our message.

Speech Habits

We are bombarded with advertising messages warning us of such social and business offenses as body odor, bad breath, and less than sparkling white teeth. We can assess ourselves and easily avoid each of those problems. But what about our speech habits? Can we assess ourselves? Will our friends tell us? We may not be aware of how we look or sound when we speak — but *they* are.

The book I referred to earlier in this chapter, *Speech Can Change Your Life*, by Dorothy Sarnoff, was published in 1970 by Doubleday. It's probably still in your local or school library. My copy is the Dell Publishing Company's paperback edition (1972) and the price (printed on its cover) is $1.50. Keep an eye out for it at used book fairs. Or maybe it's still in print. Check your local bookstore.

The book, which is in three parts, begins with the following author's note:

"This book is for you who want to sound better (Part I)... be more interesting and at ease in conversation (Part II)... or speak more confidently and effectively — without the handicap of uncontrollable nervousness in formal presentations or speeches (Part III).

"If you have speech problems, the hints that follow will help you correct them. If you speak well, they will help you speak still better.

"Before reading the book, check the distractors you would like to eliminate: Nervousness; Nasality; Stridency or shrillness; Speed, chop or slow talking; Lack of projection; Local or ethnic accents; Mumbling; Monotony; Lisping.

"Check the categories in which you would like to improve: Public Speaking; Impromptu speaking; Conversation; Capturing and holding attention; Pacing...too fast? too slow?; Convincing the listener; Speaking with enthusiasm; Using speech notes; Listening and absorbing; Communicating warmly; Telling anecdotes and stories; Handling panels and discussions; Speaking with Authority."

(These are delineated in check list form. They are reported here for two reasons: (1) to give you an idea of what the book is about, and

(2) as a list of areas for improvement for assessing your strengths and weaknesses.)

"In sum, this book can help you achieve the best possible overall speech picture for the business and social demands of your daily life," ends the author's note.

A third reason for my giving you the complete prologue of the book is because there is no way I can give you a summarization of this easy-to-read book's 350-plus pages. Nor can I write the chapter in *Letitia Baldridge's Complete Guide to Executive Manners*, that deals with executive communications. This book, too, is probably available in your library.

If you don't wish to read these two books (and both, together, will help you immeasurably to attain success to the full extent of your intelligence, talents, and education) you can do just three things:

1.) Be aware — Self and Them;
2.) Imitate and emulate those who are successful;
3.) Listen to them, and listen to yourself.

Listen! Listen! Listen!

How many ways can you say "Good Morning?" Listen to them say it. LIsten to yourself. Is your "Good Morning" light and cheerful, morose and guttural, curt or brusque? Does it reflect what your mood and feelings are, or should be, for the occasion? How about your "Hello," or "Goodbye?" Take a few minutes now and try saying "Good Morning" in ten different ways. Change the tone and pitch of your voice. Change the inflection. Put the emphasiss on different syllables. What message would each send to your receiver? Was it the message you wanted to send? Could your message have been misinterpreted? Would it have been misunderstood? Do the same thing with "Goodbye." "Hello."

The voice you have is a product of many factors — physical make-up of your speech organs — tongue, teeth, lips; your health; your personality; your early-acquired speech habits; and the influence of others. In each of these areas you can improve and/or train your voice.

First, begin by listening — alertly and aware — to others, in person, on the radio or television. Listen to those who please you most — their pitch, quality, intensity, and duration of sound. Why do their voices please you?

Every sound we hear has four characteristics:

1. Pitch — the highness or lowness of the voice;

2. Loudness — from a whisper to a shrill scream;
3. Timbre — the characteristic that lets you identify a violin from a bass fiddle;
4. Rate — whether you talk fast or slow depends on the duration of each sound that makes up a word.

Analyze *your* voice. Listen to yourself as you speak. Be aware of each of the four characteristics. Record your voice as you talk and as you read aloud. If you like what you hear, that's good. Why do you like it? If you don't like what you hear — why not? As you liked or disliked qualities in the voices of others, what do you like or dislike about your voice? Re-record the reading-aloud material. But, before you do, analyze the material's meaning. Really get into it. Read it again. Get the meaning clear in your head. Then re-record. Think about what you're saying as you are saying it. Let your brain help you to control your voice. Let emotion — controlled emotion — help you to vocalize your (or the written material's) thoughts.

Listen to a singer sing a sad, melancholy song; a lively, upbeat tune. You, too, must feel what you're saying. Especially if it's "I love you." Even if it's a single word. Is it no. No? No! NO! A command, an order, a request, an explanation, a petition, an apology, a.... Each uses the four characteristics, or combinations, of voice sounds that are appropriate to help you deliver your message.

Most of us don't require extensive analysis or renovation of our voices, as much as we need an awareness of our speech and its delivery. It we need to correct an obvious fault, there are many books in the library, containing many exercises, that will help us. But, in most cases, we will all profit by knowing our subject material, by choosing and using the proper words that express that knowledge, by knowing our receivers, and, for immediate improvement, by thinking "lower and slower" as we talk.

If you have a serious speech problem that you feel can hinder your career or social success, the American Speech, Language and Hearing Association has a list of trained speech pathologists; your nearby college or university may have a program, or can refer you to a program; and your local hospital probably has a speech therapist who will moonlight, or who knows of a colleague that's available to help you.

The one thing from which each of us can benefit is the planning and rehearsal of our important talks, conversations, and speeches.

Plan! Plan! Then Rehearse!

If I am planning an important conversation — person-to-person; one-on-one; in person or by telephone; a business or social speech; formal or informal; asking for an appointment, a date, a raise, or a favor; whatever — I make certain (as certain as I can) that my message will be received and interpreted to be precisely what I am transmitting.

I will write it first. My words *and* your anticipated words in response. Possibly several possible responses. Questions and answers. I will have several versions of my responses to your responses. Like using a roadmap I am prepared to go in this direction or that to arrive at my ultimate destination. I will use visualization, actually imagining the conversation taking place. I may be asking for a job, a raise, a date, or even refusing a job (never a raise or a date). I will plan each turn the conversation could take and be prepared to go with it or correct it. I will rehearse it until I am certain it will go — or that at least I can take it — in the direction— both in substance and style — that I want it to go. Only then will I stop by your office... your home... dial your telephone number... whatever... and I will, in all probability, accomplish my planned objective — transmitting my message, clearly and understandably, to motivate, persuade, convince, entice, educate, interest, inspire, induce, coax, cajole, etc.

If, on the other hand, we are making small talk, or holding a social or business conversation, I will speak freely, openly, and intelligently, in direct proportion to how well I know you — your character, predispositions (and the other P's), values, personality, etc., as well as the nature of the subject matter and its controversial quotient, and the depth of our personal relationship.

If you do all that you will be halfway there to being a good communicator. Halfway? The other half is being a good listener. Communication is a two-way street. To inform others we must be informed, to respond to others we must listen. To *them.*

Listening To Them

Many senior executives think it's a plus when a young executive can move easily and confidently from the role of speaker to that of listener — a time to learn. Listening is included in this chapter because it is a prerequisite to speaking intelligently. A good listener is a better speaker.

How can you be a good listener?

To repeat, communication is a two-way street. To communicate we must express our ideas, our thoughts, and our feelings to others AND we must allow *them* to express their ideas, thoughts, and feelings to us. Some people think that listening is so important to their potential success that they take the time to read *Effective Listening*, written by Kevin J. Murphy.

"Hearing and listening are not the same," Murphy said in a newspaper interview. "Hearing is when your ears pick up syllables, words and sentences. Listening is the ability to categorize and process whatever you hear and draw conclusions."

Murphy says if you want to improve your listening skills you must learn to be attentive, practice listening, concentrate on the important parts of what the speaker is saying. At the same time don't interrupt.

At a seminar I attended a few years ago, four reflective listening techniques were given:

Four Reflective Listening Techniques

1. **Encouragement**

    To show interest, to keep him talking, you encourage. You don't disagree. You use neutral words with a positive tone of voice. You intersperse such phrases as — "I see..." "That's interesting..." "Uh-huh..." and "Mmmm."

2. **Restatement**

    To show that you are listening *and* understanding, to let him know you are grasping the meaning of his words, you can restate his basic ideas, concepts, etc., emphasizing the facts. You might say — "If I understand you its..." "In other words you are saying..." "Your idea then is... ."

3. **Reflection**

    To show that you are listening and understanding, to let him know you understand how he feels, you reflect his basic feelings, i.e., "You were disturbed by this..." "This seemed to bother you..." "You feel that... ."

4. **Summarization**

    To pull the important facts, ideas, concepts, etc., together, to establish a basis for further discussion, to review, you can restate, reflect, and summarize the major ideas and feelings. You may say "These seem to be your key ideas..." "If I understand you correctly, you feel that... ."

Listening... and speaking, equals conversation. Or does it?

Conversation — Discussion Or Debate?

What is conversation? In part, it is self-expression, a providing of opportunities that lets *you* tell *them* just how you feel and what you think. And for *them* to tell *you*. It is not a monologue by him, then you, then him again. Rather, it is an interaction of information and sharing of interests — a give and take, action and reaction. It can be a discussion, or debate, or just an exchange of information and opinion. It is communication between two or more people.

There's a story about two gentlemen who meet at a company affair. Each had learned a valuable lesson (?) on the art of conversation only a few days prior to their meeting. The lesson? That everybody likes to talk about themselves so avoid talking about yourself and let the other person talk about himself... .

What makes for good conversation and what makes a good conversationalist?

Being informed. Being genuinely interested and interesting. Thinking about the other person and his or her interests. Projecting friendly actions and eye contacts. Speaking with a pleasant voice. Using correct grammar and pronunciation. Receiving and/or giving compliments gracefully. Caring for the other person and showing it. Not asking personal questions. Not interrupting. Not boring his or her listeners. Not being or acting self-centered.

A good conversationalist will guard against contradiction between what he is saying and what his actions are saying, but, above all, a good conversationalist is sincerely friendly. He, or she, speaks on knowledge and experience, not conjecture, unless so labeled. If he is not an expert on a subject, he doesn't pretend to be; he doesn't exaggerate his knowledge. He can, in fact, even exploit that very shortcoming. If, for example, the conversation centers around a subject of which he knows little or nothing, he becomes an "interested person," asking, initially, the How or What questions followed by the Why questions. He, therefore, becomes, on this occasion, a good conversationalist.

The Book Of Lists cites a poll that asked 3,000 people what their greatest fear was. Number One — chosen by more than 1200 people — was speaking before a group. (Fear of dying, by the way, was ranked sixth.)

I believe that when you learn to give a good speech you will place the fear of speaking (publicly) on the lowest rank of your personal fears.

Speech! Speech!

What makes a good speech?

To present a good speech you must first know your audience — their concerns, goals, and problems. You must know your subject material and how it relates to their interests, or solves their problems. You must then prepare your speech, choosing the words and constructing the sentences that will show them — not tell them — how the material addresses their interests or solves their problems. Then you must rehearse and practice your speech until you can deliver your message clearly and interestingly.

Know your audience. You are, by now, fully aware of the importance of knowing your message receiver(s). The more you know about him and his predispositions and the other P's, his expectations, his interests, goals, etc., the better.

Know your subject material. That is, of course, why you were chosen to speak in the first place. But, more importantly, know and show how your information pertains to their interests.

Prepare carefully — Choose your words well and choose them for speaking. Construct your sentences properly, again for speaking. Make your disclosures and points logically. Your speech text will have an introduction, a body, and a conclusion. Personally, in my planning, I write the body of my talk or speech first — the important meat — and then I write my introduction. (I find it easier to introduce them to what I will be saying after I know what I'll be saying.) Lastly, I write my conclusion. In this way my introduction does just that, introduces them to the meat of my speech, and the conclusion almost writes itself.

As you write try to vary the pace of the delivery by the length of the sentences. Use visualization. Paint word pictures.

When he gave his speech on the signing of the INF treaty (December 8, 1987) Soviet leader Mikhail Gorbachev spoke: "We can be proud of planting this sapling which may one day grow into a mighty tree of peace."

Use familiar language (even slang) to make a point. President Ronald Reagan, on the same occasion, spoke several words in Russian. On other occasions he's used — "You ain't seen nothin' yet."

Use anecdotes to illustrate a point, preferably humorous. If I were speaking about giving speeches, using proper language, even, on occasion, having to translate English into English, I might tell the story of the man who said "Ontogeny recapitulates phylogeny." Which means "like father like son."

Again. The important objective is that they understand; that they get the message.

I remember seeing a cartoon, *Charlie*, by Rodrigues, where Charlie is standing before his boss who's saying: "Don't you people in the shipping room understand plain English? I said I wouldn't tolerate ad infinitum any sub rosa deals vis-a-vis purchase orders! Don't think you can play agent provocateur and pull a fait accompli! Au contraire, mon ami — around here, l'etat c'est moi!"

I don't have do describe the look Rodrigues drew on Charlie's face. And, while this is a comic exaggeration, you may not always see the look on his or her face when he or she doesn't understand. But you probably will see the results.

When you plan and write your speech keep in mind that your objective is to give them a message that addresses their interests and concerns, and that they will understand the message. Once you've got it on paper, all you have to do is practice.

Practice! Practice! Practice!

Actors rehearse until they have the script — words and meaning — committed to memory, along with the feel, look, and action of the role they are going to play. As they say, they "get into the part." You want to do almost the same thing. Almost, because you don't want to memorize your speech word for word, nor do you want to choreograph every movement.

Personally, I prefer to almost memorize my entire speech and then bring a double- or triple-spaced copy to the podium, with the first few words in each paragraph highlined with a yellow marker. My "cue cards." I feel that this allows me to deliver a speech that is not "too pat," but rather more conversational, more natural.

Some people like to fully memorize a speech. Others like to read the speech entirely from a script. It was said of Lincoln — an acknowledged orator of his time — that he was a poor extemporaneous speaker; that he needed a written script to be eloquent. The best advice? You find the method for you and build on it. And you will build your confidence.

Knowing the subject, choosing the proper words, building your presentation, committing it to paper, and then adequate amounts of practice, will give you this most important ingredient for delivering a well-received speech — confidence. If you have confidence your material interests them, you feel at ease. If knowing you have your entire speech before you on the podium helps give you that confidence, then by all means have it there to refer to, or read from, or cue and clue you to each paragraph. And, with your script before you, and after you have practiced your speech, you will have even eliminated most of the "ers," "ahs," and "ohs." Most is fine. One or two is a very natural thing. If one comes out, don't let it bother you.

The keys? Preparedness and confidence. If I know my audience (and this applies to one person or a hundred and one) would like to know "my secret," — the information that I have — that will help them solve their most pressing, perplexing problems, then I am confident that they will listen carefully, and will appreciate what I have to tell them.

Be honest, both in your subject matter and in your delivery. I have lost my place in my notes (my highlined written scripts). I said something like this: "I've written down some interesting things to tell you... if I can only find my place... ." They laughed with me while I found my place and resumed by presentation. I wouldn't suggest doing it on purpose, but it you goof, don't get flustered or panic. Say so and correct it. It can, when it's honest and spontaneous, even warm up an audience.

As you practice, use positive imaging. See yourself successfully presenting your speech. You've taken a deep breath as you walk to the podium. People are looking at you. They are there because they want to hear what you have to say. You have your script in your mind. Not just the words, but an actor's script. With stage direction. You're playing a part. The script says you are confident and relaxed. No stage fright. You know you have some valuable information for these people. They will find it interesting. That's why *you* were *chosen* to speak to them. Your written script is there on the podium. You look out at them. You see their faces. They are waiting to learn something. Waiting to be entertained. You are, at the moment, the star.

You are now delivering your speech. You're using your voice, eye contact, and body language, to enhance the material of your speech. You believe everything you're saying. They can sense the sincerity, the truth of your words. You are speaking to *a* person in each of three areas — left, center, and right. Your words and your voice are earnest, interesting, informative, and, most important, you're being you. You ask a rhetorical question (and you see heads nod in agreement, or smiles cutting across faces, eyes looking intently at you). You make your points, buttress them with facts. You use an example, or an anecdote, a quotation, or a quote. You are using controlled gestures, making eye contact, "reaching" them.

Finally, you present your conclusions and you close to enthusiastic applause. With a "thank you" you leave the podium.

Use the same strategy for groups of all sizes, in all settings, for all occasions. A business meeting, a presentation, or a formal speech. *Prepare, practice, and visualize.* You will even find yourself doing it, in minutes, for conversation. With one exception. With conversation you must be prepared to change directions, topics, or points in seconds. But, with knowledge, awareness, and practice-practice-practice, you will find yourself at ease in conversation, be it one or two people, or small groups; you will become comfortable speaking to small or large audiences.

If public speaking is important to your career, you might consider joining Toastmasters International, a self-help, personal and professional organization dealing with communication skills — listening, thinking, and speaking effectively.

Local chapters meet at luncheon or dinner meetings which are social, hands-on "laboratory" workshops where members learn by doing — giving 5 to 7 minute topical talks with instant feedback.

If you'd like more information, call (714) 542-6793 or write, Toastmasters International, 2200 North Grand Avenue, P.O. Box 10400, Santa Ana, CA 92711.

You are now on your way to having new confidence in the way you speak—socially, in school, or in business; interviewing or being interviewed; selling a product, a service, or yourself. You can now communicate more effectively by the way you look, act, and speak.

When you *look* the part for success; when you *act* the part for success; and when you *speak* the part for success; to be completely prepared for the role, you need only *write* for success.

11

Write It Better

Public relations practitioners know that if they are to successfully communicate the image of their company, institution, or organization, they must be able to convey that image in writing — in news releases, brochures, feature stories, and the like.

Projecting a favorable image of yourself by how you look, how you act, and how you speak, are desirable skills for your P.P.R. Equally, if not more important, is the skill of writing so your reader receives the explicit message you are sending.

How you look, act, and speak, as we have seen, usually provides immediate and direct feedback, many times providing the opportunity to play up or down, modify, change, or alter speech, looks, or actions. If you're talking to a person, for instance, you can usually tell if he's comprehending the meaning of your words and even *how* he's receiving your message. If he's not understanding your message completely, you can, in midstream, so to speak, modify, rephrase, use gestures, repeat yourself, and even illustrate your words with graphics.

A friend of mine, a physician, many times has whipped out a pen and pad and has drawn a diagram of the digestive system, the urinary tract, and other parts of the body that he felt needed explaining. You may, in any way, keep modifying a conversation until the other person does fully understand your message.

When you write to someone, however, you don't have the same immediate feedback, or the opportunity to modify your message. It is there, as they say, in black and white, for him to decipher, decode, interpret, or perceive as best he can. So it behooves you to compose your message as best you can, even with more care than your spoken messages. Nowhere else is the KISS formula (Keep It Simple, Stupid) so appropriate as it is to the purpose of effective written communication.

Many times written communication is the first contact you will have with a person or organization; many times the *only* contact. Other times, written communication may be standard operating procedure, or at least part of your interaction with others. In any case, written communication is a testimony and a record of your ideas, your talent for communicating, and your intelligence. It can even provide a clear indication of your personality, character, and attitude, or, at least, their perception of these qualities.

Four Essential Considerations

Every piece of writing—a letter, a news story, a memo, a magazine feature, a resume, or a novel — is the result of four essential considerations and parts of the whole process:

1. The idea, thought, or concept, and the specific angle or direction to be emphasized;

2. The writer's interests, objectives, and goals, as well as his, or her, background and motives;

3. The reader's interests, objectives, and goals; their background, their language, and comprehension; and their Six P's—predispositions, predilections, preconceptions, proclivities, perceptions, and prejudices;

4. The medium — how and where the idea, thought, or concept will be presented to the reader.

Two Basic Formulas

While there is no single way of writing a story (interchange *story* with memo, letter, essay, report, et al) every piece of well-organized writing generally falls into one of two formulas:

1. *The Inverted Pyramid* tells all the facts — the whole basic story — in a summary lead or opening paragraph. It then gives the details of these facts in subsequent paragraphs, either as they unfold (as in their order in the lead paragraph), or as they lessen in importance to the reader.

A news story in your local newspaper (as opposed to a feature story) is a good example of the Inverted Pyramid. What the reporter did is give the reader a summary of the entire story in the first paragraph or two, and then the details in subsequent paragraphs.

The Inverted Pyramid is also an excellent formula for writing an essay, many letters, and, many times, the summary lead paragraph is, all by itself, an ideal memo.

2. *The Pyramid Formula* tells a story by unfolding it little by little. As it does it gives more and more information about people, places, and happenings as it builds to its climax or conclusion, i.e., a novel or play. It, too, can be used for an essay and for some letters.

A feature story in a magazine, or fiction, is a good example of the Pyramid, where the writer, such as Margaret Mitchell did in *Gone With the Wind*, unfolded the story of several major characters (and minor characters) as the Civil War impacted on their lives. In its simplest form, the Pyramid formula tells a story in chronological order.

The Inverted Pyramid Formula

There are four basic ways of using the Inverted Pyramid formula:

1. As a ***Straight "News" Story*** (or letter, report, etc.) where you give all the pertinent information in the summary lead paragraph and then, in subsequent paragraphs, you amplify those facts, in the same sequence as they were presented in the lead paragraph, but in greater detail;

2. In a ***Quote Story*** your lead paragraph contains a dominant point or points being made by an authority. Paragraph 2 is expository, amplifying, and transitional, paragraph 3 is another quote (either from the same authority or another), paragraph 4 is expository and transitional, and so forth to the conclusion, preferably with a closing quote;

3. A ***Fact Story*** begins with a summary lead paragraph and then adds new and more facts about the story in succeeding paragraphs, concluding with a final fact that buttresses all the points;

4. An ***Action Story*** leads with the incident itself — the act — and, in succeeding paragraphs retells the incident adding more and more detail, usually from different viewpoints or perspectives.

Your story (essay, letter, etc.) usually is a combination of these four basic ways of using the Inverted Pyramid formula. An action story with quotes, for instance; a report beginning with a summary lead, an incident, or a summary of facts followed by enlargement of, or additional, facts.

The Inverted Pyramid formula is a good way to construct a business letter targeted to the busy executive. Using this formula you will give him the summary of your straight "news", hopefully arousing his interest enough to motivate him to read the entire letter. The "fact story" approach will give him a summary lead with one or two important facts, almost compelling him to read additional paragraphs for additional facts. The "quote story" will give him an important fact as disclosed to him by an expert, a leading authority, a peer, or even a competitor. The "action story" will give him an incident and then tell him how to prevent it, cause it, or, at least, understand it.

The Pyramid Formula

The Pyramid formula, telling your story little by little by unfolding it with a beginning, a middle, and building to a climactic conclusion (fiction usually), or telling the reader what you are going to tell him, then the telling him, and then telling him what you have told him (non-fiction usually), can be used for writing an essay, a thesis, a report, etc. It is usually not the way to write a sales letter. It could very well try the busy executive's patience, even angering him for not getting to the details soon enough. If he's really busy he may not even finish your letter. A social letter, on the other hand, can use the Pyramid formula; a student's thesis could build toward the proposition being advanced for discussion; and a composition could build to a determination or climax.

Let's Examine The Pyramid Formula

The lead paragraph in a Pyramid formula story may be no more than a single sentence that *hooks* the reader. It is the opening thought of the piece, whether it takes a single sentence, a paragraph, or several paragraphs. It *tells* your reader, or hints at, what your story is about, how it may affect him or her, and, above all, it promises great things if he will only read on.

It may be just a statement telling the reader what the story is all about:

"This story (article, letter, essay, report) will show you, in words and pictures, the rewards and benefits you will get when you retire to Hazy Lazy Acres. Examine the low interest rates, the appreciation over the last ten years, and the potential return on your investment, while you do nothing except enjoy the park's clubhouse, bowling alleys, golf course, fishing pond, boating lake, and neighbors just like you."

It may summarize:

"Living in Hazy Lazy Acres is like living in a country club, but getting paid to do it. Based on the property's appreciation the past ten years... ."

It may be more direct:

"If you're one of the X million people retiring next year, you could be living...and playing...in Hazy Lazy Acres while you increase your net worth year after year. Have you thought about... ."

It may be based on news:

"The average cost of a house this year is up X% which means that a house which cost X ten years ago will cost X today. Appreciation of homes at Hazy Lazy Acres shows that... ."

It may be anecdotal:

"It was ten years ago this month that Tom and Mary Smith, two weeks after Tom retired from XYZ Company, moved into their two-bedroom dream home bordering the 15th fairway of Hazy Lazy Acres' golf course. Both avid golfers... ."

It can be startling:

"While you are reading this letter, 642 people are playing golf, or fishing, taking a boat ride, enjoying a picnic, or doing other fun things at Hazy Lazy Acres, and practically getting paid for it. You could join them in just about one month!"

It can be a question:

"Will retirement mean only that you won't have a job to go to every morning? A survey of retired people shows... ."

Any of these leads, and others, can be used to get the reader (as it addresses the concerns and interests of people nearing retirement age) interested in what you have to write about. They can even be used within your text to keep the reader interested. For instance, it can be a statement lead and then, in the text, a question can be asked, an anecdote can be told, or a news item can be referred to. As long as your story gives all the information to satisfy the reader's wants or needs, then other devices such as those illustrated can be and should be used to motivate action. You can use statistics to bring out or bear out certain points, quotations to lend credence and liven things up, and you can bring in the support of illustrations, tabulations, listings, and additional sources for completeness.

Extreme examples of the two formulas are a newspaper story (Inverted Pyramid) and a mystery novel (Pyramid). Most of your stories will be a combination of both formulas. In that way you will write a more interesting social or business letter, a compelling sales letter, a clearer precise memo, a livelier report, a more exciting essay, a concise resume — anything you want to, or have to, write that will also reveal *you* to him or her, or to them.

As you can combine the four basic ways of using the Inverted Pyramid formula, you can combine and make your own variations of the formulas themselves, to fit a specific purpose and to accomplish your own objective. This is especially true when you know your message receiver and can formulate your written message to use to advantage the knowledge you have, i.e., she loves, or hates X so you will mention or not mention X, or if you must you will minimize or maximize your reference to X.

Completeness is as important as the formula to be used, sometimes, in fact, dictating the structure. It is always necessary for the sound transmission of the idea or concept. For that we take another page from the journalist's notebook, a page that contains a formula that will not only assure that we will give the complete story — all the necessary and pertinent facts — to our reader, but will greatly improve our writing skills as well.

The Five W's And H

What your reader is interested in will be found in the answers to the six simple questions of which Rudyard Kipling wrote:

I have six honest serving-men
(They taught me all I knew)
Their names are What And Where and When
And How and Why and Who

They are the famous Five W's which, along with H, asks the questions whose answers comprise all the ingredients of the Inverted Pyramid formula's summary lead paragraph and the subsequent comprehensive story.

The Five W's are learned early in the career of every young reporter and writer. Each can rattle off the Who, What, When, Where, and Why (or How) of every story. Most can even quickly determine the order of importance to their readers.

Let's examine the W's.

WHO? Most every piece of writing is concerned with people, directly or indirectly. It is about a person, or persons, or it's about a thing that a person is involved in or with, or interacting with, or is being affected by. It's a he, a she, or a they; him, her, or them.

WHAT? What happened? What are we talking about? What do we want the reader to know about? To perceive...to understand...?

WHEN? When did it, or will it, happen? When do we want the reader to feel something? Do something? Say something? When will we act...or react? In many situations a specific "when" is vital to effective communication — the time and date of a meeting, when will the boss leave...arrive, when will the...?

WHERE? Where did it, will it, happen? Where will you and she meet? Where is the person who wrote this memo, note, letter...? Where has he gone, where is he going, where is he?

WHY? Why did it, will it, won't it, must it, happen? Why should you do something...consider something...act...react...feel...not feel...? Why do you want him, or her, to feel whatever it is you want him, or her, to feel...to do...to say? Why did it happen that way? Why did the problem, event, accident, happen?

HOW? How did it happen...how should he or she act, react, do, not do, say, not say...?

Merely seeing to it that the answers to the Five W's are included in your story (essay, report, speech, letter, etc.) will give it completeness; selecting the order of inclusion into your story will give it form and interest, and both will enhance the reception of your ideas, thoughts, and concepts by your readers.

An example—

A reporter gathers the facts for a story:

A bomb, hidden in a trash receptacle (WHAT) by a former employee (WHO) of a dress manufacturing firm, who wanted to get revenge for being fired (WHY) exploded (HOW) at the corner of Seventh Avenue and 47th Street in New York City (WHERE) at 12:30 p.m., with hundreds of people in the street (WHEN) resulted in the death of (a famous movie star) (WHO), who was walking to Broadway at the time, and six other persons.

How would a young reporter handle the summary lead and, therefore, subsequent detail paragraphs of the story?

Any one of the news elements of this example could serve as the lead sentence or "hook" to get the reader to continue into the second, third, and following detail paragraphs. The summary lead paragraph opening sentence could emphasize any of the Five W's —

Is what happened more important than who it happened to, or when it happened, or where it happened, or why? What is the second most important fact? The third? Fourth? Fifth?

Would it be "Superstar (name) one of seven people killed yesterday when..." or "During the noon hour when the streets in the garment district area are crowded with milling throngs..." or "Seeking revenge for being fired..." or "A bomb exploded yesterday in Manhattan..."?

There is no formula for choosing. You will have to assess the importance of each of the W's of your story (essay, letter, memo, etc.) to your reader, and then emphasize the most important W first, second, third, and so on. Most experienced reporters have reached a point of being able to feel a good lead when they have it. He, or she, has developed that feeling not only from experience, but from learning about his publication's readers. This story, for instance, might be written one way for the (N.Y.) Daily News, another way for the New York Times, still another way for the Wall Street Journal, a different way for Women's Wear Daily, another way for Time or Newsweek, and yet another way for People magazine.

The important point here, for you and your P.P.R., is knowing that the Five W's are an excellent way for you to assemble (if only by thought) all the elements of *your* story. How you arrange those elements will depend on your reader (the receiver) and you (the sender of the message).

Your receivers can be just as diverse as the readers of the print media mentioned above — a board, a group of employees, a group of children, a single person, et al. And, while you are not reporting news, everything you are saying should be "news" to your reader. Then you can choose which of the five W's is most important to a particular reader or group of readers' interests AND which will best serve *your* interests and objectives?

A good impression and more is in your power with the proper use of words. Using the five W's will help you organize your thinking, construct a meaningful and intelligent message, improve your writing, and provide your reader with a favorable portrait of you.

Whether by your looks, your speech, your actions, or your writing, you will never get a second chance to make a good first impression. And a good first impression is a lot easier to make than is correcting a bad first impression.

By using the five W's you will find that your messages or "stories" will be more complete, more accurate, more understandable, and easier to write. They will have a better chance of receiving the proper perception by your reader, all with a minimum of time on your part.

As you get more and more proficient in your writing, you may want to stray, on some occasions, away from the straight, direct use of the five W's. You may want to add power, or even dramatic effect to your writing, especially if it is an essay or a story letter.

Without altering the facts of the five W's you can use various grammatical construction, in addition to the Straight News, Fact, Quote, and Action variations previously mentioned, to heighten interest in your written messages.

An example—

I have long forgotten the definitions of participial phrases, noun clauses, and other grammatical terms...but I use them. And you can, too. With the same set of five W's facts. I do remember a fictional illustration from my student days. It went something like this:

WHO...David Smith, age 35, a columnist employed by the Daily Gazette, a daily newspaper... .

WHAT...was injured when a hornet flew into his car and he lost control, suffered a broken arm, and received a $1,200 repair bill... .

WHERE...Smith was driving south on the Interstate Parkway near the Cross Country Parkway interchange... .

WHEN...Monday, July 20, 10:12 a.m.

WHY...Afraid of being stung by the hornet, Smith attempted to keep his eye on the insect and the road simultaneously... .

HOW...Smith lost control when he attempted to swat the hornet with a rolled-up copy of the Gazette.

In a straight Five W's news story — or a report to the personnel director; or a memo reporting the incident; or a letter to a person who knew him or traveled the same road, or someone who had been stung under similar circumstances, etc. — it might go something like this:

David Smith, 35, a columnist for the Daily Gazette, broke his arm and sustained damages of $1,200 to his automobile when his car left the roadway and hit a tree on the Interstate Parkway near the Cross Country Parkway interchange, Monday morning at 10:12 a.m. The accident was caused when a hornet flew into Smith's car causing him to lose control.

Straight, simple, factual. Using the same facts, however, a skillfful writer might use different lead sentences to hook the reader into the story.

Same Story / Ten Lead Sentences

1. Driving on the Interstate Parkway last Monday morning, David Smith encountered a hornet... .

2. Cradling a broken arm, David Smith eased out of his damaged car on the Interstate Parkway last Monday and told how a hornet, flying around his face, caused him to lose control of his car, sending it into a grove of trees... .

3. A hornet broke a motorist's arm today. David Smith, a

columnist with the Daily Gazette, was driving on the Interstate Parkway when... .

4. Have you ever tried to drive your car and swat a hornet flying around your face at the same time? David Smith did last Monday morning... .

5. David Smith, driving on the Interstate Parkway last Monday morning, heard the buzzing of a hornet around his head... .

6. Because David Smith has two hands, and he took both off his car's steering wheel in an attempt to swat a hornet buzzing around his face, his car... .

7. To swat a hornet buzzing around his face, David Smith... .

8. A 5-gram hornet got the best of a 3,600-pound automobile and its 165-pound driver last Monday morning as David Smith, a columnist... .

9. That a hornet has a potent sting—$1,200 worth—was learned last Monday morning by David Smith when... .

10. "I don't know if it was wet, but it sure was mad," David Smith said, referring to a hornet that caused him to lose control of his car last Monday morning, sending it careening into a grove of trees... .

These ten lead sentences are not the only variations possible. Why don't you come up with ten of your own, just for fun. Then all you have to remember is to just let the lead sentence, and the subsequent sentences in the lead paragraph, fit your specific purpose, be it an essay, a report, a letter, a memo, or an incident in your novel.

Next comes the story itself. After you have decided on and constructed a good lead sentence and a good summary lead paragraph, the story (using the Inverted Pyramid formula) almost tells itself. If you've given the whole, basic "story" in your summary lead paragraph, you have only to retell it in greater detail in subsequent paragraphs, usually in the same order of importance. In this way the "story" either explains and elaborates the facts (or premise, or theory, or idea) presented in the short version, adds to, or, for shorter pieces, amplifies, minor facts not given the reader in the summary lead paragraph. Then you only have to add power.

Think AIDA

In addition to the Five W's formula (along with the Pyramid formulas for construction) for writing your term paper, letter, memo, resume, composition, or just a note, you should think AIDA. Though it has nothing to do with the popular opera, AIDA will help you make your every communication—written or spoken—sing with success.

Think AIDA as a good check list for your writing to remind you that every communication must: attract their Attention; focus on their Interest; crystallize their Desire; and motivate them to Action.

The last "A" in particular can contribute greatly to your communication because that is probably why you are writing (or speaking) in the first place — to motivate action. To get the reader to react or respond either with a physical action (to do or say something), or with an emotional action (to feel something). Or maybe both — to have the reader feel something (love, anger, pity, sorrow, etc.) and do or say something (respond in kind, kiss you or punch you...initiate or cease a lawsuit, etc.), create an impression or correct one, offer love or reject it... .

In short, using AIDA will help you bring greater strength and power to your writing by having you focus the content of your message for attention, interest, desire, and action.

Regardless of whether you use the Inverted Pyramid Formula or the Pyramid Formula, or a combination of both, you should begin your story with a plan, a blueprint — an outline.

The Outline

As anyone who has ever built a house can tell you, you may deviate from the blueprint— put a window here, move a closet there, or use a different material. You have the same freedom with your story. Your outline, after all, is preliminary, a general concept, a plan. It may be long and detailed, or short and sketchy. In any case it will be the answers to the Five W's of your story, and putting those answers (elements) into the order of building blocks. In this way your outline will contain all the elements you wish to communicate, and will order them either as a summation and explanation, or as a beginning, development of the material, and conclusion. All parts will be connected, interrelated and interactive. Each part will flow from one thought to the next. All parts will be coherent and complete.

Your outline may be nothing more than gathering up your notes, spreading them out on the floor, and arranging them to fit the predetermined concept you have in your mind. It may be a short, simple, two- or three- sentence summary of what you want to say, using only heads and subheads. Or, it can be more detailed just by answering each of the five W's and How, each in a sentence or two. It can be even more detailed by (1) stating the purpose of the piece, (2)delineating the topics to be covered, (3) listing your sources of information, (4) determining your support material, (5)choosing your anecdotes and quotations, and (6) exploring graphic possibilities. Your outline can be enlarged even further by treating each "W" as a mini-outline of its own, with its own construction, contributing to the entire outline.

All of these outlines, and combinations as well, have been used to write short papers and novels, and everything in between. Choose the outline that best suits your purpose for what you have to write — and then write it.

Write! Check! Edit! Rewrite!

You are now familiar with the things you should do when you want to communicate in writing:

1. You research your audience to learn their concerns, interests, needs, or wants, plus their language and comprehension, plus their P's — predispositions, predilections, preconceptions, prejudices, proclivities, and perceptions;

2. You determine what you want to tell them and how you want to tell them, to get what response from them;

3. You choose the formula and method for constructing your message that will best serve your purpose, at this time, in this circumstance;

4. You construct your outline;

(All of this can take five minutes, or five hours, or even five days. Sometimes you will do it without knowing it, in your mind, almost subconsciously.)

5. You write your message, carefully choosing the words, constructing your sentences and paragraphs, and using proper punctuation. (You also know where and how you can deviate from language, construction, punctuation, etc., for effect.)

After you complete these five steps, it — your memo, your letter, report, essay — is completed, and you are finished. Right? Wrong! Now — and to what degree depends on the importance of your communication — you check it, edit it, and rewrite it. If it is very important to me, I complete three additional steps — Rewrite! Rewrite! Rewrite!

Check It. Is it saying precisely and explicitly what you want to say? Can anything be misunderstood? Misinterpreted? Can your thoughts or idea or concept be perceived differently than you intended? Is the entire message coherent and complete? Have you answered every "W" that's important to your message? Are you certain of the meanings of all the words? The spelling of the words? Will your reader fully understand the meaning of the words?

Euphemisms

Is the best word really a euphemism — a word or phrase that is used to avoid saying what our society may deem as taboo? (Did he die, or pass away? Is she poor, or indigent? Are they old, or senior citizens?) Is the euphemism appropriate in your message?

Euphemisms are nothing new. Medieval Germans wanted to allay fears of the animals by calling bears *Honeyfinders*. Ancient Greeks sought to flatter the gods by calling them the *Kindly Ones*. The Romans referred to the dead as the *Gentle Ones*. It is said that in the middle ages, superstitious Portuguese sailors were responsible for changing the name of the Cape of Storms around South Africa to the Cape of Good Hope.

I have a long-time friend who began many years ago as an undertaker. Then he became a mortician. Today he's a funeral director.

Euphemisms are also used to disguise so that a failure becomes "an incomplete success," and, when the Challenger blew up (in 1986), it encountered "a major malfunction" said a NASA technician.

Many times there will be a need, or a place, for a euphemism when you want to make a word or phrase — or even a happening — more palatable to your message receiver. By all means use them to help deliver your message properly, but use them judiciously.

When In Doubt — Simplify

Winston Churchill once said his ten favorite words were: "Never, use, a, long, word, when, (a) short, one, will, do."

A shorter word usually is better than a long one; you are trying to communicate a thought or an idea, not impress with your vocabulary. Substitute for any word; change any phrase; rewrite any part, that requires more clarity.

When you are sure that everything is right, that your message will be received exactly as you want it to be, then you can edit and polish and refine. Get rid of any adjectives you don't really need, any repetitious words or phrases, awkward sentences. Check the punctuation, especially the commas. Did any cliches sneak in? Read your last rewrite for pace and flow. Check questionable spelling... punctuation...meaning.

An Expert's Viewpoint

From a book I have in front of me, *Lesly's Public Relations Handbook*, an article, "How To Write For Readership," by contributor James M. Lambie, Jr., urges us P.R. people to write for our receiver so that he can translate our message into his language — the language he understands.

Lambie points to the gist of the communication difficulty — "Language conveys meaning to the other people who 'speak' it, but to varying extents. You cannot just 'speak English' to someone else who "speaks English" and necessarily convey your thoughts to him; you have got to speak the kind of English he knows. You have got to reach his language level."

Lambie cites example after example of affected, pompous, fluffy, stuffy, sometimes unreadable, language. One example is of a bureaucrat writing about blacking out government buildings during World War 2.

"Such obscuration may be obtained either by blackout construction or by termination of the illumination... ."

And, if people must work in the building at night —

"Construction must be provided that internal illumination may continue."

Indeed!

In the article's summary, Lambie warns that "they may not have the language-experience they need to know what the writer is trying to say."

His advice: Write as you would talk:

— Use short sentences (an average of not over nineteen words).

— Avoid complex sentences.

— Avoid figures of speech.

— Prefer the common word to the uncommon, the familiar to the unusual.

— Prefer active voice to passive.

— Avoid the abstraction; prefer concreteness.

— Include as many personal references as possible.

"In applying these rules," Lambie writes, "prefer the short word to the long; prefer Anglo-Saxon words to Latin-root words; prefer the single word to the circumlocution. In observing these cautions in combination, written matter will have fewer 'affix words' and will be more easily understood."

A word about affixes. They are prefixes and suffixes that modify a root word, i.e, the root verb *serve* — one affix makes it a noun (service), another makes the noun into an adjective (serviceable), another makes a negative (unserviceable), yet another makes another noun (unserviceability). Regarding this recommendation, Lambie notes, "your mind has to remove the affixes one by one to get at the meaning of the root; then it has to build the word up again with the changes each affix makes in the meaning.

"It takes you only a split second to go through the process, but it does take a measurable amount of time and effort. The more affixes, therefore, the harder and slower it is to get meaning from the words."

Good rules, all of them, for an engineer, or a math teacher, or a physician, or maybe you.

But don't follow any rule so rigidly that it inhibits your writing, cramps your style, or doesn't project the image of you that you want to project.

I have read (and I hope I have written) 30-, 40-, even 50-word compound sentences, properly constructed and punctuated, that read clearly and easily, even melodiously. Lambie's paragraph, quoted earlier in this chapter, contained a 39-word sentence. Another in his article, with the skillful use of dashes, dots, and quotation marks, is 78 words in length.

Personally, I don't like generalizations of any kind. In this case I feel that a 19-word sentence, with dull words, constructed improperly, not punctuated properly (or not punctuated at all), can be much more difficult to read and understand than a longer, correctly constructed, properly punctuated sentence. For instance, as an exaggerated example, try this 19-word sentence:

"The young boy John ran down the street wildly screaming like Geronimo with his sister Jane on his heels."

Did John run down the street wildly, screaming like Geronimo, or wildly screaming like Geronimo? Was Geronimo with *his* sister Jane, or is Jane John's sister? Was Jane on John's heels, or on Geronimo's heels? Was Geronimo screaming because *his* sister Jane was on his heels? Just who's heels was Jane on — John's or Geronimo's? Enough! I think you get the idea.

How about: "The young boy, John, ran down the street wildly, screaming like Geronimo, with his sister, Jane, on his heels."

Both versions of the sentence comply with Lambie's rule of short sentences of an average 19-words or less. One, with proper punctuation, is understandable.

How about his sentence:

"If the corporation president wants to say — as he apparently does — not that foremen do a good job, but that they 'turn in a creditable performance'...not that things get done fast, but that they are 'accomplished expeditiously'...not that sales drop off, but that 'there is a curtailment of consumer activity'...if, to him, an end must be a termination, a use a consumption, a need a requirement, and so on... then he needs public relations counsel."

That is Lambie's 78-word sencence referred to a few paragraphs ago. Is there anything wrong with it? Is it clear and understandable? I think there is nothing wrong with it, that it is understandable, and its message is clear. That breaks Lambie's rule to avoid complex sentences. But Lambie's skill and experience allows him to break that rule for this sentence's purpose.

Another rule: *Avoid figures of speech.* Why? If you can use a figure of speech (one that the majority of your readers are familiar with; one that puts a certain picture in their mind) to make a point, use it.

Prefer the common word to the uncommon, the familiar to the unusual. Yes. But be careful in a message for a mixed audience where a word or phrase is familiar to one segment and unusual to the other. Play to the important segment, or change it to one that is common to both — but only if you can do so without sacrificing the effect or response for which you are striving.

Prefer the active voice to the passive. Most always. But not when you may be trying to create and maintain a somber feeling on the part of your reader.

Avoid the abstraction, prefer concreteness. Most of the time. But there is a place for abstraction — when you don't want to make something "perfectly clear."

Include as many personal references as possible. Yes. If they buttress your argument or support your idea. Do it when necessary, but without overwhelming, i.e., if your idea or concept does not stand completely on its own merits. If it does, you may not want to dilute it with the impression that it needs support. You may want to avoid overkill.

Lambie's rules are good rules. But consider rules about writing as guides. If you are confident that you have the skill to write longer, but well-constructed, sentences, to mix with your short sentences, and you can effectively communicate your ideas to others in this way, by all means, do so.

Let's Review The Basics

Because your written communications are so important to your P.R. — performance and response— so important to your P.P.R.— personal public relations—let's review the basics before we begin the next chapter which will give specific considerations for writing specific messages.

- Know your audience — the receivers of your message, including their Six P's — predispositions, predilections, proclivities, preconceptions, prejudices, and perception.
- Use the Five W's — Who, What, When, Where, Why — and How, to organize and research your message material, and to assist with the construction of your message.
- Know your message—receiver's language and language skills so you may choose your words skillfully and carefully.
- Use the Pyramids — the Inverted Pyramid and the Pyramid — to structure your message, for its time and place and purpose.
- Use AIDA — Attention, Interest, Desire, Action — to give your message all the punch you want it to have.
- Use KISS — Keep It Simple, Stupid — as a reminder to do just that.
- Remember that your message is vying with all other messages, distractions, and interruptions, for his or her attention; try to time the reception of your message with that in mind.
- Keep your language use active (instead of passive), spare (instead of verbose), and precise (instead of nebulous).
- Put yourself in your receiver's place. Once again, visualize. You know the circumstances and the purpose of your message. You know your receiver(s). Become him (or her) for a minute. *You* have received *the* message. How do you feel? What is your reaction? Did you receive the message that was intended? Is the effect on you, as the receiver, what you, the message-sender, wished it to be? Have you, the message-sender, accomplished your objective, achieved your purpose, received your desired response?

Effective, interesting writing is a skill you can learn and put to good use as you write your letters, memos, reports, speeches, and essays. The next chapter should help you even more.

12

Writing Memos, Letters, Speeches, Resumes...

Unlike public relations practitioners, you probably won't write press releases, feature stories, or brochures. You probably will write thousands of memos, letters, reports, speeches, essays, etc., during your long lifetime and career.

MEMOS

A memo can be a record of something, or just a note to help someone's memory. There is or should be, only two basic reasons to write a memo — to communicate something to someone in as few words as possible and to establish a documented record of the communication.

You knew that? Many people don't. They are the people who want to use the memo,(and other written communications) only to impress someone. They're the people who write "at the present time", instead of "now" or "today." They use "consequently" instead of "so," "subsequently" instead of "later." These are the people who will "eliminate the possibility of something happening," instead of "preventing it." They write "in view of the fact that... " instead of "because." They "reside," not live, in "domiciles," not homes; "commence" instead of "begin," and believe a fire by any other name is a "conflagration." They *never* use a short, simple word when a long, complex word will parade their knowledge. They have a penchant for driving people to a dictionary.

Don't be one of them!

The memo, used properly, can be an effective form of communication. It's in writing, has a name on it, establishes a record, is dated, and should convey the writer's message clearly, concisely, understandably, and to the point, always concerned with one objective — accomplishing its purpose.

Your memo can have additional impact on your message-receiver; it can provide your reader with clues to your style, your talents, and your intelligence. It can reveal your thinking, your writing ability, your personality, and, if you have one, even your sense of humor. Humor, incidently, in any writing, is a humanizing factor, but it must be used judiciously and sparingly.

Memos must do their primary job: Convey information; Establish a record of your activities or theirs; Delineate something to be done, or not done; Relate something that occurred, will occur, should or should not occur; Order or request or command that something be done or not done; Criticize, explain, or complain; Establish accountability — Communicate!

Your memo should make it immediately apparent why you are writing it and what it is about. That should be clearly expressed to your reader (whose time is being infringed upon). Your memo should quickly indicate what response, if any, is expected. Keep it clear, concise, and candid. In no other form of writing are the ABC's of writing — A-ccuracy, B-revity, C-larity — more important.

Writing a Better Memo

Before writing your memo you have, of course, given full consideration to knowing your message-receiver, his or her six P's, aspirations, problems, concerns, etc. Next, you should take a few minutes to think about our friends, the Five W's, and AIDA, as well as KISS.

Then make sure your memo contains:

1. The date;
2. To whom it is written (correctly spelled) and his or her proper title;
3. To whom, if any, copies are going;
4. The message. Answer the five W's as clearly and concisely as possible. Rank the answers in the order of importance. Choosing your words very carefully, write your message. Then eliminate at least one-third of the words. Substitute simple words for complex words. Eliminate all unnecessary adjectives. Finally, check your spelling and punctuation.
5. The closing. A thank you is in order (for his or her time and consideration, for what he did or didn't do, for what you want him to do, etc.), as well as whether a response

is or is not required. (You'd be surprised how many responses you will get if you don't make it clear that no response *is* required.)

6. Your name and title.

You may want to consider adding your "address" if it is not known by the recipient, or your telephone number or extension if a telephone reply is invited or acceptable — a P.P.R. show of consideration and thought on your part.

Memos can take several forms, from the simple, informal note — "From the Desk of... " — to the semi-formal interoffice memo — To, From, Subject — to the pre-printed memo form with routing space, reply form, in three or more parts. What they *must* be is clearly understandable and effective.

Effective writing skills have much to do with your job performance and your career. While you probably wouldn't get fired for writing ungrammatical, convoluted "gobbledygook," it could weaken, or even break, a rung on your career ladder.

Memos will probably outnumber all your other forms of in-house written communications, so keep them clear and natural, and let them project your style.

A 1970 memo by Thomas J. Watson, then chairman and CEO at IBM, asked managers to help end the "foreign language" that had found its way into the company's internal communications.

"Believe it or not," Watson wrote, "people will talk about taking a '*commitment position*' and then, because of the '*volatility of schedule changes*' they will '*decommit*' so that our '*posture vis-a-vis some data base that needs sizing will be able to enhance competitive positions.*'

"...IBM," he said, "wasn't built with fuzzy ideas and pretentious language. IBM was built with clear thinking and plain talk."

Clear thinking plus plain talk — if you write as you speak (which you should) —can equal clear, effective writing and clear, understandable memos.

LETTERS

What do your business letters, social letters, even love letters, have in common? All the "rules" of good writing apply. But more than other written communications, your letters — business or personal — should have the feel of one person *talking* to another. More and more, business letters have retreated from the "As per your letter of ..." and "Acknowledge receipt of your letter of the 15th" phrases, to a more personalized, informal reflection of the writer's, or his company's, personality.

What's the difference between business letters and personal letters?

The business letter has a "definite objective" and a "definite attitude," while a personal letter may express any of the writer's emotions, go from one subject to another, or be just a chatty narrative of things, people, and events.

The business letter's definite objective, usually, is to get the reader to respond — to buy or sell something, to pay a bill, give credit, complain, to get satisfaction, refuse satisfaction, make a donation, get a job or resign from one, etc. The letter writer — message-sender — usually is trying to influence the letter reader — message-receiver — to do something, or not to do something, the letter writer wants him to do or not do.

To use this means of persuasion the writer employs a "definite attitude" — a *you* attitude.

When you write a social or personal letter, both the "I" and the "you" attitude are used, but the "I" is predominate. I, the writer, usually tell you, the reader, what I did, saw, felt, thought, etc., relating it, of course, whenever applicable, to your interest. Generally, it will be the personal letter writer's thoughts, actions, and feelings.

The business letter writer, however, trying to induce the reader to take certain actions, must give more consideration to the reader's thoughts, feelings, concerns, and interests. He, or she, must get into the reader's mind to anticipate his reaction and response. Only in that way can he hope to gain insights that will enable him to persuade the reader that he, the reader, should act in the manner that the writer wants him to act. So, the writer must adopt the *you* attitude and write the letter to *you*, the reader, so *you* will feel that your viewpoint is being considered, that *your* best interests are being served, that *your* needs are being met.

Even when you write a dunning letter you will be more successful if, in a factual, but almost friendly manner, you point out to the reader that it is in his best interests to pay his bill, and why, even if you regret taking the step, the grief you will heap on him is far less preferable than sending you a check.

So, while you express your personality as a person when you write a social letter to a friend, the personality you express when you write a business letter is your business personality — credit manager, personnel manager, salesman, buyer, executive, etc. It must convey, on the one hand, an image of you as a fair, efficient, understanding person, as well as your title's and your company's personality. You can, with this attitude, individualize, personalize, and humanize your letters, and win your reader's confidence in your fairness, understanding, and effectiveness.

After first thinking about him, or her, and when you've got the *feeling*, you dig out your Five W's, jot down the points you wish to cover, and how, make your basic outline, and write your letter with courtesy and tact, and the understanding you want to project. Because you have chosen your words carefully, your meaning is simple and clear and your letter has an excellent chance of accomplishing everything you would like it to achieve.

Business letters, of course, should be errorless, neatly typed, spaced well, pleasant to look at, and easy to read. They must suggest, by their contents and their appearance, that you (and the company you are representing) are competent, accurate, efficient, neat, and, above all, professional.

Personal letters should be neat as well, and, at the very least, readable (although I've received some that were just decipherable). But don't make the reader of your love letter so frustrated with trying to decode your words before understanding them; before being emotionally aroused.

As for the persuasiveness of your letter's message, you must, once again, go to the fundamentals of communication — know as much as you can about your receiver's Six Ps, concerns, interests, wants, and needs, and address those that you can appropriately address. Generally speaking, whether you're writing a social, personal letter, an employment letter, a complaint—whatever—each is nothing more than communiction—message-sender and message-receiver—between you and him or her or them. The rules apply. Know *them* and use what you know.

Some General Guidelines

— Your business letters should be well-written, look professional, be well-typed; proper words should be used and they must be properly spelled; be sure to use the reader's name, properly spelled, and be sure to use his or her correct title.

— Don't be over-familiar. If the person you are writing to is someone who can impact on you or your career — a fellow or senior executive, for instance — in your first letter or memo to him you should address him as "Dear Mr. Blank, Dr. Blank, Ms, Mrs. or Miss

Blank," etc. If you want to invite him or her to get on a first name basis, sign your first name over your complete typewritten name and title. Then you can be guided by his use of salutation and closing when he answers your letter or memo. This will allow him to set the tone and style for future communication.

— Keep your personal and business letters separate. When you write a letter on your company's letterhead stationery, the receiver is getting a letter from you as a representative of the company. Most corporations enforce strict regulations on the use of the official company letterhead. Sometimes they are in print, other times they are *understood*. Senior executives in some companies may be permitted to use the company letterhead for other than business purposes, but they are expected to do so with discretion. Be safe. Don't.

— Informal business letters should contain something personal, preferably in the last paragraph (after your message has been received). This must be some tidbit with which your are familiar — the message-receiver's family, his golf game, a hobby, etc.

— A bit of humor and a bit of praise for the receiver can go a long way toward polishing your image in his or her eyes. Be sure it's appropriate and low key. Don't, however, turn your entire letter into a comic's routine or a testimonial.

— You won't, of course, use foul language, even in jest, no matter how well you *think* you know your receiver.

— Be sure to cover all points in order of their importance — the Five W's. Don't exaggerate, write simply and interestingly, edit, rewrite, and edit again for substance, pace, and readability.

—A postscript in a social letter is an afterthought; a P.S. in a business letter can emphasize a point made in the body of the letter. It, too, however, can be presented as an afterthought, making something in the body of the letter *even better*. Postscripts are often times (in a business letter) read first by busy people. In a sales letter a P.S. could make a special offer; in a dunning letter it might remind (action will have to be taken on the 15th so please...,")or it may emphasize, "I'm looking forward to visiting you on the 10th... ."

A properly constructed, thoughtful letter can persuade, cajole, praise, criticize, scold, inform, sell, complain, buy... and it can do so even while projecting the desired image that the writer and the company he works for wishes to project. But remember, your business letter is from you *and* your company. Don't be a *good guy* by making your company a *bad guy*. Don't write that "It's company policy" if it's not. Another don't — don't imply that your reader is lying, by writing "you claim...you said...according to you... ."

You can even say "no" nicely, without offending.

In *Write better, Speak better*, published by Reader's Digest Association, a book that covers many more areas of writing than letter writing, it is written that you might want to think of a sandwich when you have to write a say-No letter. The top layer is something your reader wants to know, the middle layer is the meaty filling — the reasons why you must refuse — and the final layer, like the first, is something pleasing. It is also suggested that you sugarcoat the pill. They remind you, too, that most times it is the end of the letter that's remembered longest so "leave the reader with a good taste in his mouth."

The book is probably available at your local library (and if it isn't there are many other experts waiting to help you). One in my personal library is *Lifetime Encyclopedia of Letters*, by Harold E. Myer. Published by Prentice Hall it is described as "a monumental lifetime treasury of over 500 categories of ready-to-use model letters for all occasions..." and they range from letters of reference to complaint letters, employment letters to letters of condolence.

For love letters, refer to Cyrano.

If you don't want further study, or samples of letters from A to Z, just remember that by using the Five W's you will never wonder just what it is you are trying to say; when you *know* your message-receiver you will know just how you should say it; by using AIDA you will get their attention, focus on their interest, create desire, and motivate them to action. Wrap is all up with simple words that convey your thoughts, in well-constructed sentences, and you have the makings of a successful letter— one that will raise your P.P.R. by several degrees.

NOTES

Notes, in business, are informal, brief, memos. Socially, they are short letters. Remembering all else, remember that they, too, give your message receiver clues to *you*. Be sure that it is the *you*, you want them to know.

SPEECHES

The composition of a speech may be divided into three parts — its introduction, the main content or body, and its conclusion. Many people begin to plan and write their speech in what seems to be that natural order. I suggest you try a different approach. How you will introduce your speech, or will conclude it, will, to a large extent, depend on the tenor of the contents — the body of the speech. So work on that first. Notice I said *work on*, not *write*.

First, the subject. If it hasn't been chosen for you, choose one that suits you, the occasion, and the audience. Especially the audience. Once again we must be concerned about our audience. Who are they? What do they expect to hear about? Why?

Once again you have Kipling's six honest serving-men, the Five W's and How, to help you not only write your speech, but to delineate your audience as well.

Next, you decide on the structure. The Pyramid — do you want to build, verbally, little by little, fact by fact, to a climax? — or the Inverted Pyramid — do you want to give them a brief summary of your thoughts, then expand on each point? Will you use quotes, anecdotes, quotations, humor, graphics, to illustrate your facts, and make your points?

Let's use index cards. On each, in the upper left hand corner we can write a "W" and what it stands for — What, for instance — and then write *what* we are going to say... *what* points we are going to make... *what* we will use to buttress our points... .

Compare this card with a similar "what" card for your audience. *What* do they want to hear or learn about? *What* are their feelings about the subject? *What* are their concerns, objectives, interests? *What* are their needs? Their wants?

Do this with all the W's. You will then have a good idea of how to present your subject in the words and manner that they will understand, appreciate, and maybe even think about.

Use the cards for quotes, anecdotes, or quotations that support one, or two, or more of your important points.

Review each card and begin a process of elimination and expansion by asking:

—Does *it* — the point or fact or quote —fit in with the message you want to convey?

—Does *it* advance the viewpoint of your message or will it adapt to address their interests?

—Does *it* address their interests?

What is left will be the building blocks for the body of your speech.

Some speakers, it warrants repetition at this time, will just use note cards to deliver their speech. Others will write their speech in full, word for word, pause for pause, etc., and read it. Still others will type it out completely and highline the lead sentence of each paragraph. (Their delivered speech will almost, but not quite, come out word for word.) Which method you choose will dictate how you will write your speech.

Writing Your Speech

Will you write an outline from your W-notes (or write an outline *instead* of W-notes)? Will you write an outline *just* for the body of your speech, and then write an introduction and a conclusion? No matter how you do it, or they do it, you will arrive at the same destination — a written first draft.

Now read your first draft aloud (or aloud in your *head*) circling the words that may be a problem for you to pronounce, and those that might not be fully understood by your listeners — those words that are hard for them to decipher as they make the journey from your lips to their ears. If there are such words or phrases you will have to find new words or phrases to substitute. Circle, too, any words that may be difficult for you to pronounce, but which you cannot change — a name, for instance. Write those words phonetically. While you're reading this first draft, you should edit for pace, rhythm, inflection, (voice tone rising here, lowering there), and pauses. The trials and errors you find and correct now will not haunt you when you're on the podium, or standing at the boardroom table.

Your second draft will be better. Your words are now correct. They will be pronounced correctly and correctly understood and interpreted. You will have varied your pace (rate), determined your pauses and inflections, and you will have accomplished it all while making your points.

Your next read-through will be your final edit, the polishing of your words, and the fine-tuning of your timing. Most people speak comfortably at about 100-125 words a minute. Now you can edit for time as well as make a final check on word meaning, word pronunciation, and the natural, conversatonal style of delivery that is desired.

If you think about it, an oral report at a meeting (or in school) can be viewed as a mini-speech. So can an important telephone conversation. Even asking that special person that special question. In every case, think about your message-receivers. Think about what you want to say. Choose your words carefully. Think about how you want to say it. Write it down. Edit it. Polish it. Rehearse it. Then rehearse it again. And again. Review that part of Chapter 10 on giving a speech. Visualize yourself saying the words, delivering your ideas, presenting a picture. And you will be confident that you can — as can any actor who is president, or any president who can act. Convey the message in your mind to your message-receivers in a way they can fully understand and appreciate. And they will.

REPORTS

In a very general way, a report is an accounting of something — a book report; a technical report; a business' quarterly or annual report; a report about a trip, a seminar, a project, a campaign, a...to be presented to a teacher, a group of your peers or superiors, a class, a congress, a nation, a... .

A report is evidence of work that has been done, an essential record of that work; a repository of information that can serve as the basis for decision and action. Some reports are delivered orally, but most are written reports that will allow the reader the opportunity to study the contents at will.

What distinguishes a report from an essay or a novel or any other written document or manuscript? Form? Content? Support? Yes! A report is usually the answer to a question, the solution to a problem, or the detailed, comprehensive information requested, or demanded, by someone. It is normally more detailed, more informative, and more comprehensive, than would be a note, a memo, or a letter.

Where do you begin in writing a report? You begin, once again, by thinking — about *them.* Not only the one who initiated the need and purpose for the report, but those who have a need for the information to satisfy their need for knowledge or to do their jobs better than before they read, or hear, your report.

After you have learned about your message-receiver's needs and wants (for the knowledge), their concerns and attitudes, and their feelings about the report's subject, you can choose the tone, intention, and material that will satisfy the usually mixed readership of any report. Some of them will give your report a cursory look, some will peruse it carefully, and others will scrutinize and study it long and thoroughly.

When you next have to write a report, try using these five steps:

1. Research — Gather all the material available that is relevant to your readers' needs and wants, and to the purpose of your report;
2. Select the material that presents the information objectively;
3. Put the material in a logical presentation order;
4. Delineate your interpretation (and others') of the material;

5. Determine how you will present the material as well as support matter.

You can, of course, use yor six serving-men — the Five W's and How — to gather, organize, and write your report. Answering each "W" will help you to guarantee the completeness of your report.

Unlike other forms of communication, a report, ostensibly, does not attempt to persuade anyone to any point of view. It should be, rather, a factual, objective presentation — (in my dictionary's description) "a statement of facts and/or figures ascertained by investigation." A written report, therefore, is a factual account from which others may reach a logical conclusion.

As you collect your material be sure to be on the lookout for graphics, quotes, photos, and anecdotes that will help you present a clear and complete account of your subject matter. When possible, use a graph, chart, or a photo — instead of words — to present facts. People do not, usually, read a report for pleasure, but to learn, and it's much easier and faster to examine a graph or a chart than to read a thousand words of description.

Your writing, as always, must be clear and concise, and be composed of words selected for your particular audience. Check your spelling, particularly technical words or jargon that your secretary can't correct.

Let's examine the five steps:

1. Research — How you go about this depends on the circumstances. You may use others' research, interviews, other experts' opinions, reference books, catalogs, etc., or your own. Each time you use theirs, be sure they're an authority, and use their name.
2. Selection — You will, of course, use selectivity as you gather material. Call this the final selection of material after eliminating the chaff. An editing process.
3. Presentation — Does your subject suggest a logical order or a chronological order? Everything has a beginning, a middle, and an end. Will you begin with a problem, advance to the solution, and then to the conclusion? Or will you present the solution, and then conclude what brought the solution into being? Will you present the solution, proceed to factually support each facet of the solution, and then conclude? Or will you choose from several other sequences of presentation? Only you can answer, and that answer will

4. Interpretation — has to do with the level of your readership. (This will also determine the level of the presentation and the level of the language.) It is not just a matter of style, but an understanding of your readership's understanding and familiarity with your report's terminology. Suppose, for instance, your report is for, and going to, your boss, who is the director of research and development. But it is also going to a marketing bigwig, the advertising manager, and your chief executive officer. You may, in this case, decide to write it so the advertising manager can understand it (using no unfamiliar jargon), or for the R & D man (letting the others find out what *those* words mean), or you may combine both — using technical words as necessary, but explaining them briefly the first time they're used, i.e., "the pressure of this material had dropped to 5.1 p.s.i. (pressure per square inch) against the specification minimun of 5.5 p.s.i." This is also a good rule when using and referring to the ubiquitous acronym, and the many organizational abbreviations.

5. The presentation — How you will present your material will depend on the first four steps, your knowledge of the message receiver(s), and your style. Questions about layout, structure, headlines, sub-heads, etc., can be answered by the many experts in your library. There are book reports, scientific reports, technical reports, business reports, project reports, etc. There are at least a half-dozen standard structures. But every report should contain the following in this order:

— Title page

— Introduction

— Text of report

— Conclusions

— Recommendations

— Future work to be done

— Appendix

There may be a preface or foreward, a summary, acknowledgments, references, graphics and tables, figures, index, bibliography, etc.

There are, too, as many informal reports written in some companies as there are formal reports, even more informal than memos, and still more informal as notes. The basics are the same for any of them — know *them*, know what they want or need, and give it to them in a clear, concise, understandable manner.

What's the best report for you to present — its form and its structure, its style and language, its formality or informality... ?

Look at *their* reports!

PRECIS

In school or in business you may be asked to write a precis — a very concise summary of something you've read or heard, for your professor or your boss: "Attend that seminar... listen to him speak... read that paper... and give me a written summary of what you heard... read."

A precis is a very concise, brief summary of the ideas and point-of-view of someone's dissertation, expressd in *your* words. It is not a condensation or a paraphrased distillation of what someone has said or written. It is an excellent exercise for the use of the Five W's as used by a newpaper reporter who must put all the facts into one line or summary lead paragraph of a story. In fact, a summary lead paragraph, many times, can be an ideal precis.

Today, it is not unusual for a precis to be given a broader definintion. You may be asked by someone for a precis — without his calling it a precis, for that matter — on the ideas or point-of-view of someone who has spoken them at a meeting; or as expressed at a seminar you've attended; or just on conversant knowledge.

To write a precis, read the article (or listen) very carefully. Take, make notes. Read it again if you can, taking W-notes, gathering the facts as a reporter would. Arrange the W's in order of importance, or in the author's (speaker's) sequential order. Now write your summary as concisely as possible, as a reporter writes a summary lead paragraph. As always, choose your words carefully and with knowledge of your receiver(s). Check your precis to be sure it is accurate and that the sequence of facts, or thoughts, mirror those of the author (speaker). Then edit. Eliminate as many phrases as you can. Substitute a single word wherever possible. Blue pencil all unnecessary adjectives. Then edit again. Finally, edit, edit, edit.

BOOK REPORT

Still in...back in...college? You may have to write a book report. A reminder: a book report, unlike a precis, not only describes the book you've read, but reveals your own feelings, opinions, and reactions. The Five W's can help. *Who* is the author? *Who* are the characters? *What* type of book is it? *What* is the story about? *How* are the characters portrayed? *Where* and *when* does the story take place? Why did things happen? What did you think of the story? The writing? *What* is the book's theme? Its message, if any? *What* is your opinion of the book on an emotional plane? *What* of the plot — does it make sense? *What* of the characters — do they seem like flesh and blood people? What of the dialogue — does it ring true? The setting — time and place — did it seem real? Did it come to life? Was the author successful — did you like his style? Would you recomend that others read the book — what *is* your recommendation?

If you are asked to write a one-paragraph review (not really a precis because it asks for your opinion) you can still use your six servingmen and the reporter's technique of writing a summary lead paragraph. One line or so for each of the W's and How, strung together in one or more properly constructed compound sentences — a precis with opinion added.

Many times a book is assigned for reading and a report, year after year by the same professor. If so, find out how he or she liked it and why. If you are to choose a book, you may be able to choose one of his favorites. Ask your friends, especially those a year or two ahead of you who had the same professor. Converse with the professor long before you have to do a book report. Does he have a favorite author? Why is the author a favorite?

It does no harm to share a common interest, does it?

After you've read your book and clarified your impressions, you now assemble your W-note cards and arrange them in basic outline form. Keep all the cards that are interesting and necessary, discard details that are not. Use your basic outline—

— Author.

— Type of book.

— Plot — what it's about and how it develops.

— Characters — who and what they are.

— Setting — where and when.

— Style — general characterisitics of the story and its appeal.

— Summary — your impressions and opinions

Write your first draft. Check it carefully for grammar, spelling, and punctuation. Then edit. Then polish. Read the report again. Will the reader of your report know about the book (factual) and what you thought of it (opinion)? Read it again. Vary the pace of your writing. Keep it interesting. Keep your reader (professor) interested, and your report will be successful.

TERM PAPER

As a college student some of your most important assignments each and every semester are term papers. Your task, textbooks will tell you, is to collect the facts and interpret them, and, not only write an intelligent, interesting paper, but one that is original in its thinking and conclusions.

Your research paper will draw its material from many different sources. Your objective will be to assemble facts and ideas from these various sources, study them, make your own interpretations, and draw your own conclusions about their premise. You then construct an outline, present those facts and ideas — a discussion of the subject — along with your new or different conclusions and interpretations, in a well-written, interesting paper.

You can, once again, get expert help regarding the nitty gritty of research methods, organization, and form, in the library. Your writing skills are getting better every day through your use of the Five W's and AIDA, so now, as you plan, you are ready to tailor your performance to get the response — the grade — that you want.

Before you research your subject, however, research your professor. (Or your boss if it's a "paper" for him.)

What are his or her favorite subjects? Pick one that interests you *and* him. What is his or her attitude—viewpoint, six P's—toward the subject? Do they parallel yours? If yes, fine. If not, try another of his favorite subjects, or adapt, or change your attitude, for this project at least. Is it manipulative to pick a subject that's of interest to him? Is it manipulative to pick a subject on which your attitudes, viewpoints, and predispositons mirror his? Or is it "good business" to satisfy the wants and needs of "your customer?" But first you need to know the wants and needs of *your* "customer." You have to bring a new or different interpretation or conclusion or pointof-view to the subject — what are *his* values? Do you share them? Can you?

Some may consider these tactics as being manipulative. They are. What does manipulate mean? As we discussed earlier it means "handle with skill," "influence," "manage," "adapt or change." Manipulation, then, is a *dirty* word only when you use *dirty* tactics to achieve your objectives. Don't! Do use skill, logic, common sense, consideration, and your knowledge of him or her or them; do adapt (to him or her or them), or change (for him or her or them).

In the case of a term paper it is just as easy for you to write about a subject that interests *him* as one that doesn't; to choose a subject on whose conclusions you *both* agree as one on which you are poles apart; to pick a subject which is compatible with both your values *and* his; to produce a term paper that *will* get you the grade you want.

Save your debates for the debating team!

ESSAY

An elementary school student writes a composition... a high school student writes essays...a college student writes papers and theses...a professional writes articles...an executive writes. Semantics. Basically they are one and the same — a written, based-on-fact communication on a particular subject. They are written to advance a proposition, motivate discussion, present an idea or concept, inform, educate, or to entertain. It can be a report (something he or she did), a personality sketch (about him or her), a narrative (the writer's or someone else's experience), a how-to-do something article, or even a controversial dissertation. Or it can be a combination of one or more of these types of writing.

Much of what you have read in these pages — the Five W's and AIDA, the Pyramid and Inverted Pyramid formulas, KISS, and so forth — will help you to gather and evaluate your material, organize your thoughts and present them, and even suggest an outline for the particular type of essay you're writing.

Ask yourself these three questions:
1. Who will be informed by your essay?
2. What do you want to tell them?
3. Why do you want to tell them and why would they want to hear what you have to tell them?

The answers to those three W's should give you the outline for your outline. Then you can use the Five W's for your subject outline as you have done for other written communications. Be sure to include support material such as possible interviews, anecdotes, figures, graphics, etc., all of which will not only support your thesis, but will make your essay interesting and entertaining as well.

There are many ways to help you to make your essay interesting. One way professionals do it is by carefully and creatively constructing the article's lead. They try to hook the reader with a sentence or a paragraph on the opening thought, written in such a way that the reader is forced to read on. (Take a few minutes to review the ten examples of leads given in Chapter 11.) Once you have hooked the reader you can use anecdotes, quotations, facts, and figures, as well as typographical devices such as underlining, heads and subheads, italics, short one-sentence paragraphs, to propel the reader along and sustain interest.

Before you begin — before you even pick or research the subject — take another page from the professional magazine writer's book — know your audience, your reader, whether it be one (your professor or your boss) or many. Know your reader's interests. Determine how you can satisfy your reader's curiosity, concerns and needs, with what facts and support material, presented in an informative, appealing, well-written manner.

The *successful* magazine article writer caters to an editor, and to those people the editor caters to — the magazine's readers. If he didn't, the word successful would no longer apply. If he didn't *make contact* with the reader, the reader would not read his article. If the majority of the articles in a mangzine did not satisfy a majority of readers, they would not buy the publication, would not renew their subscriptions. Multiply that by thousands of readers and you get a picture of a magazine losing readers and, consequently advertisers and money; a magazine looking for a new editor who will look for new writers.

You have a specific audience to satisfy — a professor who will judge and critique your work and reward it or not. True, this should be done objectively, but we all know that the personality of both the instructor and the student, and the Six P's of the instructor, are important factors that equate with success, in this case spelled G-R-A-D-E. Knowing the variables, why should we not use the knowledge we can learn of the instructor's Six P's. We should! We should get aware of, and familiar with, this kind of knowledge, and use it. We will be doing so the rest of our lives as we deal with people. *Up to 90% of our future success, it is said, will not come about because we have talent and intelligence, but because we are able to use that talent and intelligence as we deal with people.*

Learning how to effectively write and speak and act and look is easy. Learning *what* is more difficult. Learning what to say (and how to say it) depends significantly on learning the *what* about *them.* *What* are their values...their interests... their goals...their Six P's... their expectations... their inclinations...their needs... their... .

RESUME

One of the more important things you will probably ever write is the resume and cover letter for your first job (and subsequent jobs).

No one has ever gotten a job *solely* because their resume or cover letter impressed someone. That's true. But many have lost the opportunity to interview for a job because their resume or cover letter did not impress someone. A well-written presentation of your qualifications and experience can create a good impression and get you an interview. Moreover, it can create a favorable environment for the interview. So don't let your resume defeat you.

Your resume should be accurate, concise and clear. It should put your best image forward, telling the prospective employer all the pertinent facts about you, your education, and experience.

Structuring Your Resume

1. Name, address, and telephone number.

2. Your objective — what position, with what responsibilities, are you seeking. (This can be broad in scope, or specific if being used in a customized resume, in which case it will fill their stated requirements, and more.)

3. A brief, personal sketch — date and place of birth, marital status, children, height, weight, and health status. Some experts say put it here, some say put it at the end, some say don't give it. I prefer it at the end and say if it gives the reader a feeling of knowing you, why not? The only thing that can hurt you is your age and that is easily estimated by most resume readers anyway.

4. Education— List degrees earned in reverse chronological order; year, name of college or university. Give major or minors if they enhance your qualifications for the position. Include high school if you can "brag," i.e., valedictorian, with honors, etc., or if there is a possibility that *he* might have gone there too.

5. Military service— Some experts say no unless it was recent (in last five years), or enhances your qualifications for the job. I say it does no harm and *he* might have served in the same branch, same whatever. Include dates, honors and citations, medals, etc.

6. Employment History— Specific details of your career starting with your present or most recent position, and going back at least ten years. For each, list the name and address of the company, your immediate supervisor's name and title (some consider that trivia, I don't), and dates of employment. Describe in detail, but concisely, your responsibilities and duties, showing the chain of command to you and from you, and your contributions to the company's success.

Stress your accomplishments. State any problems you faced (especially those that are similar to the needs stated by the prospective employer), and how you solved the problem — increased productivity, cost reductions, increased profitability, etc.

Show clearly how your experience and accomplishments meets perfectly the prospective employer's wants and needs for the position to be filled.

7. Hobbies. Include them if they enhance your qualifications, or if you learn that they are *his* interests, too.

8. References— On request. Have them ready at the interview.

Do... Don't...

Don't mention salary requirements. You might be too high, or too low. You may or may not want to include service to the community, memberships in lodges, clubs, etc. Be guided by what you can learn about the company, and the person who will interview you for the job.

As companies reduce their management ranks to remain cost-effective, competition for management positions will increase. You may be tempted to overelaborate, embellish, or even fabricate as you write your resume. Don't!

Resumes are "being subjected to increasingly rigorous scrutiny by companies as employers struggle to sort out reality from exaggeration, fact from fiction," wrote Bruce Serlen in an article, "Getting To The Bottom Of Resume Inflation," in Piedmont Airline's magazine,*PACE*, August, 1986.

A survey, conducted by Ward Howell International (1986), quoted in the *PACE* article, says "a quarter of the companies polled had experienced problems with resumes."

Over 62% found fabricated academic credentials; 43% discovered discrepancies in salary history; 42% found inaccuracies in responsibilities claims; 34% found inaccuracies in accomplishments claims; and 25% omitted a criminal record.

It was found, too, that over 65% of the companies check references not suggested by the applicants; almost all contact the candidate's prior or present superior(s); and about 40% speak to the applicant's peers on his present job.

It goes without saying that if a prospective employer perceives deception — innocent or not — then your chances of getting the job are, at the very least, in jeopardy.

Do use statistics on the size of the company you worked for, and your part in it, i.e., products, sales figures, and number of employees will give credence to your story. Give specific information, but just highlight the main points.

Don't be repetitious. When you are listing more than one position, and yours is a career on the move (taking on more responsibilities and duties), the present position (and its duties) will be almost the whole story of your qualifications, with preceding positions showing how you added to your experience to get to your present position.

For instance, your present (or last position) may have 150-200 words that describe all of your talents, i.e., planning, writing, and editing sales manuals. The one preceding it may be 75-100 words, i.e., responsibility for writing descriptions for sales manuals.

A prospecitve employer is only interested in what you've done — or are doing — not in how well you think you have performed. Tell it straight as you let your record (progressively assuming more and more responsibility, promotions, titles) speak for itself.

A new graduate, with no job experience, presents a different problem. You have to highlight your practicums, work-study projects, extracurricular activities, and part-time or summer work relevant to your abilities and talents. Do not lie, but you may coat the truth with some high-gloss varnish. Put yourself in the best light. Make the most of your scholastic activites.

Writing Your Resume

Before you begin to write your *first* resume, list on a worksheet everything that might impress a prospective employer. Include scholastic or athletic honors, meritorious recognition, any positions of prominence on teams or other organizations, membership in a college fraternity or sorority (a prospective employer or interviewer may just have been a member, too). Show how your education, training, and extracurricular activites qualify you for the position; how you can contribute to the company. There is something else you can show. Enthusiasm. How exciting it would be...a challenge... work hard to... I know I can... .

There is some debate on whether to use a professional resume writer. One thought says they tend to get too extravagant describing your virtues, the other says you cannot be objective writing your own resume. I have always written my own. I have written them for others, too. Some as favors, others for a fee. If you can be objective; if you can edit, edit, edit; you can write your own resume.

Reproducing Your Resume

As you lay out your resume prior to typing (whether you or a typist will do it), you want to use enough white space so each page can be read quickly and easily. Ideally you will keep your resume to two pages in length, a single page usually is sufficient for a new graduate. Keep in mind that the reader is a busy person. He will not hire you because of your resume. Its only job is to get you an interview. It should be designed to make the prospective employer want to meet you to see if the image your resume projects (one he likes) is the same image he will perceive in person.

Laying Out Your Resume

Your resume does more than tell your career story — it can also silently say that you're well-organized, lucid, and effective. If you need more help than you get here, there's an expert waiting for you at your local library who can illustrate several examples of resume formats. Here's the one I like.

JOHN Q. BROWN
123 Fourth Street
Anywhere, New York 12345
(516) 555-1234

OBJECTIVE	At this point you decide if you want to include a job objective. If you plan on "prospecting" you will probably include one of a general nature. If you're going for that "special" job with a customized resume, your objective should be customized, too, to fit the criteria of the prospective job.
EDUCATION	Your University, Someplace,State. B.S. (Major) 1901. Honors in whatever. Your High School,Wherever,State. Graduated 1999. Honors if any. Type of diploma.
EXPERIENCE 1980-Present	Your title Company's Name Company's Address Telephone number Your Superior's name and title Here's where you tell what you are doing, how you are contributing to the company's operation, who reports to you, etc. You do it factually, letting your accomplishments, promotions, etc., along with your responsibilities and duties, show that you are

an efficient, professional employee.

Be concise and be clear, but give the entire story of this phase of your career. You should include your company's objectives and your contributions toward achieving those objectives. Use action, rather than passive words and phrases.

1974-1980
Your title
Company's Name
Company's Address
Telephone number
Your Supervior's name and title

This will be shorter than above because that position provides more responsibility and that's why you went to that company, to continue your climb up the ladder.

With this story you will give the reason for leaving. The reason should never be *more money,* but a *more interesting position with greater responsibility or challenge.*

1970-1974
Your title
Company's Name
Company's Address
Telephone number
Your Superior's name and title

Same as above, but briefer and to the point. (This completes ten years and should be enough.) If you want to include more, and it is advantageous for you to do so, go back further, but be brief.

PERSONAL
Date of birth:
Marital Status:
Children:
Height:
Weight:
Health:

BUSINESS
AFFILIATIONS
This is optional. If you have the room (you don't want to use more than two pages if possible) and you think it will help you get the interview (Did you find out that you both belong to the same organization?), use it.

SOCIAL AFFILIATIONS	This is optional. But again, if you've learned that both you and the interviewer belong to the same lodge, you may want to include it.
HOBBIES	Optional. Be guided by above.
MILITARY SERVICE	U.S. Navy, 1942 — 1946. Enlisted as RM2/c, honorably discharged as CRM (Chief Radioman), 2/28/46. Special citations, medals, etc. can be listed briefly and to the point, as can assignments and promotions.
REFERENCES	On request.

Regarding references. There isn't much sense in listing references in your resume unless the prospective employer is interested in hiring you. Be prepared at the interview, however, to give names, addresses, and phone numbers of several people who will attest to what you've written about you and your experience. Ask those people for permission ahead of time. They will appreciate the courtesy and it will give them time to formulate a written reply, or a telephone answer, should a prospective employer write or call.

Consider each job description as a summary lead paragraph or a precis and when you're working on those portions of your resume, remember the Five W's. As you answer each "W" give thought to the following which should be included:

— Additional or unusual responsibilites or duties you assumed during your employment.

— Suggestions you made that saved your company time or money.

— Examples of suggestions, systems, methods, or improvements that you made, or helped to make, that contributed to the company's growth and success.

— Recognition in the form of citations, awards, bonuses, promotions, internal or external publicity, that you received, especially for contributions "above and beyond... ."

When you are actually writing the finished product, eliminate as many of the I, My, and Me words as possible. Instead of "I performed...I did...My performance...My responsibilities... use "Responsibilities included the... Duties consisted of... Opened new territory for the purpose of... Designed new format for... ." Use action, not passive words. Steer clear of euphemisms. Do use industry jargon and technical terms if appropriate. *Think communicate!*

Finally, review your typewritten, finished resume. Is it really built of a sound list of accomplishments? Qualifications? Credentials? Are they presented factually and honestly, but favorably? Is the copy clean and laid out so it invites a reading? Check it carefully for spelling and punctuation. It is "your foot in the door." Make sure the shoe is fashionable, appropriate, and well-polished.

Customizing Your Resume

When that "dream job" comes along, by all means consider customizing your resume. To do this you research the company before you even begin to write. If it's a public company, get its latest quarterly or (better yet) its annual report. In this way you can learn about the company's past, present, and its goals and objectives for the future. If it's not a public company you may have to settle for information from its in-house publications, its sales literature, and other printed material. You'd be surprised how much of this material is available in their reception or waiting area. You may have to work even harder. But if it's a dream job it could be worth it. Does the company manufacture hardware? Try your local hardware store.

Does it produce computers? Try your local computer store. Go to the local newspaper. They probably have a file of articles printed about the company over the years. So might your local library. You may even learn something about the company's executives. Did one get an award, become an officer in a local civic group, lodge, etc., become a director of a hospital or foundation? If one did he'd have made the newspaper. Such articles usually contain a brief biography. You may learn that he or she (the very person that will interview you) attended the same college you did, or is a member of the same fraternal organization. Wouldn't that information be nice to have, and use, in your resume, or at the interview.

When you customize your resume you can slant your talents, education, and your experience, to your target company's needs. If you know who your prospective employer is and what your prospective employer's needs are, you will certainly have an edge over your competitors.

A customized resume means typing each one individually, but a page or two of typing is a small price to pay for a chance to land that dream job.

Whether you use customized resumes or only printed resumes, you can tailor your cover letter to fit each job opportunity.

The Cover Letter

Your cover letter should do much more than say "here's my resume." It may have to get the receiver to read your resume, which has to get you an interview, if you are to have a chance to get the job.

Right off be sure your cover letter says, in effect, "I understand your needs and I'm the person to fill the job." Then give an example of an accomplishment or two that you think will prove you are the best-qualified person for the job. Then show how your education prepared you to contribute to this company. After you have specifically emphasized those aspects of your talents and knowledge that meets their needs or advances their goals, say you would like to arrange for an interview. Do not be available for an interview at any time. It may give the impression you have too much time. Rather, you would like to arrange an interview at a "mutually convenient time." Be enthusiastic. It can help you get that interview if he detects your enthusiasm and interest in *his* field and *his* business.

If your experience is limited (or poor) you should, in your cover letter, stress your personal qualifications, zeal, enthusiasm, and willingness to learn or to assume responsibility.

One further hint. If you're writing to a specific person, be sure you have the correct spelling of his name and his proper title. (This may sound elementary, but you'd be surprised... .) If you are writing to a company cold (you're fishing), try to get the name of its president and address your letter to him. He probably will not be doing any screening or interviewing, but he'll be passing your letter and resume down to the right person. And that person may think about the application that the boss sent down, especially if the boss was too busy to send along a note that he didn't know the applicant.

Limit your cover letter to a single page. A short single page. Short, but powerful. The shorter the better.

Get all the help you can get when you write your resume and cover letter. Friends, books in your library, etc. Forty-plus clubs, formed to help find jobs for unemployed executives 40-years old or older, find that resumes are one of the major obstacles to placing these older executives. These men, and women, while masters at dictating letters, are almost helpless when it comes to writing objective reports on their own careers. These otherwise accomplished executives seem not to have mastered the simple art of writing a resume that gives the facts clearly, concisely, and objectively.

Now *you* can. And hopefully, you can do many things that you couldn't do before you began to read this book. Or, at least, you can do many things just a little bit better.

As I wrote many words ago, each of us, whether we realize it or not, are playing many roles. We are, if we want to be successful, always trying to project the best image we can — an image that is the prototype — in their minds — of the role we are playing.

In Part I you learned about P.P.R. Now you know you have it, you know what it is, and you know — in general — how to use it. At the very least you are aware of your P.P.R. and how it affects you even in the routine of your everyday life.

In Part II you became more aware of the basic tool of P.P.R. — communications. You learned that you were communicating with your looks, your actions, your spoken words, and your written words, and you sharpened those skills.

In Part III we will see how the knowledge of Part I and the communication skills of Part II can be used to enhance your P.P.R. and make you even more successful.

Part Three

Using The Skills Of P.P.R.

13

You & They... Specifically

It is said that a worker — for that matter a student, a housewife, etc. — relies 90 percent on know-how and 10 percent on the ability to deal with — interact with — people.

A manager, or supervisor, relies 75 percent on know-how and 25 percent on the ability to deal with people.

The man — or woman — who runs the show, whether it's a large institution, corporation, school system, public service, or business, is said to rely 20 percent on know-how and 80 percent on the ability to deal with people.

Lee Iacocca, in his book, *Iacocca: An Autobiography*, said that the key to success in management is dealing with people. The phrase he hated to see most on any executive's evaluation was — "He has trouble getting along with other people." Regardless of talent and education, this phrase, according to Iacocca, is the "kiss of death."

So, whether you're a student who must deal with teachers, other students, siblings, and parents; a teacher dealing with students, other teachers, students' parents, and school administrators; a professional dealing with other professionals, clients or patients; a salesman dealing with customers; a worker, manager, or administrators who must deal with other workers, managers, administrators, and the general public; or a housewife dealing with the butcher, the baker, and the candlestick maker (and a husband and children and in-laws) — to be successful, you must learn to — want to — deal with other people, and do it successfully.

To relate to a person — publicly or privately — you must first know about that person. You must know about all those people with whom you interact. What makes them tick? You must know of their personality and character and their interests and concerns. Only then can you truly relate. You may want to cater to those interests or concerns, especially if they are compatible with your own, or are in line with your principles. Conversely, you don't have to flout your opposition if such exists. Or, if you must, at least not in an abrasive manner.

This is doubly true when it applies to his or her knowledge, lack of knowledge, or half-correct knowledge. Unless correcting the other person *is* your job, or his incorrect knowledge will impact on your job, interests, or concerns — don't bother. You might want to try once, just once, with an "I thought... I could be mistaken, but... I was under the impression that... ." But once is enough. Especially when it is petty and unimportant, and has no deleterious effect on you or your job.

I remember sharing a table with three fellow department heads one day in the company cafeteria when the after lunch conversation turned to golf and golf courses. One of my peers belonged to a club that used the word "links" in its name although they were hundreds of miles from the nearest seashore.

"I thought links were only those courses that bordered the sea," I said, absolutely certain that I was correct.

"Oh no," he replied, "Blank Links is a true links course."

I guess, I thought at the time, that it was possible that the term had become more generic. In any case it wasn't important. Several months later when we were again discussing golf courses, he told me once again that Blank Links was a true links course, the only one in the area. I nodded. I knew, I said, he had told me. What I didn't say was that in a recent issue of *Golf Magazine*, in an article on the British Open, they gave the description of a links course — one bordering on the sea — as was the one under discussion, St. Andrews, in Scotland.

The point being made here is that there are really no reasons to win skirmishes, even battles, that have no significance other than the satisfaction of proving yourself right. And if *you* know that... why bother.

With this mindset, let's begin our excursion into the you and they of P.P.R.

You have already evaluated yourself and you have delineated those aspects of your performances that must be — can be — changed or modified to gain you the responses you want. That's P.R. — performance and response. You have determined what aspects of your performance can be changed or modified by education... by learning new or additional social graces... by changing your attitudes, or by changing your uniform — your dress, hairstyle, etc.

(If you like go back and review Chapter 3.) You may have even started to make changes or modifictions in a general way. But now let's get specific. Let's research everyone who *really* matters, in the environment that *really* matters, for rewards that *really* matter. This should be the people we listed on our Sphere II list — People Who Can Affect My Career and Finances. (Remember Chapter 5?) Since we know about those people on our Sphere I list (we may have already started doing something to improve our interaction with family members after reading Chapter 5), let's begin in the workplace with career advancement, added prestige, and more income as our objectives and goals.

Researching Him Or Her Specifically

Let's get out our Sphere II list. Using that as a guide, let's write the name and title of every individual with whom you must interact. Individuals only. Continuing relationships, not occasional. Specific, not general. If you are a nurse, for instance, it is certainly important that you relate to and interact favorably with your patients, co-workers, and physicians, (and some of them may be named here if applicable), but it could be even more important that you deal with and interact favorably with your Unit Supervisor, Head Nurse, and Director of Nursing. If you're a salesperson in a department store it is certainly important that every customer be dealt with courteously and competently, but that would go for nought if the department manager detests you and wonders why personnel hired you in the first place.

So let's list people like the unit supervisor, head nurse, and director, the department manager, et al. And when you finish — check it. Does it contain the name of *every* person who can impact on your career success? Now we're going to divide your list into smaller lists. Five names to a list. Mark one "A". Write down the five most important (from your master list) — the five *most important* people in your work life. List B will be the next five. List C the next, and so forth. As you make each list, rank the names in order of importance to prioritize each list. So now the first name on your A list is *the* most important person in your work life.

These lists will serve two purposes. One, since we cannot research every person at once we are giving priority to the most important, and, two, if there are any conflicts in the future involving people who can impact on your career success, you know immediately (if you keep your lists up-to-date) where each person involved in the conflict is ranked. If you *have* to choose sides — if someone *has to be* a winner — you know how to choose.

Ideally, by the time you finish reading P.P.R., your skills for dealing with people will be such that both the adversaries in a conflict will remain an ally. At this point in time, however, we are learning about the people who are important to us in our everyday working lives. And the first people to be learned about are the five names on your "A" List—the five most important people for you in your business or working life. You are going to write a short essay about each. (Take a peek at Chapter 12 and sharpen your pencil.)

Write An Essay About Him Or Her

Writing an essay about an important him or her (in your business *or* personal life) — a biographical sketch — will help you learn about him or her and remember what you've learned. Besides, what you learn now about researching your information, prioritizing the facts, and putting them down on paper, will come in handy in the next chapter when you plan your P.P.R. program.

First, you must learn about your subject. That's the basic tenet of public relations — you must know your public before you can truly communicate with it, be it one person, a group of people, or thousands of people.

After reading the chapters on communications, you know it is easier to write about something you know. Of course it is. That's a ridiculous statement. It is impossible to write about something —or someone — you know nothing about.

You know, too, how to use the Five W's for effective writing. Now you can make good use of them to research the five most important people (to you) in your workplace. You'll answer the Who, What, Why, When, Where, and How of each. Using the W's will make your research easier.

Let's work on the "A" List. Let's begin with name No. 1 — *the* most important person. Let's record his or her name, business address, title; home address, names and ages of spouse and children; his or her boss or superior. That's the Who.

What does he or she do for the company? What has he done in the past? What has he done that received laudatory reactions? For others? For the community? What are his interests...hobbies... affiliations...i.e., Elks, Masons, Knights of Columbus, Kiwanis, BPW, etc. What are his family interests? Sports? Other? What does he expect from his subordinates? Peers? Family? That's the What.

When did he join the company... graduate from college...get promotions... get married... ? That's the When.

Where did he come from — birthplace...prior company(s)... graduate from which high school, college? Where will his ambition take him? Higher in this company? To a different company? That's the Where.

Why and/or How— Why does he expect certain things from his subordinates...his peers... his family? How does he expect people to act and feel about him? His family? The company? The country? Why? How does he expect people to dress? To act?

Now you're saying — Where am I ever going to get all that information? My answer — You'd be surprised. The best way I can answer is to give you an example.

A Research Example

My problem: Getting to know the Five W's and H of my new boss when I joined the public relations department of a medium-sized university. He was the director. I'll call him John Smith.

By conversation with others I learned that John had joined the university almost five years to the day I did. I looked in the department's clipping book (for that year) and saw the announcement as it was printed in the local newspaper. I learned he was married and his wife's name. I learned the names of his children and could guess their age brackets. One, a girl, was in college. The other two, boys, were attending the local high school. I learned from which college he graduated. (I was hoping it was my alma mater, or even a sports rival. It wasn't.) I knew the year he graduated and his degree. (Bachelor of Arts in English). Ditto regarding his master's degree. That gave me his approximate age —most people get their bachelor's degree at age twenty-two. That guesstimate was reinforced by the estimated ages of his children. The article listed his professional and social affiliations. I learned that we would be lodge brothers as soon as I transferred from my lodge in a different city. I even learned some of his hobbies (the ones he considered important enough to list).

All of this information came from one newspaper clipping.

Now you're saying you can't look at your company's clipping book. Are you sure? You could want to learn more about the company, couldn't you. You may think your company doesn't have one. Unlikely. But let's say that that is true. Did you know you can visit your local newspaper and look through back issues, some on microfiche? If you knew *when* he joined your company you could have found the clipping in the newspaper's library. Suppose I didn't know the date, even the year. In the newspaper's library there is probably a file under that individual's name (if he is high enough on the company ladder), or a file on the company. The paper's librarian will be glad to help you. You'll probably see stories and photos of the company, him, and others. *All* useful information if you're working for him and the company, and with others.

If there is a file on him or her, or on the company, you will also learn when he was promoted, received an honor, etc. You'll learn when and where and for whom he was a guest speaker. An honored guest. Received an award.

Want more information? Of course you do. You can never have too much information about people who can have an impact on your finances, career, or happiness. Is there a company publication? If there is look over back issues to learn more about the company and its goals as well as No. 1. Don't forget observation. How does he dress? Suits, or slacks and jacket? Vested suits or not? Continental side vents in the jacket, or American center vent? Kinds and colors of shirt... ties? Style of shoes?

Does he smoke? Cigarettes or cigars or a pipe? What's his brand of cigarettes? Don't laugh. Do you think a Marlboro smoker has the same image as a Philip Morris smoker? Or is as health conscious as a Carlton or Now smoker?

Is his hair always well-trimmed? His mustache and beard if he wears one? Does he wear jewelry? What kind? Does he care for his nails? To what extemes, if any? How about the way he talks... the way he walks... the way he stands...the way he sits? How about the way he writes...have you read any of his memos, reports, letters?

All of these observations will give you hints about what he may or may not be... what he may or may not expect of others.

Does he seem to put up with bright, energetic Junior Executive, even though Junior dresses in loud sports clothes? Even though Junior smokes like a chimney in his office? Even though Junior chews with his mouth open? And if he does put up with these shortcomings because Junior is bright and energetic and talented — Is he helping Junior up the ladder, or just tolerating him for the work he gets that advances his — No. 1's objectives? If that's the case then Junior's sure wasting that great energy, brightness, and talent, isn't he?

By keeping your ears open as well, you can learn even more about No. 1 from your — his — co-workers, and even from No. 1 himself.

Has he remarked in any way about current events? Politics? Sports teams? If he's a conservative, do you really want to flout the fact that you're a liberal? Do you really want him to know you voted for the winning candidate (he hates him), or that you rooted for the 49ers to win when he was praying for the Jets? Maybe yes, maybe no. What is his attitude on such matters? How strong and how serious can he get on such matters?

What do your co-workers — maybe even subordinates — say about No. 1? Are they sincere or paying lip service... critical or complimentary...warm or cold? Do they say one thing while they are being betrayed by the tone of their voice...or a look?

Learn all you can about No. 1 from these sources and others. Did he graduate from a local (or nearby) high school or college? Have you access to high school and college yearbooks? In your local library? In the school's library? Do you have mutual friends? Acquaintances? Do you have the same insurance man, gas station attendant, mailman, grocer, bank teller...newspaper carrier? If so, you'll get to know No. 1. When you get all the information — the answers to your Five W's and How — write your essay.

Do the same for No.'s 2,3,4, and 5. Chances are you have all the Five W information on them, too. And you've added your evaluation and assessment of their general psychological attributes, too. If you haven't, review Chapters 4 and 5 and match as many definitions as possible, i.e., is he or she a Driver, an Expressive, an Amiable, an Analytical... Assertive and Responsive... etc.

Now you can write your essays. And then you can use them.

Using Your Him/Her Essays

You now know a lot about the five, ten, fifteen — more or less — most important people in your everyday work life. Use it.

As was said before, if there is a conflict between one or more of these important people, you can make a calculated choice. Suppose, for instance, there is such a conflict between No. 1 and No. 3. (They are both vp's and equally important in the company hierarchy.) The rankings of number one and three are yours — importance to *your* career. You will, of course, try to remain neutral. You never know when their order of importance in the company — and to you and your career — may change. But sometimes you cannot remain neutral. Sometimes you don't wish to. You may feel, based on your knowledge of each, that you want to side with one or the other. You may feel that you can appear to side with both. You may want to gamble. Even so, try to be moderate. (If one is your boss there is no contest.)

Then there's the thrill of debate. Many have trouble resisting it. Better to argue politics, religion, or philosophy with friends, Mom or Dad, Uncle Charlie, or your barber —but not with your boss(es). Maybe not with your barber, either.

At any rate you now have your essays — bios they're called in the public relations field — and you know quite a bit about their backgrounds, personalities, likes, and dislikes, maybe even a few of their P's, even an ideosyncrasy or two. And you've been studying their performances. Now look for both the complementary aspects and the conflicting aspects of your potential relationships. Look for them and use them. Cultivate the complementary aspects and avoid the conflicting aspects.

If you're both New York Giants fans...use it. Are you both conservative Republicans... moderate Democrats... Liberals? Use it. You both like woodworking... Fine. You're both avid fishermen... golfers... bowlers... use it.

Share your common interests. Anytime your interests and concerns complement his or her interests and concerns, why not use it to build a bond between you. The objective of your performance in these situations, all other things being equal of course, is to evoke a positive response. Commonality dictates that to be so. Common interests bind. How well depends on "all other things being equal."

What about conflicting aspects in your and his likes and dislikes, attitudes, interests, concerns, goals, expectations, and the like?

You have a choice: You can either change your performance to one that will elicit the positive response you seek; you can try to change his attitude or perception of your performance, or justify your performance to him; or you can remain neutral — unburdened by a negative response, but without the benefits of a positive response.

An Example

Let's take a hypothetical situation. You and your immediate boss are Yankee fans (that takes care of the summer), New York Giants fans (that'll take you to the Superbowl, the season of 1986-87), and both of you are crosscountry skiing enthusiasts. That gives you the opportunity to celebrate when your teams win and commiserate when they lose. Both you and he are interested in opera, modern art, and travel. Both of you are Civil War buffs. You are both golfers and bowlers.

You & They ...Specifically 215

These are your common interests. Even if you are not on the same plane of socialization with your boss or superior, not on a sharing-a-lunch-table basis, they can generate break-the-ice remarks prior to meetings, or just in an exchange of pleasantries. They can be used as positive building blocks in the construction of relationships. With your boss... your peers...the guy or girl you want to date...a teacher...a friend...the butcher...the mailman... . (The same kind of research and essay writing, with minor differences, can be used for the five most important people in your school life, your social life, etc.)

On the other side of the coin, let's say your boss is a Republican moderate and you are an enrolled Independent who refers to himself as a liberal conservative or a conservative liberal. He favors capital punishment and even thinks it may be unconstitutional to have a crime for which there is no punishment. "How many times can you sentence a murderer to life imprisonment," he asks. You are against the dealth penalty on the grounds that it is better to err in favor of the occasional innocent who may be convicted. He wears three-piece suits, keeps his shoes shined, wears white shirts, and coordinates his socks and ties. You are pretty close to him in fastidiousness, but you favor blazers and slacks and colored shirts. Your golf handicap is 9, his is 21, and you're both 125-average bowlers. He is against the Supreme Court's decision on abortion, you are against abortion personally, but you don't think you have the right to force your beliefs on others.

Some of these conflicting values, interests, and concerns, could, by themselves, wipe out many of the building blocks of positive common interests, a few could be just a hindrance, others could be turned into another positive building block. It is within your power to cultivate the complementary common interests you have, and allow the conflicting viewpoints you may have to remain dormant. Sometimes you will, sometimes you won't. Your choice.

Capital punishment and abortion are both emotional conflicts of interest, as well as intellectual differences and it is very unlikely that you could change either your performance or your boss' attitude. You would probably be wiser to remain *publicly* neutral. You may even take the same stance with your peers, for the sake of harmony, and also as a way to remain publicly neutral with your boss' viewpoint. Causes, stands, and positions have a way of becoming known in the workplace. When you need stimulating conversation on controversial issues get it from discussions with friends, preferably outside the workplace. The stakes are not as high. In either case you preserve your individuality, even though in one case you do it by *not* expressing your opinion, by not expressing *any* opinion. As Crisp wrote, "A courteous silence is more effective in keeping the peace... ."

In the Barbara Walters chapter in Readers Digest's *Write better, Speak better*, "When You Meet A Famous Person," she covers such topics as how to approach a celebrity (let good manners be your guide), be considerate (let your empathy show), safe subjects for conversation, and seven problems. If you take a walk over to your public library and read the fifteen pages of this chapter (Chapter 37), just change the title, in your mind, to read When You Meet An Important Person, and apply the information generously to your actions in your everyday business relationships. If you don't want to read it, the bottom line is...

Be Appropriate And Considerate

When it comes to how they dress, how you dress, you may want to build yet another positive building block in your relationships by *copying*, if only to a degree, those in power within your company or organization. (Remember what you read in Chapter 8.) Do all the management and administrative people dress in similar fashion to your boss? Is he reflecting the *unwritten* look or dress code for your company's executives? If he is, you may want to change your *performance* and dress the part of success in *your* company. You may want to consider if you would be just as comfortable wearing three-piece suits to the office, and blazers and slacks socially.

You might ask: What about being myself — do I have to be a total clone to be successful? Do I have to lie about myself to get along?

No. You don't have to be a clone. In dress, you may wear three-piece suits if that seems to be the *uniform* of success, but you can still express your individuality in your choice of ties, shirts (styles and cuts, color shades) and jewelry.

No. You don't have to lie. In fact, you should never lie. But you may want to *varnish* the truth. "Your point is well-taken." "That's an interesting viewpoint... ." "That could be a very appropriate direction... ." Or, you could refrain from commenting at all. At any rate, when there *is* a need for conformity, we must conform. Or move on to a place where we *can* conform.

I remember sitting in a chair in a university's barber shop many years ago. A young man entered. His hair laid across his shoulders. He wore baggy pants and an even baggier shirt. He wore no socks, only dirty tennis shoes covered his feet. He slouched in the chair next to mine and said to his barber: "Give me a haircut like his." His thumb waved toward me. Tony, his barber, looked quizzically at him. "The recruiters are coming next week," the student said, somewhat in explanation, "I've got to buy some clothes, too."

I looked over at him. My smile welcomed him into the world of reality and conformity.

The fact that you're a pretty good golfer and he's not (or bowler, or skier, or...) can be used to advantage. If you don't flout it. If he finds out you are from *other* sources (tournament results, for instance). Knowing that most golfers (bowlers, skiers, etc) want to improve, and most people like to get something for nothing, like advice, or lessons.... . Well, you can see the possibilities.

The important points being made in this chapter is that you must learn his or her strengths of mutual interests, concerns, and attitudes and capitalize on them; you must neutralize those values in which there is a conflict; and you must decide whether to use those inbetween as positive building blocks in your relationship, or let them remain neutral unspeakables.

It is true that most relationships can exist, and even grow, when the majority of common interests are positive and when the minority of common interests are conflicting and negative (and being tolerated). That is, however, usuallly the case *only* when the conflicting interest, opinion, or concern, is *not* an emotional one, such as capital punishment or abortion. In other, more intellectual and logical differences of interest or opinion, a certain amount of conflict will be tolerated when it is vastly outweighed by the common bond. You must, of course, keep a balance — at least publicly — favoring mutually favorable common interests.

You will, of course, always make a distinction (considering the risk/reward factor) between your boss, your fiance, and the clerk at the corner newsstand. You certainly did an essay on your boss, you may do one on your fiance, but you don't need to know that much about the newsstand clerk.

The same research and essay writing methods that you used to learn about the important people in your work world, can be applied to other people in your everyday life. Even toward a single person — that special person you have, or want, in your life. It can be applied to a business associate, a customer, a teacher. It can be applied *whenever* a good relationship is wanted, or needed, or is absolutely necessary.

It may seem like a lot of work — researching her...observing him...listening to them. Making notes. Getting the answers to the Five W's. And then writing a biographical sketch, an essay, or, as P.R. people call them, a bio. It only seems like a lot of work because it is. Important work. Done only for those who are important to your success. And writing things down — a list of likes and dislikes, a bio, answers to the Five W's — are important, too. Having written about him (or her) you're more apt to remember useful information and its there for you to pluck from your mind when needed. If nothing else, you've got reference material when you can't remember. Even more important, writing a bio will help you clarify and focus on the important aspects of him or her. It will help you when you plan and execute your P.P.R. program.

Your P.P.R. program will be an overall plan to achieve an overall goal, but actually it will be several programs, one meshing with another, each with objectives that will contribute to the achievement of that goal. Each can be person-oriented, people-oriented, or problem-oriented. Each will have a plan and a strategy to accomplish a desired response or result.

Let's learn about planning your P.P.R. program.

14

Planning Your P.P.R. Program

Public relations is, or should be, concerned with yesterday (what *were* our performances and their responses); today (what *is* our image now, based on our previous performances and their responses); and tomorrow (what do we wish our image to be — one year from now, five years, ten years into the future).

Visualize. Put yourself in a picture. It's one year from today. Five years. Ten. You're at work. What do you see? In your social, family, or domestic life — what do you see? If everything was exactly as you wanted it to be, what would be happening? What *is* happening? Describe the scene. What do you see? Is it the way you want it to be?

How do we get there?

What we must do first is gather all the knowledge we can about *them* — their needs, interests and concerns — our bosses, customers, clients, co-workers, teachers, patients, et al; people with whom we interact socially; family members; those with whom we have relationships within our "sphere of activity."

It is easiest to fashion a performance that will elicit a positive response for the last group. All it really takes is generous amounts of common courtesy, respect, consideration, appreciation, and a smile. Much the same — with the addition of "being there when needed" — are our family relationships. Our social relationships can range from the casual acquaintance to the friend to that very special person. Our business relationships require the most research and knowledge, both specific (about the person), and general (about the people). At any one time, therefore, you may have many P.P.R. programs working, each tailored to a specific public for a specific objective.

While we will concentrate mainly on your career P.P.R. program(s), planning is the same for *any* such program. It begins with the ten basic steps that will help you plan your program for your work life, social life, or family life.

Ten Steps For Planning Your P.P.R. Program

1. Identification of appropriate and relevant publics.
2. Assessment of your publics.
3. Analysis of all situations in which you are an integral part.
4. Identification of any problems and problem areas.
5. Definition of needs to solve problems.
6. Establishment of specific objectives and goals.
7. Development of a program to meet objectives and goals.
8. Implementation of program using appropriate performances.
9. Communication of performances.
10. Evaluation and refinement of performances.

Identification Of Appropriate And Relevant Publics

You have already identified the publics who are impacting on you, or may impact on you. You have named them, ranked them in order of importance to you (in your career life), and you have examined those publics that could impact on your important publics. For your business life you have your A-list, B-list, and so forth. If you are going to work on a P.P.R. program for your school life, your social life, or your family life, you must make similar lists for these publics.

Assessment Of Your Publics

In your business or career life you know who *they* are, how important each is to you. Your assessment of each VIP in your working life has shown you what common positive and negative interests, concerns, and opinions you share. You have written essays about each of them. You will now add more information to each one's dossier which, at the moment, consists only of one essay.

Observe and study each of them as you go about your work. Determine their personal objectives and the contribution that the achievement of those objectives will make toward the company — regarding such areas as growth, profit, prestige, image, etc. In this way you can make *their* objectives for the company, *your* objectives.

To accomplish this you can do overt research. You can ask questions. You can read your company's annual report (and interim quarterly reports if any). You can read position papers, long-range planning reports, and company publications. *You can ask your boss.* Just asking will let him know you care about the company. Your goal is two-fold — (1) you want to do everything possible to advance your company's goals and enhance its public image, and (2) you want to be recognized as a valuable asset to your company (and, of course, to your boss(es)). To do that effectively you must be aware of your role in the company.

Analysis Of All Situations In Which You Are An Integral Part

Analyzing all the situations in which you are an integral part calls for a broad-scoped study of all aspects of the business that involves your superior's success or failure; everything that affects him or her or them (your chain of superiors right up to the top); and everything to which you, in the performance of your job, can contribute. This includes analyzing the general climate of attitudes as well as the specific.

First learn, then analyze, all aspects of the business — goals, objectives for growth, plans. If you were the brand new public relations director of this corporation, you'd interview all the people who were a managment part of the corporation — board members, administrators, department heads, et al. You'd also interview people outside the corporation who are in a position to observe it objectively. These might be suppliers, service people, journalists, etc. Then you would research a cross-section of its general public — customers, potential customers, stockholders, etc. — for additional views.

Some of this work would be done through market research, such as opinion or attitude studies, or the informal research of observation — asking and listening. In any case you would soon determine a company profile.

While you are not the new P.R. director, you can, in a small way, do the same kind of research — informal conversation with some managers and workers, suppliers, service people, people who use the company's products or services. Then, combined with the official material — annual reports, company brochures, company publication stories — you have a dossier on the company. You can even write an essay.

Do that. Write an essay about your company. Nothing elaborate. Keep it brief. And then write an essay about yourself. Specifically how you *do* and how you *can* fit into your company's achievement of its objectives and goals.

A quick self-evaluation:

— Are you really and sincerley interested in your co-workers and your boss and their objectives and problems?

— Are you able to work with others to achieve common goals and objectives?

— Do you really try to understand the other person's point-of-view or, as the old Indian saying goes — Walk in the other person's moccasins for a couple of miles?

— Could you be a better listener and, like the television commercial says, "be surprised at what you were missing?"

— Do you really try to keep learning — about your job and the other person's job?

— Are you really enthusiastic? (You have to like your job and your company to be really enthusiastic. If you're not, you don't, and you should change jobs or company — for them and for yourself.)

— Are you taking the initiative preparing yourself for the next job with more responsibility?

— Do you resist change or welcome it?

— Do you resist new ideas or are you willing to experiment?

— Do you take yourself too seriously, or do you get some fun out of your work and life?

You have identified your appropriate and relevant publics — those people whose lives and work and success that you affect, and who can affect you. You have delineated and analyzed the situations of which you are an integral part — situations in which you can affect them, their success, and your company.

Now you must define any and all problems — real and perceived — in which you are, or may be, a principal.

Identification Of Any Problem And Problem Areas

"Problem — A difficult or perplexing matter; a troublesome person; a proposition to be worked out."

Problems are either covert, or overt. Our first task is to discover those P.P.R. problems hidden from our view, after which, all of our problems are overt — plain to view — *our* view.

To uncover problems with which we are not aware, even though, possibly, we may have suspected —"he seems a little cold and distant...she never seems to really open up..." — we must first analyze his or her state of opinion.

Is he or she envious — of the way I dress, look? Does he or she feel in competition with me? Does a superior *seem* to be overly considerate... attracted... favoring... benevolent... interested... in me and my welfare? Am I consciously promoting favored treatment? (Or does my work warrant it?) Does he or she fear me; am I qualified to do his job? Am I demotivating people? (Review Chapter 6 regarding the 12 ways to motivate and the 6 ways to demotivate people.) Is he or she in a position to do me harm? (Probably. It's not difficult for another person — a co-worker or a subordinate — to start a rumor, insinuate, or imply, and it's not hard for a superior to make life just a bit harder, or stand in the way of a favorable response from others.)

Define these personal opinion problems. Write them down. Get specific. Be subjective and objective. Are any of his or her opinions legitimate, imagined, or fabricated? Is there a personality conflict? Jealousy? Is it just a misunderstanding?

Gather all the views you can. Now you have uncovered all hidden problems. Now you are aware of *all* your problems. Even potential problems.

Make comparisons from among the views that you have learned each of them have. True, many are guesstimates made from observations, brainstorming, remembering incidents, remarks, etc. But if you feel them, and know them, then they are real. They must have substance. And you can learn. You can see better which of their interests and concerns parallel yours, as well as which are different. These differences may be genuine differences of opinion regarding strategy, values, goals, etc.; they may be a product of ignorance and/or misconception, or some of their P's; they may be the result of personality conflicts, jealousy, or even competition, real or imagined; or they may arise because of some cause-and-effect relationship.

All you have to do now is determine into which category each problem lies, and then determine which public relations strategy you want to use to surmount, overcome, or solve each of them.

Definition Of Needs To Solve Problems

Analysis of your problems and problem areas may indicate that certain performances must be changed or modified to improve his or her attitude toward you. Or, you may have to "educate" them. Often the change or modification of your performance may only involve eliminating causes of one mis' — misconception, misunderstanding, misinterpretation, misperception, or misjudgment.

The first thing to do is to cut the problem down to size:
1. *Identify the problem.* Once you can delineate the problem clearly and concisely, preferably in writing, you are halfway there to solving it. Remember, too, that opinion is not fact. He, or she *thinks* something about your performance and *that is your* problem.
2. *Get all the information you can get.* Maybe it's mostly subjective. If you *feel* it, it is probably so. If you see it, or have been told about it, it *is* a problem, and in more than one mind. Keep an open mind. Don't *think* thoughts or come to conclusions that support your own P's or ideas. Be objective.
3. *Determine the possible solution(s).* Be creative. Review if you must, Chapter 2, where you read that you cannot pull your own strings without pulling theirs; how others see you, in Chapter 3; learning about them in general in Chapter 4; and public opinion, in Chapter 5. If you've got a good memory just jog it a little.

Establishment Of Specific Objectives And Goals

Before you can begin to solve your problems (or potential problems) you need a list (preferably in writing) of the possible solutions to those problems, as well as long-range objectives with regard to your respective publics in general. These might be groups—the mailroom staff, the steno pool, your subordinates within your sphere of operations (department, section, etc.), your peers, your supervisors, the top brass, *the* company. These may be few in number, or large, but if you interact with them, you are forging your reputation—your public image.

What are your objectives? They should be delineated with a perspective that they will serve as guides over the long term. If you view them only with an eye on the short term, they will not provide the continuity of direction over the long-term unless you continually modify and revise them. Delineate the long-term objectives and goals and you will easily see the short-term strategic milestones along the way.

Your goal should be the achievement of some thing at some time in the future. For instance, in your business life this goal may be appointment to Regional Sales Manager in five years. Your objectives (long-term) should be those accomplishments along the way that will get you to your goal, hopefully, in the allotted time period. Your short-term objectives should be the solutions to those problems which are *now*, or can become, stumbling blocks to reaching your objectives and, consequently, your ultimate goal.

(In your social life your goal may be to marry him or her in X years, to improve a relationship within a family by Christmas, or to get the garbage pick-up men to start putting your cans down gently ASAP.)

Write down your goal or goals in your business career life. Be realistic with both your ambition and time. Then write the objectives you must reach along the way to reach your goal. Now review your problem list and add their resolutions to your short-term objectives.

Development Of A Program To Meet Objectives And Goals

With your new-found awareness and understanding of what people think of you — the negative debits or problems *and* the positive assets — and with a clarification of performances that affect your publics' opinion, you now have a base upon which to develop your program — activities that will explain "you" and, at the same time, overcome misunderstandings and promote goodwill.

This is not to say that your personal public relations program will be a rigid roadmap to success. Professional P.R. practitioners are always prepared for the unexpected, the curve in the road. You too must remain flexible as the driver would be following a roadmap. Your program will probably have to be modified as time and circumstance may require. Keep your perspective broad while drawing up your program, and you will find that the changing day-to-day problems will fit within the framework of your broad objectives.

Planning and developing your P.P.R. program involves laying out in detail those various things you will do, and not do, and those things necessary to communicate those actions, reactions, or inactions to the key people (your publics) that you have listed in your objectives.

For instance, let us say that it is your responsibility to review and record and facilitate the payment of expenses for a sales force that operates from your office. You must review their monthly expense report to see that each item is an approved expenditure, that each item is within the limits with regard to amount, and that each item is justified. In short, you are the company "watchdog," and the facilitator for getting reimbursed, and you are somewhat in the middle. Your P.P.R. program may outline the activities and actions and attitudes you will take to get, keep, or improve your reputation for fairness, amiability, and competence from both sides — both of your publics — those who get paid and those who do the paying.

You may have one problem person. One that wants to play the

game of padding the monthly expense account. The "gyp sheet" he calls it. He's not really dishonest, but rather he considers it one of the "perks." You can't and don't. You may have to draw the rein here, or enter the "game" there, by your interaction with him. You have to determine an action and attitude that solves this immediate problem now, and sets a tone to prevent the problem in the future.

Implementation Of Program Using Appropriate Performances

The tools of public relations — knowledge of your public's interest, concerns, and needs; knowledge of motivational and demotivational buttons; knowing what makes *them* tick; and awareness of the concept of performance and response — are then used to carry out your planned P.P.R. activities.

In the case of the "gyp sheet commando," for instance, you may wish to use one of the best public relations tactics, the truth, with a coat of varnish shining brightly from it.

Not — "You cannot do this ..." but "Do you really want me to send this upstairs for approval?" Not to say "No!" but to bring him or her into the picture and let him or her say "No!"

You may even enlist the aid of others in an oblique way — having the financial administrator issue a copy of the company policy on expenses reimbursement, or a memo regarding it.

You will do well, in any case, when you are in such a situation, to bring him or her into the boat with you. And when you get him there, give him an oar.

I remember a hospital administrator, a vice president for clinical services, who was having problems passing the word down from the CEO, the Board , etc., to the physician. Now physicians hardly ever hear the words no, or can't, or mustn't. And this young administrator, fairly new in the job, had to tell Dr. Soandso that he could not have the program he wanted to start...tell Dr. Whozis that he was not going to get that new piece of equipment this year... advise Dr. Whatshisname that he couldn't have that, do that, buy that, and so forth. He was the messenger of bad news to the hospital's physicians. And, as the joke says, the docs were ready to kill the messenger. At least with words. Both to his face and behind his back. Yes. People can be very vicious, even otherwise and compassionate physicians when caught in a cost-cutting squeeze. My advice to this young executive was for him to put the physician into the decision-making middle, or, at least, into the middle of the lack-of-capital problem. Like the Indians' said — Let him walk a few miles in the moccasins.

He did.

Instead of delivering a "Sorry, we don't have the money... we can't find the money...etc., he told one physician about what a great idea it was that he had for a screening program that would, over a period of time, bring in new customers, and enhance the hospital's image. He relayed how the hospital administration and the board members would like to do it — have he, the physician do it. (He also knew that the physician would increase *his* income if he could begin the program.) Then he told the doctor about the problems in starting the program. How the hospital could provide space, but not the $22,000 piece of equipment. The hospital budget could not afford it at this time. Did the physician have any idea how the money could be raised? Could he possibly help raise it? Could he possibly buy the equipment and maybe the hospital could rent it from him?

He handled all future idealistic, well-intentioned (for the most part) physician requests for new programs and equipment the same way, sometimes even steering the physician to a possible source of revenue to purchase the equipment he wanted, i.e., an opthalmologist got a new operating microscope for the hospital (and his use) via the Ladies Auxiliary.

Consideration for the other person? Yes. Consideration for the other person's interests, ambitions, goals, concerns, needs and wants? Of course. But more than that. Consideration for the other person's feelings. Assuaging his ego, his disappointments, his failure to fulfill his expectations. Putting yourself in his or her place for a minute. Understanding. It doesn't cost a dime, and it can pay dividends forever.

Would that kind of consideration solve any of your immediate problems? Would that kind of understanding, which allows you to commiserate rather than degradate — consciously or subconsciously — change their response to your changed performance? Isn't it a question of attitude.

Attitude, according to the dictionary, is "a position or manner indicative of feeling, opinion, or intention toward a person." It's a state of mind. You control yours and you can understand theirs. And that's important. Because attitude affects how you look, how you act, and what you say. It affects how you feel. And it does the same for them — the people you have to interact with. In school ...at work... at home... socially... .

You have the *most* control over your own attitude. You can be positive toward yourself and toward others. Work at it. Be open-minded. You may even learn one small something, one new way of doing something, that may make your job just a little bit easier, and make you just a little bit more successful.

Another way to be when you are implementing your program of action is enthusiastic. Be enthusiastic. It may rub off on them. Listen to others — their interests, concerns, opinions. Try to understand not only their point-of-view, but how they feel and act — and why. It will make it easier for you to work with them to achieve common goals.

But public relations is more than just attitude and consideration. It's identifying with their *special* needs, ideas, objectives, and purposes. It's recognizing that they are entitled to respect and dignity and individualism. It's accepting that they have a right to their own opinion, which, incidentally, you have the right to try and change.

Public relations is friendliness. Being polite to the other person...being a good and interested listener...praising him or her...being courteous...giving a smile — especially to those who don't have one of their own.

And public relations is understanding. Knowing and understanding. Your company — its purposes, its principles, its programs, its goals — and all the people that make up your company, or school, or church, or organization, or institution, or .... .

If you are to successfully initiate and execute a planned career P.P.R. program, know your part in your company. Keep informed about your company. Do your part to make your company successful, help others do the same, and you will be successful. If *they* know it.

Communication Of Performances

After planning and implementing your P.P.R. program — after you've done the research and learning who your publics are and what they're all about; after analyzing your interactive situations; after defining your problems; after establishing your specific objectives and goals; after changing, modifying, or clarifying your performance(s) — you then come to the second function of public relations. You then must "tell" them about it. You must communicate.

You know now you've been communicating with them and they

with you, not only in the manner of which you were aware, but by how you look, speak, and act. And you are going to keep giving them little bits of information about yourself by the kinds of clothes you wear and how you wear them; and by how you do your nails and your hair; and by how you act in the office, in the cafeteria, and at the company picnic; and by the words you speak and how you speak them; and by the words you write and how you write them. So since you have to, why not give them those little bits of information consciously, in a way that they will perceive you in the way you want to be perceived?

That's what you need to do if you are to accomplish that which you have planned. It's vital to your personal public relations. You must communicate properly and effectively. (You might want to review parts of Part II.)

And especially you must keep them informed. People will put up with almost anything as long as they're told about it, and why. Try to give *them* what you'd like to get — cheerfulness, politeness, patience, punctuality, understanding, friendliness, and consideration. As the Clint Eastwood character might do if he had a change of attitude — make *their* day. And they might *make* yours.

Evaluation And Refinement Of Performances

Conditions, situations, and circumstances are constantly changing. You are contributing to these changes, and you are affected by them. So conscious, periodic evaluations of progress are necessary. You change, modify, or improve a performance and you get feedback. "I like the way you... That was a good method you... You're looking very professional today in... You look different... good... lose some weight or something?"

Or you get negative feedback. "Can't we do this a little bit easier... a bit faster... slower... ."

In either case you've gotten feedback — a response. One that will determine whether an adjustment is necessary. It is important to continually get these readings from your publics — verbally, a nod of approval, a thank you, a reward, or, conversely, a negative message. In this way you can assess the results — the response—to a performance and adjust your performance, and your program.

Sit down weekly (at the beginning), and then monthly, and quietly think about your performances and *their* responses. Do a mental (or in writing if you prefer) progress report on yourself. Get out your list of program performances and the objectives you wanted them to meet. Are they doing the job? Do they require change? Modification? Increased emphasis? Keep *your* P's out of your thinking. Is the response suitable? Desirable?

Did the "problem" disappear when you put your solution (changed or modified performance) into effect. If it did you had the right idea. If it didn't, try a new approach. Maybe it partly alleviated a negative situation. What can you do to complete the solution?

I can tell you the story of two young secretaries who worked almost side-by-side in a university department. One, Mary, dressed very fashionable and chic. The other, Jane, was rather dowdy. Jane was never too friendly to Mary until she, offhandedly, began to tell Jane about her shopping prowess and almost secret places to shop. This led to a shopping excursion or two. Advice about clothes asked for by Jane, and given by Mary, followed. And then friendship.

Now you may have been using many of the concepts and techniques of public relations for many years, but you just haven't been doing it consciously. Or on such a broad scope. Or you didn't have the labels.

Now you can do it consciously, and using the labels will give you a mental (or written) check list to make sure you do.

Your P.P.R. plan must remain flexible, too, to respond to changing needs and to keep your program in line with your objectives and goals.

Let's review the steps to planning and executing your program of action to earn understanding and acceptance among your select publics.

A Review —

The planning of your P.P.R. program begins with you:

— A comprehensive analysis of your history;

— Your role in the marketplace — (business, school, corporation...);

— Services you can offer to your company — clients, patients, customers... ;

— Your publics; their needs, wants, interests, concerns... ;

— Your strengths and weaknesses;

— Your publics' perceptions of you;

— Your objectives — what do you want to accomplish? When? How? Your priorities?;

- The formulation of a program for attaining your objectives and goals;
- Communicating your performances properly, effectively;
- Controlling and monitoring your progress; taking corrective action when necessary.

The planning of your P.P.R. program continues with them:
- Examining their needs, wants, interests, concerns, etc.;
- Assessing their attitudes of you; of themselves; the circumstances; and the integration of attitudes — yours and theirs;
- Acceptance or modification of their performances; your performances.

And then:
- Delineating your objectives and goals; setting priorities; short-range and long-range;
- Determining rationales;
- Determining techniques and methods;
- Implementation of your program; communication;
- Evaluation and refinement of your program; preparedness for adjustment and changes.

What you are doing is constructing an ideal, and focusing on those parts of the ideal that need immediate attention with follow-up continuous observant care — refinement, adjustment, adaptation, change, or modification.

You are delineating your objectives and goals. Each should be focused on one public, each should have a rationale, and each should have a method, or methods, for accomplishment. Each should contribute to the *whole*.

Each objective of your overall plan should state a need relating to one of your publics, and should answer these questions:

Why does the need exist?

Is it really a need or a want?

Can you perform to accomplish the desired result?

How can you perform to accomplish the desired result?

Be specific. But do not cast your plan in bronze. Be prepared for detours. Make it a blueprint for action, a roadmap for your trip. Be objective. Don't be optimistic... or pessimistic...but realistic. Work for yourself as if you were a P.R. professional working for YOU.

Be A P.R. Professional Working For YOU

Imagine that you are a one-person public relations agency and YOU are your only client. This visualization can help you maintain an objective point of view. You are charged with keeping YOU happy with your professional advice, counsel, and recommendations, even the administration of your P.R. program for YOU. You, as a professional P.R. practitioner will depend on YOU, your client's success, for your own success.

Before you give out any news about YOU, you will determine the objective of such a communication. You use the Five W's and H:

> WHY should you transmit *this* message to them?
>
> WHAT do you hope to accomplish for YOU?
>
> WHO should get the information contained in this message?
>
> WHAT goals or objectives of YOU will be advanced by the transmission and recepton of this message?
>
> WHAT is the receptivity for YOU's message?
>
> WHAT will happen if you don't give out the information regarding YOU?
>
> WHEN is the best time to transmit YOU's message?
>
> WHAT is the best method of transmitting YOU's message?
>
> WHAT is the best medium to transmit YOU's message?
>
> HOW do you anticipate they will respond?
>
> HOW will you respond to their response?
>
> HOW will you accomplish what you wish to accomplish?

You are probably familiar with the concept called management by objectives. Think "public relations" instead of management as you read the following description:

"First, you set management goals (which are ideals), then you determine objectives (specific and measurable) which are milestones along the way to reaching a goal. You remain flexible so you can change as a situation might change. You listen. You watch. You assess feedback. You change, adapt, or modify as needed. You reach your goal. Success!"

Yes. It's a lot of work. You may want to start small. One objective

Planning Your P.P.R. Program

at a time, but focused on *the* goal. And, as you see first-hand that the results are worth the effort (and as it gets easier as you do it) you can add more and more objectives to your plan, all, of course, focused on *the* goal.

Whether you're planning a P.P.R. program at this time, or not, you now know you have it. You know what it is. You know how to use it. At the very least you are aware of it and how it affects you even in the routine of your everyday living. And, consequently, even if you don't formally structure it, you have a mental picture of what your everyday interaction with them should be to enhance your P.P.R.

But there are other, more special times, when you might want to make specific plans to utilize your P.P.R. Public relations practitioners call these — Special Events.

15

Both There And Here

Chapter Six, *Motivation— Are There Buttons to be Pushed?*, belongs here. It could be very helpful for you to read it now, as you put your P.P.R. plan(s) into action. Remembering what makes people do the things they do could help you do that.

It would also be good if Chapter Six was here so you could read it before you read about using your P.P.R.— and everything you've learned about it— for those "special events." Like getting that first job, or the tenth one; starting the new job, working for that new boss or being that new boss; meeting that very special person; moving to a new neighborhood; or going to that party, wedding, or funeral. Yes. It could help you at these special times to remember those motivational (and demotivational) buttons they have.

But Chapter Six is important right where it is. Up there in Part I it helps give you a basic picture—a foundation of knowledge —of public relations. It helps you to get to know *you* better, get to know *them better*, and what makes you both tick. And all of that is very important background information to know when you read Part II, about communicating with them. So Chapter Six is necessary right where it is.

It could have been put in both places. It could have been Chapter Six *and* Chapter 15. Then you would have read it back there as you built your foundation, and you'd be reading it here where it could help you use your newly acquired P.P.R. skills.

But that seemed like a waste of a perfectly good resource—trees. Why not just suggest you go back and read Chapter Six again. Consider it suggested. Unless you've got a terrific memory. If that's the case, turn the page and learn about your P.P.R. and the Special Event.

16

The Special Event

Public relations practitioners practice good P.R. on behalf of their clients in their everyday interactions with their client's publics. They routinely act — disseminating good news, assessing feedback — or react, using all the techniques of public relations for their client's best advantage. In addition to these routine practices they look for circumstances that will lend themselves to "staged" occurrences that will attract favorable public attention — a national happening that could attract millions of people, or a tea party that may be of interest only to a handful of people (but the *right* people). Regardless of audience size, each event requires research, detailed planning, and complete preparation to be fully successful. P.R. people call these legitimate, if staged, happenings a special event.

You will not have to look very hard or long to find your special events. Most will find you. Your first job (or *new* job), finding it and starting it; meeting that special person, the first date, and a relationship or marriage; going to a party, a wedding, or a funeral; your birthday or anniversary or his/her birthday or anniversary; anything that will help you convey an image of you, or a message about you, from which you will benefit.

Just as the P.R. practitioner must conceive, plan, and execute the special event so that it runs smoothly and effortlessly (and gets the desired results) so too must you plan and execute *your* special event.

Always remember that the special event is a communication. You do not want to communicate your warts or blemishes to your public(s). Just the reverse is true. You want to conceal, or at least minimize, those imperfections with the make-up of positive images. I have written it before (and will probably write it again) — even when the truth has a negative connotation, it can be made more palatable if it's coated with the varnish of understanding and empathy.

But a special event, by its very nature, is positive. We, for the most part, control it. Yes. We should be aware as we research and plan our event that something can go wrong during its execution. But we can be secure in the knowledge that we are prepared to meet those contingencies because we know our objective and we know him, or her, or them. All things considered, we will plan accordingly to maximize success and minimize error, and to overcome any error if and when it should occur.

Let us also remember the basic tenets of P.R. — performance and response. Whatever we do or say, we are performing to elicit a certain favorable response from the receivers of our message. If we don't get the desired response we must change our performance, or we must explain our performance in such a way that the receiver will change his or her response, from one that is negative or neutral to one that is positive.

With this in mind let's look at some special events and examine the research and planning that goes into each of them, knowing that the same basic actions and principles will apply to *any* special event.

Getting *The* Job

Thinking of a new career? A first career? A change of careers? How will you choose the first job — the one that's right for you?

You can have someone — a career counselor — test, evaluate, and analyze your interests, talents, aptitudes, and personality, or you can do it yourself.

If you choose the first option, be sure to check the qualifications of the career counselor. In his book, *What Color Is Your Parachute*, author Richard Bolles says they fit into one of three categories: sincere and skilled; sincere but inept; insincere and inept. By his reckoning you have a one in three chance of putting yourself in good hands.

Bolles' book will help you with your self-analysis, containing as it does, not only information and advice, but self-analysis programs.

At the very least, since you have already started to learn about the unique you (Chapter 3), you may just want to write an essay about yourself, answering that question — If everything was going well for me in my career five years from now, what would be happening? Factor in your education, past and future, ditto job experience(s), and temper your visualization with reality.

If you're presently a student, you have had, and do have,

professional guidance counseling available. But even there, evaluate him or her very carefully. I know of one student who got his bachelor's, master's, and doctorate in physics whose first job (and future career?) was as an apprentice leather artisan. That's what he *liked* doing.

You will probably work for forty years. Mark Twain said — "Work consists of whatever a body is obliged to do, and play consists of whatever a body is not." If you can get paid for doing what you *want* to do, you will not only enjoy your work, but will probably be more successful. *You* must make the choice, whether its choosing a career, or changing one. Evaluate well. Get help if you need it (but you might want to do it faster than our physicist/leather worker). Go to the library and read Bolles' book, or others that will help you self-evaluate *you*, and your interests and goals.

Any of these roads will bring you to the point of researching the market — the industry and its trends and opportunities, size of company, location, your level of entry, etc. — that will best serve your career goals.

You have already evaluated yourself. You know what you have to offer. You have read about and evaluated your image regarding speech, body language, writing, dress, actions, etc. You have a working acquaintance with your P.P.R., its concepts and its techniques.

Your next step is to search out companies where your needs and theirs will provide a mutually beneficial relationship. You learn about these companies from business friends and acquaintances (whether those companies are presently looking or not), trade journals, placement services, as well as those companies that have advertised for someone with your qualifications and experience, and/or education. They comprise your "hit list."

It is for these companies that you will write your resume and cover letter *after* you research them. Before you write your resume you may want to review those parts of Chapter 12 that deal with resume writing and production, so you can design yours to *sell* the product that is you.

It goes without saying that you will only apply for a position for which you are fully suitable without stretching your qualifications to the breaking point. The operative word here is *suitable*. More often than not, it is *not* the person who is best qualified for a job who will get it. It is more likely that the person who can convince others that he or she *is* the right person for the job, will get the job. Being suitable and qualified will help you *keep* the job.

Once you have determined your career direction, and you've chosen those companies that fit your goals, you must then research those companies.

Researching A Company

It may seem elementary, but remember that for you to get *that* job, someone must hire you. And that someone, whether a personnel officer or some other executive (even the top man), is another human being who also has his or her own P.P.R. And he or she has certain predilections, predispositions, and, no doubt, a few other P's, centered around, or seemingly independent of, his P.P.R. In any case, to some degree more or less, he knows that he will bask in the sunshine of your success, or, heaven forbid, stand in the shadow of your failure. You (now) know, and he might, that his P.P.R. will be affected by how well he does, or doesn't, fill the open position in his company.

Would this suggest to you that whether or not he likes you can be equally as important as how well you can actually do the job? Do you think it may actually influence his perception of how well he *thinks* you can do the job? These are, somewhat, rhetorical questions. He may very well be predisposed, not to you personally, but to the image you are projecting at the time of the interview. How you are dressed, how you speak, how you act, the expression (or the lack of expression) on your face as you listen, and a myriad of other things that make up the impression we call image. Remember, too, that *what* he perceives is *what you are* to him.

So when we are speaking about researching the company, we are also speaking about researching *them* that make up the company. We can even learn how you fit in.

You have evaluated yourself long before you ever heard about this dream job. You are fully aware of your strengths and weaknesses. You know how to maximize your strengths and minimize or eliminate your weaknesses. How about your attitude and qualifications for this particular job, in this particular company?

Can you do it? Can you do it well? For this company? Are you sure? What is this company all about? What are its goals? Their goals (the people of the company)? Can you contribute to the achievement of its goals... their goals? How? Why do you want to? Would an association between you and it... you and they... be mutually beneficial?

How do you get the answers to these questions, and others?

If it's a public company get their last two annual reports as well as any interim quarterly reports. Study the president/chairman's narrative report to the stockholders. It will tell you where the company has been, where it's at, and where it wants to be going. Your local library has many of the larger companies' (and local companies') reports. The universities, the hospitals, will have theirs. If all else fails call the P.R. department, they'll be happy to provide one.

Use the business directories — Polk, Moody's, Thomas' Register, et al. They're available in your library, too. They'll give you some facts about the company — how many employees, key officers, products and services, sales volume, etc.

Ask your local stockbroker if he has any reports on the company (an S & P report or a pink sheet). Ask them for their impression of the company — its growth, performance, etc. — for investment purposes. They'll be glad to help; you may be a client some day. Especially if you get that great paying job.

Check your local newspaper's library. (They used to call it "the morgue." Some still do.) If it's a local company (hospital, college, etc.) they'll have a file on it, and its key officers and directors. Even if the company is large *only* for the town, city, or area in which it's located, stories will have been written about it and its people.

If it is local — even within a hundred miles or so — visit the company itself, its offices, its plant. Ask for a copy of its company publication. There's probably a copy in the reception waiting area. They may even have a house organ — an employee newspaper. Keep your eyes open. Make a mental note of the ambiance, the environment, the interaction of people. Is the atmosphere formal or informal? How are the various levels of employees dressed? Make a special note of how the company's executives dress — one of them will be interviewing you and you'll have an idea of how to dress. Speak to an employee or two, even if only the receptionist. You might be surprised as to just how easy it is to talk to an employee about his or her company and the people who work there. Are there any sales brochures on the tables? Learn about the company's products or services. If you're there near quitting time study the employees as they leave work. Talk to a few of them. Tell them you're a candidate for employment. Ask about the company. There's nothing wrong with showing your interest.

Many newspaper stories carry personal information about an executive in a story about that executive's promotion, award, or if he just talks at a Chamber of Commerce breakfast or luncheon meeting. These particular stories will usually tell where he or she went to school and degrees earned; social, business, and civic memberships;

marital status, including children and names; church membership; hobbies, etc.

Each story can open avenues of possibilities that could enhance your chances during your interview, especially if you pick up knowledge about *the* executive — your interviewer. Is he an Elk, Mason, Rotarian, Knight, Moose, Lion; a member of a club or society or professional group? Are you a member of the same organization? Does he play golf? Did he ever play in a local tournament? Is he a club champion? Does he bowl? Play racquetball? Ski? You can see the possibilities. It only requires some searching. And, when all else fails, just be honest. Ask the company employees, the secretary at the local Chamber office (a very good source of information about the company). Ask the security man outside the company's building, a local newspaper reporter, the company's own public relations department.

The more you learn about the company and its people the more comfortable you'll be during your job interview. Isn't it much easier to speak with someone you "know" than with a perfect stranger. Of course it is.

When you complete your research you'll know better how to dress and how to act. You'll have a good idea about the interviewer's concerns for his company and, therefore, himself. You'll know how you can contribute to the company and how you can be successful in the job. That knowledge will help you show him how you can make him (the interviewer) successful in *his* job by filling the position with a highly qualified, motivated, likable person — YOU.

What if you cannot get in to see how they act and dress? What then? Then you might go over to your local library and read parts of *Winning The Job Interview Game* by Jo Danna.

Among other things, Dr. Danna has a chapter (6) titled "Polish Your Image," which covers wardrobe, grooming, body language, speech and voice tone, as well as your energy level, intelligence, and state of health. If you feel like reading more, Chapter 7 discusses the tricks of body language; Chapter 8 is about speaking more effectively; and Chapter 9 discusses how to improve your interview skills. Sounds like a lot of work? If this is *the* job, it just may be worth it.

If you just want to stay curled up in your chair with *P.P.R.*, you should still do pretty well if you remember what you read in chapters 6 through 10. You must have re-read chapter 11 and 12 carefully because you've got a job interview coming up — your resume and cover letter did their jobs.

You have found the company that you have determined is right for you. You know the criteria the company places on the job. You feel confident you can meet all the requirements. You have learned what qualities and qualifications the company is looking for in the candidate that fills the position. Now you will prepare for projecting those very same qualities to one person — the interviewer.

Preparing For A Job Interview

Remember first that the interviewer's primary concern is filling the position with the person who will become an asset to the company. That's his (or her) job. He is concerned with doing his job and doing it well. He knows what skills, talents, and qualifications are necessary and/or desirable to do the job well. He will probably interview several candidates who are A-plus in these categories. Can you picture yourself as one of them? If you can, and you are, the final choice of the interviewer will depend on *his* personal values, as well as *his* predispositions and other P's. If there is something about red hair that somehow (even subconsciously) annoys him, and you're a redhead, guess what? If he's short and you're a six-footer, he may, without actually knowing it, resent you. Is he dressed conservatively? Are you? Do you smoke? Does he? (Of course, you won't smoke during the interview even if he does.) Will his personality blend with yours, clash, or be neutral? Wouldn't it be nice to know about him and his partialities before you met him? Of course. That's why you did research.

During the interview you, and he, will be communicating. He'll be sending messages, verbal and otherwise, and you'll be his receiver. You'll be sending him messages with your words, your looks, your actions, and your manners.

If your research couldn't go far enough, then what? You can't really communicate like a friend, but must as a stranger. What do you do?

All you can do is be neutral and react. As you learn, by reading his actions and listening to his words, you can begin to perform in such a way as to receive positive, favorable responses from him.

How?

You question him about the company and the job. About the goals. You put yourself into *his* picture. If experienced, stress accomplishments that *fit*; if just out of school, how your education prepared you to contribute to the company's goals. Keep it active. "I have done... that resulted in... and it solved... ." Visualize yourself doing the job. Be enthusiastic. Show how you can do the job if given the chance.

Chances are none of his predispositions and other P's with regard to physical image will kill your chances for the job. Sure, it would be nice if your physical image coincided one hundred percent with his preconceived image, because all other things being equal — skills, talents, experience, and qualifications — the candidate that best reinforces the interviewer's image of the person to fill the position, will probably be the person who fills the position. At the very least, because you became aware, and have P.P.R. knowledge, you will be projecting at least some of the image that he, the interviewer, has in his mind. You will be projecting an image similar to his — a company (business) image.

While you can be neutral, or safe — you *will* dress business-like, you *will not* smoke, you *will* be well-groomed, you *will not* discuss anything controversial, you *will* make good eye contact, you *will not* fidget, fuss, or crack your knuckles, you will... you will not.... You will, however, be interviewed, and that adds up to questions (from him) and answers (from you).

Interviewers And Interview Questions

Dr. Danna's book discusses two basic types of interview questions — the factual (Why did you or why are you leaving your last position?), and the psychological (What have you learned from past mistakes?). She gives many examples of each. She cautions against the open-ended question (Tell me about yourself?) which can not only lure you into telling your life story (you talk too long and tell too much), but is designed to elicit information about your personality, attitudes, etc.

"Mention only those aspects which demonstrate your suitability for the job," Dr. Danna writes. "The interviewer may also want to see how focused your thoughts are. Be concise."

Robert Half, in his book, *The Robert Half Way To Get Hired In Today's Job Market*, writes "...the interviewer is playing out his or her role in the game: Paying attention not only to what you're saying, but to how you're responding.

"The interviewer is making an evaluation, computing nearly everything you say and do, the better to judge whether your ability, experience, education, and personality fit the job and the company. The interviewer *knows* you're doing your best to create a positive impression. The interviewer *knows* that as hard as the two of you may try to make the interview seem natural and unforced, the interview is, by nature, an unnatural and forced situation. Much of how the interviewer evaluates you will be determined not so much by the qualifications you enumerate and the personal qualities you exhibit during the interview, but by your *interview performance in general*. How you play the game!"

You have an edge. You've done your research. You've thought about playing the role. You feel comfortable because you know about the company and its executives. Now you'll learn more about the questions and answers that will probably make up a large part of your interview.

Half writes that he has, in his files, nearly 300 of the most frequently asked questions. In his book he's picked 25 that get asked most frequently in job interviews. For each question he's tried to suggest what the interviewer might be looking for, then suggests a strategy for answering it. Reading these Q and A's is certainly worth a trip to your library.

The first question Half lists — he calls it the typical ice-breaker — is *Tell me about yourself?*. (Danna cautioned against this open-ended question.) But what do you do if he asks it? You answer it, concisely. Half's next twenty-four questions range from what you think of the company, to your career, to what you liked best about your last job. Following Question No. 25 and its answer, Half then gives an additional list of questions you should be prepared to answer. These range from "What motivates you?" to "What was your favorite subject in school?" to "What are you doing now to improve yourself?"

"The object of the job interview is not to 'tell' the interviewer about yourself," Half writes. "It's to communicate to the interviewer... your ability, your willingness, and your suitability (to do the job)."

Robert Half, about whom the book jacket says — "Get the inside story from the man who has found jobs for over 100,000 people," might be worth a trip to your bookstore or local library if *that* job is *the* job for you.

The bottom line?

No matter how much you learn from these books, or if you read no books on the subject at all, you will still be ahead of most of your competition if you apply your newly acquired P.P.R. techniques:

Know the company, its people and its objectives; know yourself; be aware of how you can be of value to them; be truthful, to yourself and to them. (Being truthful, however, does not mean you must volunteer negative truths if they are none of their business. It also does not mean you cannot present a negative truth, when that is necessary, in a favorable or positive manner. "Yes. I was fired at that time. I learned much from the experience... that one must be patient, and understanding, and flexible.")

Rehearse ... Practice ... Role-play

A week or so before your interview, write a script. His part and yours. Anticipate questions and answers (which will lead to other questions and answers). Be creative. You know the general questions. Now formulate your answers.

You know he's used your resume to develop questions about your education and your experience. You wrote you *can do*, he's saying, *show me*. He's trying to determine if you lied by omission, if you've over-gilded the lily. If it's not your first job he wants to assess why you left your last job. Is it career advancement? Is this job on your "increasing responsibility track?" Have you been job-hopping? Is it justified? (Good reasons for leaving your last job are career-oriented — greater opportunity, responsiblity, challenge and, correspondingly, reward. Bad reasons are personality conflicts, reorganizations, work force reduction, or the obvious hedge — by mutual agreement.)

Write your script. It's not a waste of time, but a way to focus clearly, and plan. Cast yourself in the role. Put yourself into the interview picture. Visualize. You're dressed in the style and manner the interviewer is — appropriate for the company and the position. Your research pays off. Shake his hand firmly. Make good eye contact. You've addressed him by name. You pronounced it properly. (A difficult ethnic name? Learn it phonetically.)

You react to his actions. He motions to a chair as he sits. You sit. He's comfortable. So are you. (You're comfortable because you're confident.) Your resume, on the desk in front of him, gave the basics — the steak, baked potato and vegetable. During the interview you will add the sour cream and chives, the butter and the sizzle.

He asks the first question: "Tell me about yourself?" You tell him. You've answered that question a dozen times. Your reply is informative, yet concise. Your voice is businesslike, confident, yet friendly and warm. He continues to ask questions. You've "heard" them all before. And you've answered them before. Many times. Your answers are complete, but concise. Your voice remains pleasant, without a trace of nervousness betraying you.

You ask him questions about the company, and the position. While he answers you show interest with your eyes, agreement with a nod, warmth with a smile. You don't interrupt. More questions from him. Your answers are direct, conveying factual information. You very rarely, if ever, hedge with "I believe... You're probably right...I could be wrong, but... ." You might soften some assertions with "Has the company ever considered... Would you say... ." Each answer (and each of your questions, for that matter) conveys to the interviewer, your qualifications, skills, talents (I can do the job exceeding your expectations); your interest in the company (I want to do the job for this company); and that your image fits into the company's image (Look at me and how I comport myself).

You do not fidgit, tap your fingers, fold your arms across your chest, or grip the arms of the chair nervously. You do not smoke (even if he does), jiggle your foot, or scratch your head. You do not tug at your collar or lapel, rub your nose, pull your ear, or rub the back of your neck. You do not, in fact, do anything that will distract him (or her), or detract from your answers or actions. You are comfortable because knowledge and practice made you that way and because you know that you are the best person for the job.

You have written the script and played the role in your mind. You have smoothed out the rough spots and polished your performance. Now rehearse. Rehearse. Rehearse. If you have a few friends who can help, give them parts to play. One can be the interviewer. Others can be critics or advisors. Rehearse not only your words, but your body language messages as well. Imagine, visualize, and rehearse. P.R. people use this type of role-playing, for instance, to prepare a client for a press conference. You will find it valuable, too.

Research, prepare and rehearse, and you will (even if you do not get the job) have a good interview.

After The Interview

After completing your interview you thank Mr. Interviewer by name for his time and consideration. As you stand up you tell him (if you are) that you are interested in the job and the company. As you shake his hand you tell him that you are confident that you can contribute to the company... that you would do well for him and the company. As you leave you feel confident that the interview went as well as the half-dozen times you visualized and rehearsed it.

That very evening you write a brief (no more than a single page) hand-written letter to Mr. Interviewer. In it you thank him for the interview and restate your interest in the position and in the company. You mention one or two key points discussed during the interview, and a solid reason or two testifying as to why you can do the job and be an asset to the company. A week or so later you will telephone Mr. Interviewer to ask if he received your letter.

If your candidacy was rejected, accept it. It happens to everyone.

It's no disgrace to maybe come in second or third in a field of twenty or thirty candidates. (At least I didn't think so when I came in second out of thirty-three.)

Learn and profit from the experience. Look over your script. Add, subtract, modify. Visualize the interview. Did it go according to the script? As you rehearsed? As you visualized? Where is improvement necessary? Did you rate an Oscar for your performance? A nomination? How could your performance have been better? Did everything you said and did evoke the response you wanted? If not, why not? Did you respond properly to his words and actions? If not, what would have been a proper response? A better response?

Call Mr. Interviewer. Ask him if he would take a few minutes to comment on and give you suggestions to improve your interview techniques. You'll be surprised at his willingness to do this ego-satisfying chore. You might be doubly surprised if negotiations break down, or something comes up, so that the successful candidate cannot ultimately take the position. Or if Mr. Interviewer asks you to consider a different positition (now or at a future time).

Then put that interview, that job, out of your mind. Find that opportunity for an even better job — *the* job. And get ready for your next job interview.

But wait. You got the job. You were the Number 1 pick. You successfully negotiated your terms — salary, perks, benefits, etc. (Of course, while you negotiated you were fully aware of your P.P.R.) Your performance was such that you got the response you wanted. You start next Monday.

Starting The New Job

It took a bit of work to get the job; now it will take a bit more to start it right. But it will be worth it.

Learn as quickly as you can all the nitty-gritty details of your new job — the parameters, your responsibilities, as well as others' responsibilities that can impact upon your performance. In this way you will know how and where you can "take the extra step." It is the extra steps that enhance your P.P.R. by showing your superiors that you are as concerned and interested in the welfare of the company as they are. But you want to take these steps without infringing on the P.P.R. of others. An added bonus: there is nothing a company (executive) appreciates more than a new member of the staff "delivering" from Day One.

Learn not only about your job, but enough about *their* jobs — their duties and responsibilities, goals and objectives — so that you can determine how you can interact favorably (non-threateningly) with them in a mutually beneficial and advantageous manner. In this way you will be, even indirectly, helping them to be successful in doing their jobs. You'll become a valuable member of the team.

There is a time to take the initiative and there is a time to follow your boss' lead. Knowing when to do either is a skill that shows you know how to be a team player. These types of people, according to *Personnel Journal*, a national publication, tend to ask a lot of *why* questions because they are interested in expanding their knowledge of the business beyond specific job duties. Be a *why* person for success.

In the same article they say that companies are looking for the job skills, but also for the employee who can help them grow. They want employees who can take constructive criticism in a positive way. People who can take responsibility, and people who want to continually improve and increase their contributions to the company. Be a contributor for the company's —your—success.

They want employees who have the ability to effectively present their ideas to other employees, superiors, customers, and their publics. They want employees who can manage their time, and who can remain adaptable. They want people who are assets to their company. Become an asset and you'll become a success.

And companies want employees (according to a survey by Hodge-Cronin & Associates in a *Forbes* article) who have a sense of humor. Their study found that 97% of more than 700 chief executive officers interviewed said they would — all things being equal — just as soon hire a candidate with a good sense of humor.

It's more scientific than it seems. According to Joseph Boskin, a professor at Boston University, researchers have found that people with a well-developed sense of humor are good problem-solvers. A study found workers who have the most fun at work are likely to be the most productive. Learn about *their* sense of humor and other things — learn about them.

About Your Co-workers

Learn as much as you can about each of your new co-workers — your peers, and each of your superiors. Learn as much as you can about the basics: the schools they attended, degrees earned, and career progression. Have they been a member of the firm (the faculty, the staff, whatever) since college graduation X years ago, or is this their second, third, fourth, etc., company affiliation? This will give you clues as to the depth and width of their experience, as well as their vision, within and outside the company.

Learn of their lodge, club, and society memberships; business, social, and civic affiliations; marital status (spouse's name, number and names and ages of children); hobbies, sports activities and interests (participant and spectator), and other recreational leisuretime activities. All of this information will help you not only to understand him, but will direct your attention to areas of common interests for conversation. These could also be areas of future interaction should you care to pursue new interests. Going in that direction could even provide multiple benefits, i.e., you may find you enjoy "whatever," while at the same time "whatever" gives you another common interest to share with Mr. Important.

As you gather the knowledge of your workplace VIPs — from listening to others, or even to him or her; reading company biographies, house publications, and local newspaper stories; talking with mutual friends, co-workers, etc. — determine his (or her) wants, needs, goals, objectives, fears, and concerns, especially as they relate or interact with his (or her) job.

There are, of course, generalities.

Everyone wants to be successful in the eyes of his peers, his subordinates, and especially his superiors. We all want to be seen as competent, efficient, even as a *star*, whether our superior is only the Assistant to the Assistant Department Manager, or the Chairman of the Board. We all want acceptance... recognition... compliments... even, symbolically, applause.

He or she or they — too — want to excel, to do the job to perfection, to be Miss, Mrs., Ms, or Mr. Perfect. If you can do your job in such a way as to help him do his job just a little bit easier, or just a little bit better, or both — that's a positive performance to him. You become valuable to him. His response will be positive. He may even develop the tendency to nurture, help, certainly appreciate, one (you) who is the least bit valuable to him and his success.

If you can do nothing that adds to his success, or failure, (you will after all be interacting with *many* co-workers), that's neutral. Even if you remain in this neutral status regarding work, you may still develop positive responses on a social-work level, or even on a social level. He could be, after all, your superior sometime in the future. Possibly even in a different company.

I remember reading a story about a man who was scheduled to make a presentation to a large corporation for a multi-million dollar package. When he walked into the board room he found himself facing an executive vice president who looked familiar. You've guessed it. He had been the vp's boss some twenty years before. In the Marines. And he had done him a kindness. What's the point? Good human interaction is what life is all about. It also happens to be good business.

Of course, you cannot do everything that makes everyone else's job easier. But, on the other side of the coin, you can do nothing that makes his job harder, or his success more difficult to attain. Even if this performance is a positive performance for you, and makes your job easier or more successful, it will remain a negative performance to him, UNLESS you bring him into the picture.

"Jack, the boss wants me... Jack, if I do what the boss wants me to do, it could impact on you... Jack, how can I do (whatever) the boss wants me to do and not affect your... or at least minimize the impact... .'

In these case, you may even change a potentially negative response from Jack into a positive, because you showed Jack you understood and you cared.

If there is a performance (yours) that would have negligible affect on the accomplishment of your job, while having a negative impact on his, you may want to weigh the cause and effect, the advantages and disadvantages, as compared to alienating your peer (and what that might mean to you in the future). This would be especially true if he knew you had alternatives and neglected to use those that would not adversely impact on him. It goes without saying that where there is no benefit (to you) at all, you will not do it at all.

With those of your peers with whom you will maintain a neutral working position, you may want to weigh the advantages and disadvantages of establishing a workplace social relationship (lunch, either in or out, being a member the bowling team, coffee-break conversations, etc.), or even developing an after-work social relationship, with or without spouses or opposite-sex friends.

The ability to interact socially with your fellow employees — subordinates, peers, and superiors — can be a big plus for career advancement. Limited social relationships might also be developed with your superiors (a round of golf, attending a party, a luncheon, a semi-business function, etc.). These relationships with those you consider important to your well-being or success with the company can build future P.P.R. benefits. You are building an account of goodwill that you may draw on someday.

Nowhere else is the opportunity for social P.P.R. enhancement greater than at corporate social, or quasi-social functions — the annual picnic and Christmas party, recognition or testimonial dinners, retirement parties, et al.

John T. Molloy, author of *Dress For Success*, writing in *Success* magazine, wrote, that when he was writing *Live For Success*, he "interviewed several hundred executives and over 70 percent of them said they often learned more about a person at the Christmas party than they did working with that person all year."

But be careful. Very careful. The way that you learn about them, they can learn about you. Be sure *they* learn what you want them to learn.

People with whom you have lunch, play golf, or go bowling; with whom you go to parties, dinners, the theater, sometimes accompanied by spouses or friends, can become friends. And people are more tolerant, more understanding, about the shortcomings of their friends. So be a friend.

Friends have an inclinaton to want to believe good things about their friends, do not say bad things about friends, and don't allow others to do so either, or they correct them when and if they do. Friends are nice to have, especially when related to the workplace where, inevitably, you may have some enemies among your subordinates (there is always someone who hates the boss); and among your peers (jealousy can be a big culprit here). Fortunately, you usually do not have enemies (unless you foolishly make them) among your superiors (except on that rare occasion when you got the job that the 2nd vice president wanted for his brother-in-law). Normally, your superiors are only interested in what you can do, and do do, for them and for the company

The thing to remember about superiors is — If you refuse to take that extra step on occasion (stay late, do that little something above the call of duty, etc.), they *will* remember. They'll also, most times, remember when you do. If they don't however, you can remind them the next time, about the last time — "Sure, I'll stay and help out. You know I always try to accomodate you for the benefit of the department (the division, the company). I'll just take a minute to phone and cancel a dinner date (bowling, visiting my mother-in-law, whatever)."

You are making *him* look good (to *his* superior) by helping *him* meet a deadline, make a quota, complete a report, or reach a goal. He may not say it, but he *knows* it. And he knows that you know it.

One thing to remember. Managers, department heads, vice

presidents, all got where they are because they've got something. And that something is the ability and talent to deal with people. And they know what's going on down below them on the corporate ladder — they've been there. They know that dealing with people is the most important skill of any administrator. There are, they know, two ways to get to the top—you can claw your way up, or you can have those below you lift you to the top. They know if your superior can motivate you and others to produce his performance is A-1. If, on the other hand, he is doing the job himself, even if he's doing it extremely well, his performance *as a manager* is not up to par. Their response to these two extremes of his performance will be appropriate, as should *his* response to *your* performance be appropriate.

When you start that new job, it will be advantageous to take the time to think about your P.P.R. — personal public relations. Once again I remind you to think of P.R. as standing for performance and response. Think about his and hers and their P.P.R. in the same way. Think of them interacting and impacting on each other.

In your new job you must learn about each of them. What makes them tick? What are his objectives and goals? What problems does she face in reaching her goals? What are the ramifications of his success or failure? What would either of two (or more) possible results mean to his security, his well-being, his career.

By thinking of his and your P.P.R. interacting, you will see the importance of trying to perform in such a way that will help him in reaching his goals. His goals become your goals. And, if you're fortunate, your subordinates will do the same for you (or you should get subordinates who will). In this way, everyone in the company, and the company itself, is able to reach the pinnacle of success. And that includes *your* success. Especially if you don't trip along the way.

Six Common P.P.R. Stumbling Blocks

There are always stumbling blocks to avoid in any climb to the top of the success hill. Most are easily avoided by the judicious use of common sense.

1. Whether at a company function, or in a strictly social situation with any level of co-worker — subordinate, peer, or superior — do not drink too much. Certainly, do not drink to any point which makes you lose control over your tongue, your actions, or even your thoughts.

2. Office friendships with members of the opposite sex can give the appearance of "other" male-female relationships. (This could be especially true when between subordinate and superior.) There can

254   P.P.R. (Personal Public Relations)

be a bit too much envy of the relationship by others; positive work relationships can turn negative when two co-workers share too much of their personal lives; the home may not be able to compete with the excitement of the office and result in spouse resentment; and a superior/subordinate relationship can cause jealous reactions. In this area of office life, be guided by the concepts of P.P.R. and tread softly and carefully, keeping "image" in mind.

3. Don't take the negative side when discussing contentious organizational issues. There can only be one winner in a debate; don't turn discussions into debates.

4. Refrain from conversations (or at least don't join in) that criticize another person on a personal or business level. Ditto for criticism of company policy. What you say may be misconstrued, misquoted, misunderstood, or mistaken, and can be "passed-on" that way, even sounding worse when taken out of context. If you must criticize a company policy, activity, etc., do it officially and properly.

5. Don't divulge confidential corporate matters to others and don't pump others for this kind of information. This does not, of course, preclude your keeping your eyes and ears open for the indiscretions of others.

6. Do not embarrass your boss — in the office, on the golf course, at a party — anywhere, ever.

Common sense and an awareness of P.P.R. — yours and theirs — will prevent you from tripping over these and other stumbling blocks. This awareness will allow you to recognize stepping stones, too.

Six Common P.P.R. Stepping Stones

While you want to avoid stumbling blocks on your path to the next career rung of your ladder, you should seek out and use (in addition to your everyday efficient use of P.P.R. concepts and skills) those positive steps that will serve to enhance your image.

1. Volunteer to help with those special company (institution) events: participate in the organization of, the recreational activities of, even the cooking at the company picnic; assist with the organization and the "fun-stuff" program for the Christmas party; help with the nitty-gritty of any company social event. You may be working shoulder-to-shoulder with Mr. Important himself. At the very least, it will help you to keep from becoming invisible.

2. At business-social events, introduce yourself to senior executives (and their spouses when possible). Express appreciation for the event and your "being here." But be sincere. If you can't say

it honestly, don't say it at all. Say what you *can* honestly say that's complimentary.

3. Bring your spouse to company social events. It's an excellent way of showing you're a family person and that Spouse not only supports your career, but fits into your company's environment.

4. Join in and add to positive conversations about the company (or absent executives), but do so only when you can be sincerely complimentary. Otherwise nod and smile a lot.

5. Be a social asset. Dress for the occason and act appropriately for the occasion. Reflect the company's image. Contribute to the social success of the occasion.

6. Listen for favorable comments or criticisms of your company, department, or self. This is valuable information which you may be able to build into positive stepping stones later to advance your career.

If you're a professional, small businessman, merchant, etc., *you are your company* and the community provides your "bosses," your environment, and your events... your stumbling blocks or building blocks.

There are some situations and actions that are not stumbling blocks or stepping stones per se — but they can be either.

Neither Stumbling Blocks Nor Stepping Stones

There are some interactions, especially with your boss, that can trip you or boost you as you step along your career path:

1. How's your attitude? You can be responsible for a good or a bad relationship with your supervisor. (Good, if you practice good P.P.R.)

2. Can you "read" your boss? — When he looks too busy, when he seems receptive, when he's in a good mood or bad. Keep an eye on your colleagues, especially the "old timers." They may read *him* better.

3. Can you do things to make his job easier? Should you? Are you expected to? Don't say yes — or no— unless you're sure.

4. Learn to use his criticism constructively to do the job that meets his expectations (a good response to your performance), or, in a diplomatic, factual fashion, set him straight (educate).

5. Be candid with your boss — sometimes.

6. Talk about your boss behind his or her back, in a positive or negative manner, depending on whether you want to stay or leave.

If there is a personality conflict between you and your boss, and you cannot cope, and he is always going to remain one step ahead of you on the organizational chart, you may want to consider sharpening up your resume and interview techniques, keeping your eyes and ears open, and finding a new boss. One way to do that is networking.

Networking

You should have, or should be, building a network of peers. To do this you join professional, trade, and civic organizations that provide you with the exposure and contacts you need to advance your career objectives. To advance your professional objectives, too, if you're a lawyer, doctor, etc. First, you join, then you become active. Officially active. You join in all those organizational projects and programs. Socially active. You choose several colleagues that are *like you* to establish going-to-lunch, playing golf, or dinner-out relationships. You build your relationships with care. Gradually. You let them develop naturally through the course of working with, or interacting with, your peers. Be sure you build your network on sincerity, integrity, competence, and a sense of caring, and he or they may do the same. Don't be concerned about showing interest. Be interested. Be interesting.

Networks are valuable in the development of a career. They can make your professional life richer and more enjoyable, and they can be there when you need them. So, when you have a boss you cannot live with, you can draw on your contacts — business associates, fellow alumni, lawyers, bankers, accountants, sales people, et al, especially those among them you can call a friend. Networking, when done properly, is an excellent way to practice your P.P.R.

Networking *is* a good way to find a new boss. But suppose a new boss comes to you. You've been at the company for five, ten, fifteen years or more; he, or she, just started.

You've Got A New Boss

During the last year for which I have figures — 1986 — about five times a day, every day (in the United States), a group of employees got a new boss. The first resolution you should make if you get a new one is to remain calm, cool, and collected — and alert. And be yourself.

Why did you get a new boss? Was the old boss replaced? Did the old boss go on — voluntarily — to bigger and better things? Was he popular with the employees? A tyrant? Was getting a new boss the result of a merger? (There were over 4,000 mergers — each worth $1 million or more — in 1986.) Was the new boss the result of the company foundering — a company in trouble that needed a savior? Did the new boss bring any key people with him. Whose jobs can they fill? Don't guess. Be sure. Don't jump to conclusions.

Each of these reasons and situations for your getting a new boss casts a different light on the situation. The best thing for you to do is determine the situation and be patient. Consider your alternatives. Updating your resume, if nothing else, will be an exercise in reviewing *you*. Keep your networking activities up to par. Ignore all rumors. But be prepared.

If he didn't make sweeping changes (in one firm every director and vice president was out in three weeks) — grandstanding, it's called — then the transition will probably take place in an orderly fashion.

If he did grandstand — a tactic that many consider counterproductive and not good management — you have either survived, or you're busy researching new companies.

If you are looking for a new job, go back to the beginning of this chapter. Start sharpening up your job-hunting skills, and get an even better job. If you've survived, go back only part way — you'll want to research your new boss.

First, keep your eyes and ears at-the-ready. Listen to what he says — in person, at meetings, by directive — he wants. New dedication. New vigor. New directions. This or that attitude. Teamwork. Whatever. Learn and analyze his style. Go back to Chapter 5 and review general types; to Chapter 6 for a refresher on what motivates him. But, while you're being alert to change, be yourself. You're apt to be angry and disturbed, psychiatrists say, about a big change in your work life. It will pass. In the meantime, stay cool. Be patient. Anxiety is likely to be endemic. Don't allow it to become hostility. Don't anticipate. And don't suddenly become a yes-man. Just do your job, be yourself, and watch. And while you do, research him (or her).

You research him the way you've researched this company and its executives a long (?) time ago. The public (or in-house, or both) announcement of your new boss' appointment probably contained a lot of information about him — college, degrees, former company, etc. With that basic information you research him using the same methods you've used before (earlier in this chapter). Newspapers and company publications (where he came from), college yearbooks, business directories, etc.

Get to know as much as you can about him (before he got there) through research, and as much as you can (since he got there) from observation, and put your concept of P.P.R. to work. Remember, he has P.P.R., too. He has interests, and goals, and problems to overcome, and — a boss or bosses to please. In many ways, he, and you, are in the same boat — you both have a new boss.

You Are The New Boss

When you're the boss you've got double-trouble. You're the boss to dozens, (a department); hundreds, (a division); or maybe even thousands of employees, (a company); and, you're an employee, with a boss, or bosses of your own — a Vice-president, President, a Board of Directors and its Chairman, even stockholders. You've got to satisfy your employees' expectations, as well as motivate them, in order to satisfy your boss' expectations, and you must do both successfully in order to satisfy your real bosses — your customers.

That's a tall order.

All the concepts, techniques, and skills of P.P.R. that you've read about, of course, apply, from determining and learning about your publics, to communication. And, as many experts say, 80 to 90% of your success will be dependent upon your ability to deal with people AFTER you put a solid foundation into place.

Where do you start? That depends. Why have you become the new boss? Are you replacing an incompetent? (You have to do better; have to remedy his mistakes.) Are you replacing a boss that did extremely well leading the company and is now retiring in glory? (You have to do as well or better.) Are you replacing a boss that was very popular with the employees, unpopular, indifferent? Were you hired because you're a "hotshot" who's expected to bring the company roaring into the industry's forefront? Are you the board chairman's son who just graduated from business school?

First things, first. You will be surrounded by rumors. Some good, some bad. Kill them. You must communicate, frankly and honestly. Give them the truth. If you were hired to save this faltering company from collapse, say so. Tell them how you will do it, how they must help, and how that will save the company... *their* company. Don't make promises you cannot hope to keep, or you have no intention to keep.

Tell them exactly what you expect from your managers, and, therefore, what their bosses (your managers) must expect and get from them. If you have the time, tell them that changes will be made slowly. Give them the whole story. If you don't, they will fabricate one of their own.

Employee resentment will rise in direct proportion to the number of rumors that are circulating. Consider an inside telephone extension number for employees to call, anonymously, to get the truth about rumors. Put out a "Rumor Of The Day" memo debunking a rumor, or clarifying the truth about a rumor. Don't communicate with your employees or staff by way of public media. (One executive heard his job was eliminated on a business review tv program.)

Be truthful. One case I heard about was of a group of managers being told that no one would be brought in from the outside. This the day before his wife showed a house to an executive who was joining the company.

Do not mislead. Again the truth. Tell it like it is. If it's going to be a great opportunity... tell them so by all means. If it's going to be a great opportunity *if*... tell them that, too.

The truth will always come out. Better if you're the source and it comes out the way you want it to come out. And, when the dust settles, and you get down to doing *your* job, apply generous doses of your P.P.R. You make *your* performance(s) — your company's, your division's, your department's — such as to elicit the response(s) that you want from *your* publics. You get your publics — managers, staffers, employees — to cooperate. You use P.P.R. to effectively and successfully deal with people.

I remember reading an article about John, a top-notch salesman, who "moved at the speed of light." He became president of the company. And six months later the Board knew it had made a mistake. He couldn't get people to cooperate. His style of management alienated people. He was fired.

Your performances, of course, will be varied, for various publics — top management, middle management, staff, support staff, etc. Each have different expectations regarding their contributions to the company, the nature and tenor of their relationships, and their rewards. These you must know, for yourself and for your company.

One of the benefits of being a boss, however, is you don't have to do the research yourself. You have a P.R. department and/or a personnel department to do the research for you. At the very least you have a secretary. Through them you will learn about *their* concerns and interests and goals, and you will use that knowledge to further your (and the company's) interests and goals. You then have to concern yourself only with *your* images. That's plural.

Even if there are only shades of difference there will be one image to your Board, another to your top-line executives, still another to middle-managers, and yet another to rank and file employees. And, to project those images, you employ P.P.R.

P.P.R. is people-oriented.

P.P.R. —minded Bosses

P.P.R. —minded bosses do not show arrogance toward their subordinates, nor do they belittle their subordinates' efforts. They do not betray another's trust for any reason. (If they do they can only do it once.) They have enough confidence in others to delegate, and if they don't they will get others in whom they can place their confidence. They have the courage to admit when they've made a mistake, and they know that other people are not infallible, either; that being a good manager is not being mistake-proof, but making many more good decisions than bad. P.P.R. —minded bosses are leaders. And leaders care about people.

P.P.R. —minded bosses are concerned, too, with their style and methods of management, if only in principle:

1. He, or she, sets a reasonable number of key goals and targets for his employees to focus on; employees know his future expectations from them and for them, and from and for the company.

2. He consistently stresses their achievements of these key goals in his day-to-day activities. He helps to identify specific problems and specific problem behavior that may be hindering goal achievement, and he solicits solutions.

3. He recognizes, appreciates, and applauds each small achievement victory along the way, if only with a simple well-placed thank-you or well-done.

4. He makes his employees feel needed, important, appreciated, and cared about.

5. He communicates 1, 2, 3, and 4, effectively and efficiently — saying what he means and meaning what he says — over and over again.

As a boss you don't have to purr like a kitten, or roar like a lion; you don't have to generate euphoria, or cause stress-related ailments; you only have to consider, understand, appreciate, care for, and treat your employees as you wish they — *your* bosses — to treat you.

Nothing spectacular is required; nothing but your everyday consistent, solid, dependable, considerate, competent, even friendly, treatment.

Patients, Clients, Customers

Solid, dependable, considerate, competent, friendly treatment is the right prescription for a physician to give his or her patients; is the best evidence for a lawyer's concern for his clients; and is absolutely the greatest gift a merchant or a businessman can give his customers. That is, if each would be successful.

How?

By applying the same concepts and techniques recommended to employers and employees, professors and students, husbands and wives, parents and children, people and people:

1. Know your publics — patients, clients, and customers — as people with feelings who will respond to your performances — your concerns, your praise, your appreciation, your consideration, etc.

2. Know your publics' needs and wants, how they want them met, how much they will, can, pay, give, to have them satisfied. (Emotional needs may only require a smile or a kind word. Don't always think money.)

3. Play your role to meet their expectations. They know, in their minds, how a physician should look, sound, and act. Look, act and speak like the physician (lawyer, merchant, salesman, etc.) that you are.

4. Treat each of them like the patient, client, customer that they are, with the consideration and respect that they expect and deserve.

5. When in doubt remember *you* before you became what you are — how you expected to be treated by your physician, lawyer, merchant, dentist, businessman, salesman, auto mechanic, serviceman, et al. Treat *them* that way.

And on those rare occasions when something does go wrong, and you have an irate patient, client, or customer, then what?

That's when your P.P.R. awareness really comes to the fore. Irate people demand to be heard. Listen. Make an attempt to agree with something they feel, even if you only agree that it should never have happened. Empathize with him or her. Put yourself in his moccasins. Feel what he feels. Then, when things are calmer, clarify the situation, solve the problem, and close the action. Ask if there is any other way you can help. Thank him or her for bringing the matter to your attention and for helping you to rectify the situation. You might even call back in a week or two, when necessary, to check on the status of the problem, and its solution.

I once heard a businessman say that the best, most loyal customer (or client, or patient, or...) was one who had had a problem, and had had that problem taken care of, in a timely, friendly fashion.

Starting College

Starting college is a lot like starting a new job. While usually not as crucial to your well-being as an employee-employee, or an employee-employer relationship, you have some important publics to consider as you begin — or continue — your education.

Important to you are the faculty. All faculty. More important, at least for now, are the professors (and instructors, even TA's) who will not only be teaching you, but grading you. The ones who'll be giving you the grades that will, someday, be a part of your transcript. Important, too, are the faculty members that could be teaching you (and grading your work) in the future. At the moment (if you are a freshman) your slate is clean; only you can make enemies.

Another public is your fellow students — classmates, dormmates, roommates, and others such as class and school officers, fellow members of clubs, and teammates.

Where do you start? You already have. You're learning about P.P.R. You only have to apply your newly acquired knowledge.

Professors are easy to research. There's the student newspaper, the college newspaper, the catalog, the local newspaper. One or all should have a story or information about the professor when he, or she, was appointed, promoted, etc. You may even find a student publication that "rates" the school's faculty. If nothing else, stop by the college's P.R. office. Tell them you'd like some general information about Prof. Whozis, and why — you feel that knowing your professor(s) will give you a perspective on their academic objectives and values.

Ask several second-year students how they liked Prof. Whozis. Compare their answers (those who liked him, those who didn't, and those inbetween).

Talk to the professor himself. Friendly talk. How-are-things-going kind of talk. Occasionally ask a question about the subject not normally covered in classroom work, a theory's application, for instance, in an everyday life situation.

Keep what you learn about Prof. Whozis in your mental file to build rapport and to prevent you from making a P.R. faux pas. For instance, if Prof. Whozis is a hunter, and you're a hunter, that's a mutual interest to build rapport on. But if you're a member of an anti-hunting group, you really don't want to make disparaging statements about hunting. Either way you'd be glad you picked up that little piece of information. There are dozens of other activities and interests and issues you can, in your mind, substitute for hunting.

Can you use any knowledge you've learned about Prof. Whozis' P's, especially his predispositions, to give your work the best chance of getting its best grade? Like choosing certain books or authors for reports, choosing certain viewpoints for certain theories, taking certain sides on certain social issues, or remaining neutral? Can anyone be totally objective? Consciously, maybe. How much subjectivity is found in the difference between a B+ and an A? Why not use any legitimate edge you can.

You will probably learn *about* your fellow students *from* your fellow students, directly or indirectly.

You can use matter-of-fact information — He's a Yankee fan... She loves modern art... He's a Chinese food freak... She hates pizza... — to start conversations, make friends, or just build upon.

Gossip is another story. Don't believe it. Don't pass it on. Don't let it color your mindset — your P's — in any way. Like Sgt. Joe Friday used to say in TV's Dragnet: "We just deal in facts, maam."

Remember, too, it may just be a college classmate who's the head of the search committee looking for a new corporate CEO, ten or twenty years from now, that you recognize when you enter the boardroom for your interview.

It may be in college, too, (it's happened before) that you meet that very special person — Miss Ideal or Mr. Right.

Meeting That Very Special Person

You've seen him... you've seen her... in class, at the office, in church, at the library, the hardware store, the supermarket, the mall, wherever. You would like to meet her. At least you think you would. You wonder if she could be Miss Ideal; whether he is Mr. Right; or just if she, or he, would be a good, new friend, nice to know, fun to be with. Will you ever know? That's up to you. But first you must find out if you really want to. You must do your research. Research again? Yes. Unless you're psychic.

Certainly, there is a physical attraction. Not that she has to be Miss America, or he Mr. Hunk. Maybe just interesting. Something caught your eye — his looks, her walk, a smile, a gesture — something that made you say — "I'd like to know him... I think she'd be fun to know."

We're not talking here of marriage. We're not even discussing whether or not you want to get married. There aren't too many people — men or women — who deliberately planned — at least not consciously — a campaign to get married. Most of us, it seems, just want a someone, or several someones, with whom we can share our successes. We'd like someone to participate in our fun times. Even someone who can commiserate with us when we fight disappointment. We may even have different someones for each of these happenings. Specialists, so to speak. When we find one that is important for each, and more, Pow! that's when it happens. It being a commitment, a relationship, even marriage.

The steps are always the same. Attraction, getting to know *about* him or her, getting to *know* him or her, developing a relationship, and, ultimately, the success or failure of the relationship. Mind you, the step progression may stop at any point — you may decide after you get to know *about* him, you do not want to get to know him. After you get to know him you may not want to develop a relationship. Even then, a relationship can succeed *or* fail.

Like a successful business that fails after years of success, so, too, can a friendship, a relationship, a marriage. People change. Circumstances change. Environments change. Maturity. Values. Viewpoints. Whatever. Ideally, a relationship should last forever if built on the solid foundation of knowledge of each other's values, dreams, goals, and expectations; on mutual trust and respect, friendship, common goals, and that undefinable state of mind called love. But sometimes it doesn't. Then, because P.R. — performance and response — is alert to change, remains flexible, and is prepared to adapt; favorable performances and responses can result.

Careers change, jobs change, values change, relationships change, but each experience contributes to the living of life. And living is something each of us wants to do. And part of living is meeting the Mr. Right or Miss Ideal — ideal mates, ideal friends, ideal neighbors, etc. — and that begins by learning enough about a prospective ideal to determine if we indeed want to get to know him or her better. We have to experience their performances before we can respond, and they have to experience ours. Action, reaction, and interaction. Will she be a Scarlet to your Rhett; he an Antony to your Cleopatra, or will you, together, be a Laurel and Hardy?

First things first.

While you go about fully involved in the business of everyday living — business activities, skiing, partying, studying, jogging, traveling, shopping... in church, at the mall, in the supermarket, at the library... etc. — be aware that you might see or meet Mr. or Miss Prospective Friend. Of course, you won't go out looking — you're not lonely, or desperate for company. Or are you? If you are, there's nothing wrong with looking.

Harry Reasoner, relating a short story on radio, told of a friend, Buzz, and what he, Reasoner, called "love among the melons." It seemed that Buzz went to the local supermarket to meet women. He'd zero in on date candidates (those without wedding rings) in the fresh produce section. Harry said, that Buzz said, his success rate was very high, when he, Buzz, stopped making dates around the melons; didn't go to the supermarket at all. It seems Buzz met his wife while picking out a melon. She now did all the shopping.

How about at the office? It is now more likely you will meet your future spouse in work, rather than school, social, or neighborhood settings, according to a research report quoted (1988) by the Bureau of National Affairs, a private Washington, D.C., publisher.

Whether you first see X at work, or someplace else — even in a supermarket by the melon counter — there are things to learn, beginning with X's name. You have to know about this person, just as a corporate P.R. person must know about one of his publics, before you can relate to him or her. You need to learn enough to determine if X will be, or should be, one of *your* publics.

Learning About Miss Or Mr. X

Your first objective is to change X to a name. If X is a co-worker, even in a different department or division; if he or she is attending the same school, maybe even taking the same courses; if you're both members of the same church or club; if you are members of the same hobby group, bowling league, whatever — you probably can easily learn X's name.

If X works in a pharmacy, a department store, a hospital, etc., he or she probably wears a name tag.

If all else fails, ask someone who might know (a clerk, a co-worker, a mutual friend).

"Who is that... Do you know... Is that Mary Doe who checked those books out?" you might ask the librarian. "Wasn't that John Smith who just..." You might even ask X. "My name is John Smith," extending your hand, "I'd like to meet you but there's no one here to introduce us."

However you get it, once you have X's name, many avenues of information open to you — a high school or college yearbook, a newspaper, a student directory, a company directory, newspaper articles (local, daily, weekly, or company publications), a church bulletin, club notes, and city business directories.

City business directories, for instance, (available in your local library), while primarily for businesses, contain the names, addresses, telephone numbers, occupations, (hints as to marital status), of most of the residents of the city and its suburbs. They're cross-indexed. If you know X's name you can learn his or her address, phone number, occupation, and you can guess at marital status. You can even learn if she lives with her parents, and if there are brothers or sisters at home.

Do you know only X's telephone number. The directory will give you her name, address, occupation, and all the rest. Know the address and nothing else (you just happened to see her enter her house) — look up the address listing and learn all the rest.

One of the three components — name, address, or telephone number — will give you the other two... and more.

Let's take a for instance:

You've just picked up Granddad's prescription for him at the local pharmacy. The pharmacist is a nice looking, pleasant young man. You wonder if you'd like to get to know him. His name is John Smith. (If he has no name tag — he should — you might ask — "If my grandfather has to call you, who should he ask for?" He wears no wedding ring. You guess his age as the late twenties. That's all you know. What next?

(Incidentally, this pharmacist could be a nice looking, pleasant, young woman, and nothing would change.)

Go to your library and get out the city directory. Under Smith you find Michael and Lenore, and children Marie and John. The pharmacist's father, Michael, is a carpenter. His mother, Lenore, is a housewife who works part-time at the local supermarket as a cashier. Marie's a secretary at XYZ Company, and John is, as you know, a pharmacist. John lives at home. If he was married his wife's name would be listed.

Now you know John's address and telephone number. You know where Marie works. You could call John. It's being done, but it's risky — he may not like aggressive women. If John is a Joan, and you're the "aggressive" male, you might call. In either case, knowing his address and neighborhood, you could accidently bunk into him — at a neighborhood store, on the street, in church. If we're talking about John, you could also flirt with him in the pharmacy. If Joan, you would flirt with her. You have to choose the medium and method, as would any P.R. practitioner. You may even elect to learn more.

Is there a pharmacy college in commuting distance. You might be able to see its yearbook. It will be in the college library, and most colleges open their library to the people of the community — it's good "town and gown" P.R. This could lead to other avenues of information. Does the yearbook say he is an avid golfer, bowler, tennis player. If he is, does he enter local tournaments? Check the newspaper if he does. He may have won something. Last, but not least, do you have a mutual friend or acquaintance? P.R. people sometimes support one public to get a favorable response from another. So can you.

If you really try, you should be able to learn about any X's — male or female — name, address, telephone number, and marital status. You should be able to find out X's interests, such as hobbies and social activities; determine his or her public personality; learn about things you have in common or do not have in common. You will be able to learn one thing for sure — whether you want to know *more* about X. If you find that you do not, you just continue your everyday living, enjoying all the things you enjoy, until another X comes into view — a public that matters.

Meeting Miss Or Mr. X

If, however, this particular X is becoming more and more interesting, you must then arrange meeting — through a mutual friend, acquaintance, or relative; by *accident*; or even directly by introducing yourself.

An introduction is most acceptable. Have you managed to meet John's sister? Anyone else? You could meet by accident, but that will only put you both in the same place at the same time; one of you will have to approach the other. A smile given and a smile returned may do it. So may direct eye contact. (There are so many ways to communicate.) You may have to introduce yourself. Make polite conversation, asking for help or advice, or you may want to consider a cutesy — ice-breaker — remark.

Most surveys put thumbs down on the cutesy remark approach. The direct approach is thought by some people to be too aggressive for a woman to use. (Most women do not have the ability a female seahorse has — all she has to do to incite the romantic action of Mr.

Seahorse is to turn her head.) The safest approach, it is thought by many, is the neutral approach. At the library — "Can you tell me where I can find a book about...?" (Especially great if you hit a favorite subject.) In the supermarket — "What's the best meat to use for beef stroganoff?" (Or you can drop a can, maneuver a shopping cart collision, or just back into X. Believe it or not, all have been done. You may even want to hang around the melons asking for advice on how to pick a ripe one.) In the shopping mall — A plea for help: "Could you help me pick a gift for my father/brother/sister/mother?" At a party or dance — "What's the name of that song... who's band is that?"

The beauty of the neutral approach? You really are not leaving yourself open to rejection. Only to possibilities.

If you're a man, or if you're a woman who wants to try it, there's the direct approach. If you use it, keep it sincere and honest.

A survey conducted by psychologist Dr. C. Kleinke, University of Alaska, asked 650 men and 831 women to rate 200 opening lines. The best conversational move with a stranger of the opposite sex? "Hi!" It shared the spotlight with "I feel a little embarrassed about this, but I'd like to meet you" and "I don't have anybody to introduce me, but I'd really like to get to know you." (Both are close to my personal favorite: "My name is... I've seen you here several times and I keep wondering if, after we got to know each other, we might become friends."

Dr. Kleinke's survey, announced in January, 1988, reported that neither men nor women like "cutesy" lines, but women disliked them most. And men never seemed to realize that.

But let's say that your approach to X (or X's approach to you, for that matter) develops into conversation. Now your research becomes even more valuable. You can lift all that information you've gathered from your mental file and get some favorable P.P.R. underway, and build a relationship.

Building A Relationship

X loves corn, hates broccoli; is into skiing and bowling, hates golf; collects coins, not stamps; loves Westerns, hates Whodunits, etc. etc. etc. If you share some of these likes and dislikes and interests, so much the better. (You probably share most or you wouldn't have decided to meet X.) Build on those you share. Of course, on those you don't share, you won't even bring up the subject. The neutral ones remain neutral. Later you can decide if X is worth your cultivating an interest in yoga, or jogging, or origami, or whatever?

The Special Event

At this point, if you want the relationship to grow, you will become even more aware of your P.P.R. Which of *your* performances gets a positive response from X, and which a negative? And you know your options — change a performance or justify it to change a negative response. If you do not, or cannot, change a performance, can you educate X so as to neutralize his or her response, or even change it to one that is positive?

How about X's performances? Are there more that generate a positive response from you than negative? Can you change an X's performance so as to change your negative response into positive, or, at least, neutral? How about X's performances and responses with regard to others with whom you both interact — are they positive or negative or neutral? Do any of X's negative responses affect *your* P.P.R. with these people? With your family? With close friends and relatives?

Are X's performances unpredictable, irrational, or erratic? Does X's words say one thing, actions another? Is X self-centered, inconsiderate of other people? When things go wrong is it X's fault, or others?

Or is X truly interested in, considerate of, and concerned about others? Is the relationship mutual. Will... can... X become your friend? Your good friend? A very best friend? Your spouse? Any of the above? None of the above?

If a relationship with X becomes more desirable, what can you do to make the desire reciprocal (if it's not), or more so if it's lukewarm?

Be responsive. That means being truly interested and concerned about X — goals, wants, needs, feelings, dreams, thoughts, problems, opinions, likes, and dislikes. Conversely, X must respond in kind — being truly interested and concerned about you.

Your reception of X's responses — feedback — and its analysis, will determine your future performances:

1. Continue to build your relationship with a continuation of positive performances as you learn more about X by direct observation and interaction.
2. Change those performances (you can) that elicit neutral or negative responses from X.
3. Educate X in order to change neutral or negative responses to positive while observing X's response to your education strategy performance.

All three of these courses should be used if your objective is to reach the corporate P.R. person's unattainable pinnacle of success — 100% positive response.

Does all of this sound too calculating and manipulative for you to do? Think about it. You *are doing* all of these things now. Without thought. Without purpose. Without direction. Without regard to outcome.

Why not do it with thought, with purpose, with direction, for the outcome you want to achieve?

Of course, when you think about meeting that very special person, you know that people don't plan on falling in love. It just happens. But shouldn't you also concern yourself with the relationship after the honeymoon is over; after, as they say, the blush is off the rose? Good P.R. is planning for future interaction with a public.

Leo Buscaglia, the renowned exponent of love, said, in an interview: "I'm always warning people that if they're going to form a deep relationship of any kind, leading in any direction, be it finally consummating in a marriage or whatever, that they should look at that person when they meet them and say, if that person remains this way for the rest of their life, is that enough for me? Because if the answer is no, then watch out.

"...What I mean is that I think love oftentimes plays almost no part in what draws people together, at all. I think our first attraction to a human being, the majority of people at least, is a physical attraction. And then they think that's really enough and everything will follow naturally. Well, it doesn't follow naturally, because it's a very different thing. And they don't even like the other person, which is even more frightening. And as they get deeper and deeper involved, they hate the person more and more, and so then they marry them."

Parents, Spouses, Children, Siblings

It should be easier to deal with, and interact with, our spouses, parents, children, and our brothers and sisters. Right? Wrong! It's not easier. Why? We expect more from them, and we give less to them. And when we both do that — we've got problems.

We expect them to understand us, be considerate of our feelings, be friendly, selfless, tolerant, and just plain nice to us. Why not? Blood *is* thicker than water, isn't it. They know us for all, or most of, our lives. They love us. They are family. We can let our hair down with them, be ourselves, relax, not have to *always* be on our best behavior. We can even forget our manners.

But, unfortunately, they have the same expectations.

If they satisfied our expectations, and we theirs, we'd have an ideal relationship. But we know that all interfamilial relationships are not ideal. Many are far from it. How come?

Knowledge is missing. Real knowledge of each other. P.P.R. knowledge.

I suggest that those interfamilial relationships that are ideal — husbands and wives, parents and children, brothers and sisters — are that way because *they* got to know more about the other person.

Family members, it seems, all start out the same. Mostly we learn about each other by observation and interaction. Some go no further. Others add to that knowledge by applying general principles — motivational factors, for instance. But those of us who get even closer, who really confide in them, really talk to them, really communicate, go further. We get to know more, as if we researched each of them. And that's not hard to do. We have the luxury of being able to do so just by asking questions, and listening to their answers. No reading about them in publications or asking others. We can learn much about *them* easier than we can a prospective employer, a new boss, a co-worker, a new friend. We can, if we really want to, learn about their interests, concerns, needs, wants, fears, hopes, and dreams.

An Exercise

Pick a member of your family — Mom, Dad, Spouse, Sister or Brother — with whom you'd like a better relationship. For the moment imagine he or she is not related, just Dick, or Jane, or whatever. You might want to review chapters 4 (Getting To Know The Consumer... Them) and 6 (Motivations — Are There Buttons To Be Pushed). You may even want to review parts of chapter 5 (Your Publics — Who Are They?) Now:

1. Bring to the forefront of your mind all the general knowledge you have of him or her. Successess and failures. Hopes and fears. Interests and goals. As well as general personality traits, types, etc.

2. Research further. By discussions. Really get to know his or her likes and dislikes, objectives, interests. Keep your eyes and ears open, with mutual friends, for clues about him or her.

3. Assess and evaluate. Are there any performances of yours that seem to get a negative or neutral response from him or her. Can they

be changed to get a positive response. Can they be explained (if they cannot be changed) to neutralize a negative response?

4. Assess and evalute his or her performances in the same way. What performances of his drives you up the wall? That's a negative response. Does he or she know it? Recognize it as such?

5. Delineate your objective(s). Be specific. Don't say "I want to improve my relationship with Dick." Say, "I want to improve my relationship with Dick in this way, that way, by doing this, or that.

6. Design a P.P.R. program to accomplish your stated objectives, by certain means, within certain time periods.

7. Communicate. You may communicate *before* (We have not been getting along too well. Not nearly as well as two brothers should. I'm going to try...); *during* (How're things at work... What's new in your life...); and *after* (Thanks for whatever... What did you think of...).

8. Assess... Evaluate... Adapt... Change... Performances. Responses. Actions. Reactions. Attitudes.

In general, we want to become more interested, more considerate, more aware of them (and they, hopefully, will reciprocate). If we expect more *from* them, we'll give more *to* them. We will praise them when praise is due. And we will tell them — matter-of-factly — when their performance displeases us — and why — and we hope they'll do the same. We will always, of course, remain civil, speaking to them (with the same respect) as we speak to our co-workers, bosses, even strangers. Because young people tend to become what we tell them they are, we will be positive with them (if they are young) so they will be positive with themselves. Because older people need consideration, too, we will appreciate the good they do, or try to do. We will not take affront if they do not do things, or say things, that *we* consider the right thing to say and do. We will treat all events a little special, and special events — Christmas, birthdays, graduations, anniversaries, etc. —very special.

We will treat them — our parents, spouses, children, siblings — as members of a very important public. And they'll do the same for us.

The Party... The Wedding... The Funeral...

A party is nothing more than another setting in which you're having fun, building relationships, and where you may even meet a special him or her.

If there *is* someone there to meet, the big difference is that there will be someone at the party — a mutual friend, the host or hostess — who can introduce you to each other. Of course, if you already knew that the "Special One" was going to be there, you'd have done your homework. You will already know what subjects interest him (or her); what topics of conversation will pique her curiosity; whether he is shy, or outgoing; and the best approach to take to get to knew her better.

You will have the opportunity to meet many new potential friends at parties. If it is an initial sighting or meeting, you will have to decide if you want to, indeed, know him (or her) better. To do this you will take notice of his (or her) dress — conservative, modish, coordinated, moderate, loud, etc. He is, as we know, communicating a personality, a style, an attitude. You are the message receiver. Assess your overall impression, feeling, opinion, intuition, in addition to the physical attraction.

If you decide to pursue the opportunity, you will use neutral conversation to draw out his interests, her concerns: "What do you think of... Have you seen... read... heard about? I really wonder about... ."

There is usually a purpose for a party — a holiday, a birthday, an anniversary, a housewarming, etc. There is usually a host or hostess, or both. You, therefore, have subjects for neutral conversation. The event: "I just love the Christmas season. Isn't it nice to help Jane celebrate her birthday. Have you known her long?" The host or hostess: "Have you known the Smiths very long? Don't the Joneses make a beautiful couple... have a lovely home... know how to have a party... ?"

Neutral conversation, even chance remarks, can give clues, not only to interests (and non-interests), but to his or her predispositions and other P's.

Does he have a predilection for the president (governor, mayor, etc.)? How does it influence his reception of that person's administrative decisions and policies? Does she have an inclination to be pessimistic or optimistic? How does that color her perception of events? Get to know your public.

Once you discern these nuances of personality and values, you will either decide to go on to the next opportunity, or proceed with this one, going from neutral conversation to topical conversation of interest to him, or her.

Some may consider this a mild form of pandering. Would you rather attempt to discuss a strong military with a pacifist, abortion with a right-to-life advocate, or the taste buds titillation of a sizzling steak with a vegetarian? Regardless of which side of the issue you stood, the results would be that if you could not tolerate this difference of opinion or values, you would have to move on without fully exploring the full potentiality of this friendship. If you could, you would probably, at the outset at least, refrain from antagonizing the other person.

Is it pandering?

Barbara Walters relates a story in *Write better, Speak better* about attending a dinner party where she was seated next to then Indiana Senator Birch Bayh. She was, she said, discussing his possible candidacy for the Presidency when a friend, Lola, was introduced to the senator as dessert was being served.

" 'Tell me, Senator Bayh,' she (Lola) began, starting slowly, 'how are the tomatoes coming along?' " The senator, Walters wrote," laughed out loud and asked how on earth she knew that he used to grow tomatoes and still loved to. Lola, who now had his complete attention, explained that she knew that he was going to be at the party and that she'd looked him up in a reference guide she had at her house, much as she would study a libretto of an unfamiliar opera before going to see it. She also knew a good deal more about the senator and was so refreshing and complimentary because she had done this homework that I lost the senator for the rest of the dinner. But it was worth it for the experience."

When it comes to becoming an interesting conversationalist or person; meeting Miss or Mr. Right; or just meeting a new friend, all of the concepts and techniques of public relations that are now in your repository of skills, apply. Especially the concept — performance and response.

Getting to the party itself is yet another facet of your personal public relations that requires research and planning.

You were invited, either as a good friend, a casual friend, a job-related friend, or possibly as a friend of a friend. In which category you fit depends your P.P.R. problem and its solution. You either know or should find out about your host/hostess' likes or dislikes, personal dress mores, home, etc., to determine the strategy of your performance, as well as the choice of a gift if one is consideration.

If the party is a wedding reception you should even know a little about the couple's religion. If it's different than yours, learn a little about the marriage ceremony itself. It's true that you can always follow others in attendance, but even that is easier when you have at least an idea of what is going on. It could even pay dividends to know your host/hostess' religion if the party is of the small dinner variety.

In some Jewish homes, for instance, you don't smoke on the Sabbath (sundown Friday to sundown Saturday). If they keep a kosher household you shouldn't ask for butter for your rolls, or cream for your coffee.

Knowing the couple's religion at a wedding may also prevent you from commiting a faux pas in the selection of a suitable gift. What of the cost or value of a gift? It should be commensurate with the importance or status of your friendship, as well as your financial situation.

Your choice of a thoughtful gift for any occasion, even a gift which is relatively inexpensive, can help stimulate a relationship in a meaningful way. When you share, in some way, in someone's happiness, you become a closer friend, and a relationship grows.

And when you share his or her grief with someone, that, too, can help nurture and bind a relationship.

Depending on your relationship with the deceased; your relationship with a close relative, friend, or even a distant relative of the deceased; or your job-related relationship with the deceased (co-worker, boss, subordinate, customer, etc.); will depend your degree of commiseration and its manifestation. You may send a note or letter or card of condolence; a Mass card (Catholic); a fruit basket to the home of the deceased's family (Jewish); or flowers. You might make a donation to a charitable organization; attend the wake or funeral services, or both. You may serve as an usher, or a pallbearer, or give the eulogy.

In any case your expression of sympathy should be appropriate to your relationship with the deceased, or the deceased's family.

At a wake, a pressing of the hand, a brief embrace, a few words, are all that is needed. A simple "I'm sorry." Do not attempt to console with "She's no longer in pain... Isn't it better... It's God's will." Don't try to tell the bereaved how he or she feels. At that particular time and place, in that particular circumstance, you really don't know.

Is a wake or a funeral an appropriate place to meet new friends? Modern funeral homes have lounges for smoking, talking, or just leaving the chapel area for quiet thoughts and reflection. You may very well be introduced to someone who could become a friend, maybe more. It has happened. That person you meet is probably a caring person, just as you are. And, although the setting is subdued and the mood somber, quiet conversation, even laughter, can and does take place in the lounges, outer lobby, and gardens of funeral homes.

If the opportunity arises, there is no reason not to participate. Whether at a party, a wedding, or a funeral, or some other place where people congregate, you have only to be prepared — as you go about the business of living your life to the fullest — to meet a new friend and/or enhance your P.P.R.

Especially to enhance that P.P.R. that can be impacted upon by others.

17

Your P.P.R. Through Others

Someone — a secretary, a co-worker, a friend, an acquaintance, a colleague, a relative, a lodge brother, a professor, a family member, whoever — is saying something *in your name*, doing something *for you*, saying something *about you*, that is, will, or can affect your image — your P.P.R.

Furthermore, the act, word, or deed, can have an impact on the receiver, so that the receiver's predisposition toward you changes, leading him to alter his previous responses to your previous performances. It can even color his responses of all future actions by you, or by others on your behalf.

For instance, many dignitaries and celebrities lauding Bob Hope's good works and humanitarianism would exhibit disbelief that he charges hospitals upward of $45,000 for a one-night performance. That's the business-side of Bob Hope. As his business manager writes, he does about ten personal appearances a year. That's an annual income of a half-million dollars a year for this business activity. Many of Hope's publics would have a hard time believing that this personification of humanitarianism can also be a materialistic businessman. People talk well of Bob Hope. And that's good for his P.P.R.

On the other hand we have Frank Sinatra who does do benefits — for hospitals and other charitable causes. But his image, built over many years, is, in general, the opposite of Bob Hope's. So much so that even his good deeds (which rarely become known) can be viewed suspiciously, his motives ulterior. With his public's attitude it would be very easy for someone *to do* something — even something positive — *for* Sinatra, unbeknownst to him, that could put a strain on his credibility, or *to say* something — positive or negative — *about* him that could put a new stain on his image. In either case, the mindsets of anti-Sinatra publics could be reinforced.

Maybe not as public, nor to such a degree as Hope and Sinatra, you, too, must be concerned and aware of the affect on your P.P.R., of the remarks or actions of others about you, or on your behalf.

Now, if bad things can happen to your P.P.R. when well-meaning friends do things for you, just imagine what your enemies — even mildly antagonistic people who "just don't like you" — can do.

You must try to give neither the friend nor the enemy the excuse, the wherewithall, the reason, or the ammunition to do something for you or against you — unless you can control it, or at least control the perception of it.

How?

You do as Mr. Hope does. You accept the plaudits and you don't "rock your publics' perception boat." You don't do as Mr. Sinatra does — unless you want to promote the image of being an independent, tough, do-it-my-way kind of guy.

The impact on your P.P.R. by other people can be found anywhere you interact with other people — by your enemies who can distort the truth or hint at negativism, or by your friends who think they are "sticking up for you." In school, at work, in your neighborhood, wherever. Some may be purposefully spiteful, or even malicious — a jealous rival — others may be innocent, but destructive, motivated by a friend's considerate kindness. Awareness, as with all P.R. problems, is the first line of defense. Reaction, as always, is the truth.

What can be seen from the examples of Bob Hope and Frank Sinatra?

What you *really* are is not important to him or her; what is important is *what* he or she *perceives* you are. If you want their positive responses you must conform to his or her positive perception of you. You must project a public image that matches the one they picture. Or you must change the negative picture that shows up on the screens of their minds into one that *is* positive.

You must, that is, if he or she is the one who can advance or impede the progress of your career; make your life happy and contented, or miserably troubled; give you a raise or curve your grade; give you love or give you hate; give you sustenance or take it away. In short, if he or she can give you happiness or discontent.

There is yet another way that he, or she, can affect your personal public relations. In a more devious, cunning way. How? By saying something positive about you that is really negative. "I know for a fact that he has never... No matter what you hear she doesn't... ."

Mario Cuomo, Governor of New York, commenting on the Reagan Administration's problems with the Iranian arms deal, late in 1986, said he hoped "the trail ended before it got to the very top." He called on members of his party (the opposing Democratic Party) to cooperate with investigations to help restore the nation's credibility. He said in a radio interview:

"I'm hoping that we'll never learn that he (President Reagan) had real complicity and deceit. I don't want that to occur and I don't think that's good for the country and it would displease me personally."

He said also that some top officials must have known what was going on "because it's just unthinkable that you'd let anybody make deals with the Israelis and make deals with the Contras who are only lieutenant colonels," (referring to a leading figure in the investigation).

Now the governor did not *say* that President Reagan had real complicity (in the deal), or was being deceitful... he didn't say that the President let someone who was only a lieutenant colonel make deals with the Israelis... or did he?

"I'm praying that we never learn that he (Reagan) knew all about this," Cuomo said. "I'm hoping that all the suspicions that you know you'll hear over the next few days about 'Can it be that the trail ended before it got to the very top?' will be wrong."

Those are the words that Cuomo used to fuel the fire of doubt and curiosity of a public who heard and read them.

The President of the United States, of course, has a public relations staff to correct and counter such curves thrown in his direction. You, on the other hand, are your own public relations person. You must be aware of the actions and words of others that can affect your P.P.R. When you find it, if it is positive, you can build on it as any good P.R. practitioner would do. If it is negative, in any shape, form, or guise, you must, as would any public relations practitioner, correct it by educating that particular public by your words and deeds.

Either is accomplished by practicing good personal public relations — good P.R.

18

Good P.P.R.— The "Can-Do" Edge

If you ask newspaper editors what makes good P.R. they're likely to answer by telling you what makes a good P.R. practitioner — he (or she) can get the answers from top managers, he knows his company well, he can find information (they need) quickly and efficiently, and, he's honest.

In a survey done by James K. Gentry, director of the business journalism program at the University of Missouri-Columbia School of Journalism, and reported in the Washington Journalism Review, in July, 1986, business editors said:

"A good P.R. person is someone who understands your needs and responds to them promptly."

"...the person is knowledgeable about the industry he/she works in as well as his own company."

"...has a way with people, prepares good basic (news) releases..."

"The good P.R. person is someone who can write clearly and concisely and has a good news sense."

"Is someone who can translate corporate gibberish into understandable English."

They also talked about good P.R. being responsive, truthful, conscientious, and cooperative.

Bad P.R., many believed, was when a company thought that if they didn't answer questions about negative news, it would go away. Bad P.R. was not responsive; wasn't even well-informed about the company or its industry; thought they could hide the truth; wasn't capable of answering questions about something, and was, of course, not conscientious or cooperative.

For those who can remember (in 1982) a good example of excellent P.R. was the handling of the Tylenol tragedy. When people died after taking cyanide-filled Tylenol capsules, Johnson & Johnson's director of corporate public relations, F. Robert Kniffin, mobilized the company's forces — removing the product from the shelves, getting the investigative wheels turning, advising the public truthfully and often (not playing down the seriousness of the event), and taking steps to prevent reoccurrences and to restore public confidence — all under the company's credo that put responsibility toward customers (their public) above all else.

That was, of course, reactive public relations, but much of its success can be attributed to the foundation of public trust and confidence built by the company long before the crisis. The building of such a foundation is good basic public relations.

Corporate public relations today is, or should be, involved in the complete analysis and understanding of *all* the factors that influence people's attitudes toward a company, its products, and/or its services. These people — their publics — may be employees, customers, stockholders, suppliers, etc. Learning the attitudes of these publics, the company is able to see where it is understood or misunderstood, what is perceived and what is not perceived about it, what is liked and what is not liked. Its goal is to discover its public's Six P's — proclivities, predispositions, preconceptions, predilections, perceptions, and prejudices — plus one more — preferences.

Analyzing the research data, the company can then predict, and many times, even prevent, future problems of misunderstanding, misperception, or misconception. It can, in fact build on its public's positive opinions by formulating responsive policy. Should this be modified...this changed...this strengthened...? Then, planning and programming activities that fully explain the company and its products, it can overcome negative images and promote positive images.

All of this is then communicated to the company's publics by carefully worded and packaged messages, transmitted by appropriate media, to the chosen receivers.

Following this the company listens to feedback, reassesses its policies and programs, makes adjustments, and then continues this *on-going process of public relations.*

You are *your* company and you, too, can build your public relations in this way. It will not only build and enhance your P.P.R. — but it can provide a favorable environment should *you* have to respond to a crisis.

Sometimes good P.R. must even overcome negative, bad P.R. This requires a turn-around of public opinion and requires more work and greater effort to produce favorable responses.

A good example of this is the P.R. program of the Soviet Union in 1987-88. Under a headline, "Soviet Union Becoming Model Of Cooperation," an Associated Press story (1/21/88) says that the Soviets, once regarded with suspicion, have launched a vigorous P.R. campaign to promote the U.N. as an effective world forum — they've paid their back dues, called for a U.N. naval peacekeeping force in the Persian Gulf, is seeking to use the 159-member organization as a vehicle of its foreign policy, and is saying "nyet" less often.

The new approach, the story said, contrasts sharply with the Soviet conduct of the past and is being met with skepticism in the West. This is often the case when a P.R. turn-around is attempted because motives and sincerity are questioned. It is, as former Speaker of the House Tip O'Neil said on a Larry King show (2/88), "tough to shake a bad image."

In the face of this skepticism, however, the Soviet ambassador says that his delegation "would continue on that path."

This, too, is the proper P.R. approach — breaking down the barriers of resistance and suspicions with continued favorable, positive performances.

Is it working?

The ambassador of Canada called the new Soviet performance and attitude "a complete metamorphosis." In an interview, he said that "It augurs well for future collaboration."

Based on these opinions and examples, good P.R. is positive activity undertaken by an organization to promote a favorable relationship with its publics — *before* a problem arises, to build trust; *after*, to build upon trust.

Good P.P.R. then is doing the same — performing favorably and in a positive fashion to promote favorable relationships with *your* personal publics.

First, you learn what constitutes a good performance in *their* eyes— one that will produce a favorable response. Then you learn the skills, even the nuances of that performance. Then you perform, and communicate that performance by words, looks, and actions. You get feedback from *them.* You modify. You adapt. You improve, change, or explain your performance. And so the ongoing process of living — of P.P.R. — goes on.

Good P.P.R. starts with you. Note what the editors said about good corporate P.R. people; the good ones. Do the same for your publics.

- *You* understand their needs and you respond to them.
- *You* stay knowledgeable about the industry and the company you work in as well as your most important product — you.
- *You* have a way with people. You, too, can prepare good basic "news releases" — messages about you.
- *You* write clearly and concisely and your have a good news sense.
- *You* know what's important for them to know about you.
- *You* express yourself well.
- *You* are responsive, truthful, conscientious, and cooperative.

Examples of good P.P.R. can be the result of good manners — a thank you or a thank you note; of consideration — not doing something that impacts adversely on another; of altruism — caring about the welfare of others; of courtesy — kind and thoughtful behavior to others; of empathy — identifying with another's needs, desires, values, etc.; *and* the communication of these qualities to *them.*

A good example of P.P.R., is told in a newspaper story (1/24/88):

Sally Kirkland, star of the critically acclaimed "Anna," called John H. Richardson, critic with the Los Angeles Daily News, to say thanks.

"Thanks for what?" Richardson wanted to know.

For being a member of the Los Angeles Critics Association, Kirkland said, which made her a co-winner of its best-actress award. Kirkland, who, the critic wrote, was subsequently nominated for the Golden Globe award for best actress and was "well on her way to an Oscar nomination," apologized for not calling sooner, explaining that she had been hospitalized with a brief illness. She was, she said, grateful for the award which had boosted her career, and she was calling all twenty-eight of the critics involved.

Richardson wrote that he told her her action was definitely unstarlike. "She seemed surprised. How refreshing." He wrote.

Sally Kirkland was appreciative of this "boost" to her career. She knew enough about *them* to know that people like to be appreciated. She did. And she was. With the award. So she was calling all those responsible to say *thanks.* To show her appreciation. To enhance and build her P.P.R.

To enhance your P.P.R., in this or any way, you must first know about *you*. You must realize that you have potential — talent, aptitude, skills, and ability. You must use these qualities. Furthermore, you must not allow any one to deprive you of them, by words or actions of any kind.

Young Tom Edison was considered a dolt by his teachers. Even his father. In his later years he said:

"I never got along at school. I don't know now what it was, but I was always at the foot of the class."

He was almost convinced, by others, that he was a dunce. He was even afraid to tell his mother about his difficulties in school. Afraid that she, always kind and sympathetic to him, might lose her confidence in him.

"One day I overheard the teacher tell the inspector that I was 'addled' and it would not be worthwhile keeping me in school any longer. I was so hurt by this last straw that I burst out crying and went home and told my mother," Edison said.

"Mother love was aroused, mother pride wounded to the quick. She brought me back to the school and angrily told the teacher that he didn't know what he was talking about, that I had more brains than he himself, and a lot more talk like that... I determined right then that I would be worthy of her and prove that her confidence was not misplaced. My mother was the making of me."

Actually, Edison was the making of himself. He believed his mother's words. He refused to let others deny him the gifts he had. That day in school, standing beside his mother, he got the winning edge — the slight advantage. He got the confidence, the will, the self-esteem. The "Can-Do" edge.

We see this concept at work when we see a football team score with only seconds left on the clock, when a horse wins by a nose, when a basketball team wins by a single point, when a golfer chips in on the 18th for a one-stroke victory, when a pinch-hit home run in the bottom of the ninth wins the game, when you get the job or promotion over others, when you get the award, when you get the girl (or the guy).

In an article in Success! magazine, January/February 1987, written by Auren Uris, Prof. Aaron Levenstein of City College of New York, was cited as an early propounder of this winning edge concept as a guide for managers who traditionally operate in competitive situations.

Managers my foot. We all operate — live — in competitive situations. And we all want any advantage we can get. I know you do. You're reading P.P.R. to get your winning edge — your knowledgeable "Can-Do" edge.

How do we get the winning edge? Uris' article tells us to focus on *them*. The better we understand our competition — strengths and weaknesses — the more effective we can be. Look for *the* edge. Learn his or her most important needs and fill them. Use your advantage, i.e., your knowledge of him or her.

"Make sure you get the prize money'." The article ends. "Winning gives you a victory. Exploiting the victory gives you the benefits."

It's nice to be a winner. But if you want to be one, you've got to act like one. You've got to be confident and self-assured based on knowledge of them and of you. You've got to be interested and interesting, caring and concerned, people-oriented and goal-oriented — and you've got to communicate those features of you.

And this is true whether you're a man or a woman. P.P.R. knows no sex. Catherine R. Stimpson, professor, dean, and vice president of New Jersey's Rutgers University, speaking at Russell Sage College, in Troy, New York, said there was no such thing as a woman's or man's nature.

"The only difference between the sexes," she said, "is pregnancy. Many things that appear to be different are not inherent, but learned."

So, everything written about P.P.R., its concepts and its techniques — whether referred to with a he or a him, a she or a her, or a he/she — was and is truly meant for you, him or her. There's really no difference.

Start today! Visualize! Visualize who you are and where you're going. Do it now! It's not too soon. Nor is it too late.

Thomas Watson, Jr., 40 years old at the time, joined a company that manufactured meat slicers and punch-card machines. Just one year later he became president of the company. Nine years later, in 1924, he renamed it — International Business Machine Corp. In his later years he was asked when he visualized IBM getting so big. His reply: "Right at the beginning."

Top-notch performers, many human relations experts say, are those people — men or women — who are determined to make the most of themselves to reach their full potential. They can *see* themselves being successful. They know they can do it.

Knowing and using your P.P.R. can give you the "Can-Do" edge. Decide now what *you* want to be, how *you* want others to perceive you, how successful *you* want to be, then shape an image of you that can—like the metamorphosis of the butterfly—become the real you.

In the final analysis you have only to do what movie superstar Cary Grant said he did:

"I pretended to be what I wanted to be and I finally became that person."

That's not as easy as it may seem. To pretend to be someone or something you first have to learn about the model—the prototype—in order to fit the mold; you have to learn about yourself—your talents and intelligence—to form the model; you have to learn about them—their values, interests, concerns, needs, and wants—to make your model valuable to them; and you must effectively communicate what you're doing and what you've done—your performance—so they know and value the image that is you—their response.

But that's P.P.R.! And you've just spent hours reading some 80,000 words about it. And now you are prepared to be as in control of your life as you want to be... as successful as you have the potential to be... and as happy as you have a right to be.

May God grant you good luck, good health, and good fortune as you live your life to the fullest.

About The Author

John A. Chestara is a P.R., veteran with almost 40 years of experience in newspaper, corporate, university, and healthcare public relations, both in the United States and abroad.

Over the years his career has ranged from Vice-President for Public Relations for Seaboard Publishing Corp., Associate Director of P.R. at Fairfield University in Connecticut, Director of Public and Professional Relations for the Department of Postgraduate Medicine of Albany Medical College, Public Relations Account Executive at Rensselaer Polytechnic Institute, Director of External Educational Affairs for the Albany-Hudson Valley Physician's Assistant Program, Director of Community Relations for an upstate New York hospital, to the owner-manager of his own public relations firm.

During his career he has been among the pioneers who have made a strenuous effort to take P.R. out of the "publicity flack" category and into its true function — understanding, evaluating, and communicating with people to promote favorable relationships.

Now semi-retired, he is a public relations consultant to a publicly-held, listed corporation, as well as others in the commercial and healthcare fields.

Bibliography

Amy Vanderbilt's Everyday Ettiquette, by Amy Vanderbilt. New York: Bantam Books, Inc., 1974.

Book Of Lists, The, by David Wallechinsky and Irving Wallace. New York: William Morrow and Co., 1977.

Counseling and Psychotherapy, by Carl Rogers. Boston: Houghton Mifflin Co., 1942.

Dress For Excellence, by Lois Fenton and Edward Olcott. New York: Rawson & Associates, 1986.

Dress For Success, by John T. Molloy. New York: Warner Books, 1976.

Effective Listening, by Kevin J. Murphy. New York: Bantam Books, Inc., 1987.

Gone With The Wind, by Margaret Mitchell. New York: Macmillan Publishing Company, 1936.

How To Increase Your Word Power, by the editors of Reader's Digest. Cincinnati, Ohio: Writer's Digest Books, 1987.

Human Behavior, by Berelson and Steiner. New York: Harcourt Brace Jovanovich, Inc., 1964.

Iacocca: An Autobiography, by Lee Iacocca with William Novak. New York: Bantam Books, Inc., 1986.

Introductory Psychology, by Anthony Davids and Trygg Engen. New York: Random House, Inc., 1975.

Language Of Clothes, The, by Alison Lurie. New York: Random House, Inc., 1981.

Lesly's Public Relations Handbook, edited by Philip Lesly. **Englewood** Cliffs, New Jersey: Prentice-Hall, 1978.

Letitia Baldridge's Complete Guide To Executive Manners, by Letitia Baldridge. New York: Rawson & Associates, 1987.

Lifetime Encyclopedia Of Letters, by Harold E. Meyer. Englewood Cliffs, New Jersey: Prentice-Hall, 1983.

Live For Success, by John T. Molloy. New York: Bantam Books, Inc., 1983.

Manners From Heaven, by Quentin Crisp. New York: Harper & Row Publishers, Inc., 1985.

McCalls Book Of Everyday Ettiquette, A Guide To Modern Manners, by Margaret Bevans, with the editors of McCalls magazine. New York: Golden Books, 1960.

Office Politics: Seizing Power/Wielding Clout, by Marilyn Moats Kennedy. Chicago: Follett Publishing Co., 1980.

Public Relations In Action, by Robert Reilly. Englewood Cliffs, New Jersey: Prentice-Hall, 1981.

Pulling Your Own Strings, by Wayne W. Dyer. New York: Avon Books by arrangement with Thomas Y. Crowell Company, 1979.

Robert Half Way To Get Hired In Today's Job Market, The, by Robert Half. New York: Bantam Books, Inc., 1987.

Speech Can Change Your Life, by Dorothy Sarnoff. New York: Dell Publishing Co., Inc., by arrangement with Doubleday & Co., Inc., 1972.

What Color Is Your Parachute, by Richard Bolles. Berkeley, California: Ten Speed Press, Revised edition, 1988.

Winning The Job Interview Game, by Jo Danna. Briarwood, New York: Palomino Publishing, 1986.

Woman's Dress For Success Book, The, by John T. Molloy. Chicago: Follett Publishing Co., 1977.

Write better, Speak better, by the editors of Reader's Digest. Pleasantville, New York: Reader's Digest, 1972.

Index

A

ABC's of writing (see Writing)
Abortion, 215
Act, How you, 98
Actions, 131-143; Four basic reasons for, 131; subconscious, 132; from ignorance, 133; unconscious, 134; body, 135; eye, 136; facial, 136
Action Story, 163, 168
Administrators, company, corporate, school, 63, 66, 69-70, 102-03
AIDA (see also writing), 170-71, 177, 180, 185, 193-94
Alexander (the Great), 31
Ambition, 85
American Heritage Dictionary, 29
American Medical Association, 127
Amiable, The (personality type), 73
Amy Vanderbilt's Everyday Ettiquette, 140
Analytical, The (personality type), 74
Aristotle, 47
Assertive (people), 75
Associated Press, 283
Associations, Business, 64, 256
A's Three (psychological) Anxiety, Affiliation, Achievement, 53, 85
Audience, not clearly defined, 108

B

Baldridge, Letitia, 140-41, 152
Bayh, Birch, 274
Baylor College Of Medicine, 106
Berelson and Steiner, 113, 116
Bergman, Ingrid, 20
Blue Cross/Blue Shield, 60
Body Language (See Actions; See Communication)
Bolles, Richard, 238-39
Bonaparte, Napoleon, 31
Book Of Lists, The, 156
Book Reports (see Writing)
Boskin, Joseph, 250
Boss, 26, 30, 31, 57, 63, 71, 142 (learning about 71-74; you've got a new 257-58; you are a new 258-60; P.P.R.-minded 260-61)

Boston University, 250
B.P.W. (Business and Professional Women), 211
Buckley, William, 105
Buddha, Gospel of, 49-50
Bureau of National Affairs, 265
Burns, Robert, 45
Buscaglia, Leo, 270
Business (See Company)
Buttons, Motivational (See Motivation)

C

Caesar, Julius, 31
Canada, 283
Capital Punishment, 215
Career Projection, 33-46
Carlton (cigarettes), 212
Censorship, 107
Charlie, by Rodrigues, cartoon, 158
Children, 270-72
China, 108
Christ, Jesus, 52, 86
Chrysler Corporation, 13
Churchill, Winston, 37, 173
City College of New York, 285
Claiborne, Liz, 125
Classmates, 66-67, 262-63, 265
Clients, 65, 261-62
Clothes, Language Of, 121-29
Club Members, 62, 256
College, starting, 262-63
Communication (see also Story, Message), 30; People who can affect, 61-69; Four basic ways we communicate, 97-99; Roadblocks to, 106; Absence of a clear purpose, 107; Psychological considerations, 113; Nonverbal, 121-143 (by body action and positioning, 135; by eyes, 136; by facial expression, 136; by gestures, 136-38; by design, 138; by manners, 139-42); Speaking, 145-60 (choosing words, 146-49; sound of voice, 145-51; speech habits, 152); Listen (to yourself), 153; Listen (to them), 154; Reflective (four) listening techniques, 155; Conversation, 156; How to plan, write, present a speech, 157-60; by writing, 161-78 (Memos, 179-80; Letters, 181-85; Notes, 185; Speeches, 185-87; Essay, 194-96; Resume 196-202; Cover Letter, 203-04); of performances, 229
Company, 63-64 (See also Boss, Co-workers, Publics, Public Relations); researching a, 240
Competitors, 65, 261-62
Conflict, in public opinion, (See public opinion)
Congress, 86
Conversation (See Communication)
Cook, John E., 105
Corporate (See Company)
Counseling and Psychology, 42
Cover letter (See Writing, Resumes; see Communication)
Co-workers, 25, 26, 30, 63-64, 69-71, 248-52
Cox, Debra Gae, 121
Crawford, Joan, 19, 20
Crisp, Quentin, 141, 142, 216
Crosby, Bing, 19, 20

Cuomo, Mario, 279
Customers, 25, 65, 261-62

D

Danna, Jo, 43-44, 45, 242
Davids, Anthony, 89
Davis, Bette, 43
Dell Publishing Company, 151
Dialogs, 119
Doubleday & Company, 151
Dress For Excellence, 127
Dress For Success, 122, 127, 252
Driver, The, (personality type), 72
Drives (see Motivation)
Dyer, Wayne W., 23-27

E

Edison, Thomas A., 37, 285
Educational Assessment, 35-37
Eastwood, Clint, 229
Effective Listening, 155
Einstein, Albert, 37, 88
Elks (B.P.O.E.), 211, 242
Emerson, Ralph Waldo, 139, 140
Emotions, 54, 79, 86
Employees (see Co-workers).
Enemies, 62, 65
Engen, Trygg, 89
Erikson, Erik, 42
Essay (see Communication; Writing)
Etiquette (see Manners)
Euphemisms, 173
Expressive, The (personality type), 73

F

Facial expression, (see Communications)
Fact Story, 163, 168
Family relations, 24, 26, 27, 61, 270-72
Federalist Papers, 31
Fellow workers, (see Co-workers)
Fenton, Lois, 127, 128, 129
Finances, People who can affect, 63-68
First World Assembly Of Public Relations Associations, 29
Five W's and H, 166, 167, 168, 169, 170, 171, 173, 177, 180-94, 211, 218, 232-33
Forbes (magazine), 249
Ford (automobile), 114
Ford, Henry, 79
Fortune (magazine), 30
Foundation For Christian Living, 89
France, 140
Franklin, Ben, 31, 47
Frede, Ralph E., 106, 116
Freud, Sigmund, 42, 53
Friends, relations, 24, 25, 27, 62, 66, 67
Fundamentals of Human Behavior, 48-55
Funeral, The, 275
Funk & Wagnall (dictionary), 118

G

General Electric, 36
Gentle Persuasion, The Art Of, 80, 89-90

Gentry, James K., 281
Germans, 173
Golf Magazine, 208
Gone With The Wind, 163
Gorbachev, Mikhail, 157
Grant, Cary, 287
Greeks, 173
Griswold, Denny, 28
Grooming, 126

H

Habits, speech, (see Communication)
Half, Robert 244-45
Happiness, People who can affect, 61-62
Harding, Warren, 86
Harvard Medical School, 127
Hippocrates, 42
Historical Figures and public relations, 31
Hodge-Cronin & Associates, 249
Hope, Bob, 19, 20, 277-78
Hospital's primary publics, 60
How To Increase Your Word Power, 147
"How To Write For Readership," 174
Human Behavior, Fundamentals of, 48-55 (Perception, 49; Motivation, 51; Incentives, 52, 53; Drives, 53; Three A's (anxiety, affiliation, achievement) 53; Emotion, 54; Seven Basic Motivating Instincts, 54; Learning experience, 55); 113-116

I

Iacocca: An Autobiography, 207
Iacocca, Lee, 13, 14, 207
I.B.M., 181, 286
Image, Image-making, Images, 19-21; Celebrities, 19-21; Influence of past, 20; Influenced by Six P's (see Six P's); Consultants, 21; Dressing for, 21, 121-29; Projecting, 21, 161; Sound of, 150
Incentives, 52-53, 81, 89
India, 140
Interpersonal relationships, 30
Introductory Psychology, 89
Inverted Pyramid Formula (see Writing).
Italian(s) (See also Romans) 117

J

JAMA (see Journal, AMA)
Japan, (Japanese), 117, 140
Jesus Christ, 52, 86
Jefferson, Thomas, 31
Job Interview, 25; Preparing for, 243-44; Interviewers, Interview Questions, 244-45; Rehearsing for, Practicing for, Role-playing for, 246-47; After the interview, 247-48
Job, starting a new, 248-52
Johnson & Johnson, 282
Journal of the American Medical Association, 127
Jung, Carl, 21, 75

Index

K

Kennedy, John F., 146
Kennedy, Marilyn Moats, 40
Kiersy, David, 76
Kiersy's Theory of Four Temperments, 76-77
King, Larry, 283
Kinney, Thomas J., 36
Kipling, Rudyard, 166, 186
Kirkland, Sally, 284
KISS, (Keep It Simple, Stupid), 161, 177, 180
Kiwanis, 211
Kleinke, C., 268
Kniffin, F. Robert, 282
Knight - Ridder (newspapers), 79, 121
Knights Of Columbus, 211, 242
Kroc, Ray, 37, 43, 44

L

Lambie, James M. Jr., 174-77
Language, 22, 30; Know the other person's, 102; Faulty selection, 108; Semantic, 109; Faulty arrangement (words) 110; Clothes, 121-29
Language Of Clothes, The, 121
Lauren, Ralph, 125
Lead sentences, (see also Writing) 170-71
Learning Experience, 55-56
Lee, Thomas, E., M.D., 127
Lesly's Public Relations Handbook, 174-77
Letitia Baldridge's Complete Guide To Executive Manners, 140-41, 152
Letters (see Communication, Writing)
Levenstein, Aaron, 285
Lifetime Encyclopedia of Letters, 185
Lincoln, Abraham 31, 88, 90, 158
Lions International, 242
Listen (ing) (see Communications)
Live For Success, 252
Look, How you, 97, 121-29
Los Angeles Critics Association, 284
Los Angeles Daily News, 284
Lurie, Alison, 121, 122, 125, 126, 129
Luther, Martin, 31

M

Managers (see Adminstrators, Boss)
Manners From Heaven, 141-42
Manners (see Communication)
Marlboro (cigarettes), 212
Marvin, Lee, 20, 116
Maslow, Abraham, 88
Masons (Freemasons), 211, 242
Medicaid, 60
Medicare, 60
Meeting That Very Special Person, 264-65; Learning about, 265-67; Meeting, 267-69
Memos, (see Communication, Writing)
Message, Transmission of, 99; Packaging of, 104; Conflicting, 109; Unattractive packaging of, 111; Bad timing of, 111; Lack of useful

information in, 112; Incorrect premise or assumption, 112; Your voice becomes the, 145
Miami Vice, (t.v.), 127
Mitchell, Margaret, 163
Molloy, John T., 121, 126, 127, 128, 129, 252
Moody's (Business Directory), 241
Moose (Fraternal), 242
Motivation, 51-56, 79-93; Drives, 53, 81-86; Business spends on, 79; Buttons to push, 81-83; 84-86; Multiple drives, 83-84; Conflicts, 87-88; Needs, Drives, Incentives, 89; 12 ways to motivate, 90-91; 6 ways to de-motivate, 91
Murphy, Kevin, J., 155
Myer, Harold E., 185
Myers-Briggs Type Indicator, 75-76
Myers, Isabel Briggs, 75

Mc

McCalls Book Of Everyday Etiquette, 140
McDougall, William, 54
McGovern, George, 116

N

Napoleon Bonaparte, 31
NASA, 173
Neighbors, 62, 65, 68
Nelson A. Rockefeller College of Public Affairs and Policy at State University of New York at Albany, 36
Networking, 256

Newsweek (magazine), 168
New York Daily News, 168
New York, Governor of, 279
New York Times, 168
New York University (Graduate School of Business Administration), 121
Nixon-Kennedy Debate, 146
Nixon, Richard M., 115, 146
Nonverbal communication (see Communication)
Notes, (see Communication, Writing)
Now (cigarettes), 212

O

Office Politics: Seizing Power/Wielding Clout, 40
Olcott, Edward, 127
Olivier, Lawrence, 43
O'Neil, (TIP) Thomas P., 283
Organization, Fraternal, 62; Business, 64; Student, 67
Outline (see Writing)

P

PACE (magazine), 197
Parents, 61-62, 271-73
Party, The, 273-76
Patients, 65, 261-62
Peale, Norman Vincent, 89-90
Peale, Ruth Stafford, 89-90
People (magazine), 168
Perception, Fifteen Fundamentals of, 118
Performance and Response, 13; Four basic options, 14, 22, 28, 32
Persian Proverb, 56

Index

Person, Know the other, 102-03, 220, 250-53, 265-67
Personal publics, identifying, 61-77, 220
Personalty, 21, 40-44, 71-77
Personnel Journal, 249
Persuasion, Art of Gentle, 80, 89-90
P-factor (see P's, Six important)
Philip Morris (cigarettes), 212
Physcial assessment, 34
Physicians, Dress Survey, 127
Piedmont Airlines, 197
Plato, 119
PLUS, Magazine Of Positive Thinking, 89
POLK, (Business Directory), 241
Porchia, Antonio, 147
Portugal (Portuguese), 173
Positive Reinforcement, 90
Praise, 79
Precis (see Writing)
President of United States, 31, 59-60, 86, 88, 90, 105, 106, 115, 146, 157, 158, 279
Professor (see Teachers)
Pronunciation, 149-50
P's, Six important to image, to communication, 20, 57, 91, 97, 101, 102, 104, 106, 115, 116-119, 157, 162, 172, 177, 180, 183, 193, 195, 282
Public Image (s) (see Image)
Public Opinion, 57-59; Conflict of, 58; Changing of, 59
Public Relations, definitions, 13, 22, 28, 29, 219; for individuals, 13; corporate, 282
Public Relations In Action, 113
Public Relations News, 28, 29
Public Relations (personal) Programming, 219-33
Public Relations Quarterly, 105
Publics, 14, 22, 30-31, 47-48, 57-77, 220, 221
Pulling Your Own Strings, 23; Victim/Non-victim examples, 23-27
Pyramid Formula (see Writing)

Q

Quote story, 163, 168

R

Reader's Digest, 21, 148, 215
Reagan, Ronald, 106, 157, 279
Reasoner, Harry, 265
Reilly, Robert T., 113, 114, 116
Rembrandt, 38
Reports (see Writing)
Research (ing) (him, her, them), 209-13, 220-21; a company, 240; co-workers 250-53; a special person, 265-67; family, 271-73
Responsive people, 75
Resume (see Communication, Writing); Inflation, "Getting To The Bottom Of Resumé Inflation," 197; reproducing, 198-99; layout, 199-202; customizing, 202-03
Richardson, John H., 284
Robert Half Way To Get Hired In Today's Job Market, The, 244-45
Rodrigues (cartoonist), 158
Rogers, Carl, 42-43
Romans, 173
Roosevelt, Eleanor, 88

Rotary, Rotarians, 242
Russell Sage College, 286
Rutgers University, 286

S

Sarnoff, Dorothy, 147, 151
Saint Peter, 52, 86
School board, 66
Scotland, St. Andrews, 208
Self-actualization, 42, 88
Self-assessment, 33; Physical, 34; Education, 35; Abilities, 37; Special talents, 38-40; Personality, 40-44; Six questions for, 44-46; In career life, 222
Serlin, Bruce, 197
Services, Business, 64;
Services, Providers, 68-69
Siblings, 270-72
Sinatra, Frank, 19, 20, 277-78
Six P's (predisposition, predilection, proclivity, preconception, perception, prejudice) (see P's, Six; see Perception)
Social Learning Theory, 42
South Dakota, 116
Soviet Union, 60, 157, 283
Speak, How you, 99, 145-160 (see also Communication)
Speech Can Change Your Life, 147, 151, 152
Speech, planning, writing, presenting (see Communication, Writing)
Spouses, 270-72
State University of New York, Albany, 36
Stereotypes, 35
Stimpson, Catherine R., 286

Story (communication), Straight news, Quote, Fact, Action, 163, 168; Lead sentences for, 170-71; AIDA formula for, 171; Outline for, 171-72; Five W's for, (see Five W's); Inverted Pyramid, Pyramid formulas for (see Communications, see Writing, see individual listings)
Straight "News" Story, 163, 168
Students for Democratic Action (SDA), 102
Subordinates, 30, 64 (see also Co-workers, Adminstrators, Boss, Publics)
Success! (magazine), 122, 285
Sullivan, H.S., 42
Supervisors, superiors (see Co-workers, Administrators, Boss, Publics)
Survey-Top Four Motivators, 79

T

Teachers, 66-67 (see also Publics)
Term paper (see Writing)
Thomas' Register, (Business Directory), 241
Time (magazine), 168
Toastmasters International, 160
Todd, Mary, 88
Traits, personality, 75, 76, 77
Transmission of ideas, 99; Roadblocks to, 106-07; Censorship of, 107; Absence of clear purpose for, 107; Choosing the wrong channel for, 110; Timing of, 111

Index

Trustees, 66
Twain, Mark, 147, 239
Tylenol (see Johnson & Johnson)
Types, personality, 41-42

U

U.N. (United Nations), 283
United States, 140
University (College), 36, 60, 69-71, 102, 106, 191, 262-63, 268, 281, 285
University of Alaska, 268
University of California, 106
University of Missouri - Columbia School of Journalism, 281
Uris, Auren, 285-86

V

Vanderbilt, Amy, 140
Voice, Sound of, 145-53; Four characteristics of, 152-53 (see also Communication)

W

Wall Street Journal, 168
Walters, Barbara, 21, 215, 274
Ward Howell International, 197
Warhol, Andy, 126
Washington, George, 31
Washington Journalism Review, 281
Watson, Thomas J., 181, 286
Wayne, John, 20
Wedding, The, 272-73
What Color Is Your Parachute, 238-39
Wilson, Flip, 21
Winning The Job Interview Game, 242-43, 245
Woman's Dress For Success Book, The, 121
Woman's Wear Daily, 168
Words, choosing, 146-49, (see also Communication, Writing)
Word Power, How To Increase Your, 147-48
Write better, Speak better, 21, 185, 215, 274
Write (writing) How You, 98, 161-78; Four essential considerations of, 162; Inverted Pyramid formula, 162-64, 165, 177, 186; Pyramid Formula, 163, 164-66, 177, 186; Four story types - straight "news," quote, fact, action, 163; Five W's, 166-69, (see also Five W's and H); Lead sentences, 169-170; AIDA formula for, 170-71, (see also AIDA); Outline for, 171-72; Checking and editing for, 172-73; Euphemisms, 173; KISS formula, (see KISS); Review of basics for, 177-78; Memos, 179, 180; ABC's of, 180; Letters, 181-85; Notes, 185; Speeches, 185-87; Reports, 188, 190; Five steps for, 189-91; Precis, 191; Book reports, 191-93; Term paper, 193-94; Essay, 194-95; Resume, 196-202; Cover Letter, 203-04; Research for, 210-13 (see also Communication)
W's, Five (and H) (see Five W's

Are you reading a borrowed copy of *PPR*.? Would you like a copy of your own... to be used as a reference book... or just to read now and then to renew your awareness in their... and your P.P.R.?
If so, just send your check for $19.95 to:

SAGE PUBLISHING COMPANY
26 Moonlawn Road
Troy, New York 12180

We'll take care of postage, handling, and (if necessary) sales tax.

If you prefer to use your VISA or MC, please include your card number and expiration date. And please print your name and address clearly so we can send you your personal copy of *PPR* by return mail.